GW00371245

THE TEST MATCH CAREER OF

TED DEXTER

Derek Lodge

Foreword by Robin Marlar

THE NUTSHELL PUBLISHING CO. LTD.
TUNBRIDGE WELLS

In the Spellmount Cricket list:
The Test Match Career of Geoffrey Boycott
by C D Clark
The Test Match Career of Sir Jack Hobbs
by Clive W Porter
Cricket Anthology
by Samuel J Looker
Cricket at Hastings
by Gerald Brodribb

First published in the UK in 1989 by
THE NUTSHELL PUBLISHING CO LTD
12 Dene Way, Speldhurst
Tunbridge Wells, Kent TN3 0NX

© Derek Lodge 1989

British Library Cataloguing in Publication Data
Lodge, Derek
   The test match career of Ted Dexter.
   (Test match career series).
   1. Cricket. Dexter, Ted, 1935-
   I. Title II. Series
   796.35′8′0924
   ISBN 1-871876-30-3

Design by Projects Thirty-Seven, Paddock Wood
Printed in Great Britain by
Courier International Ltd, Tiptree, Essex

DEDICATION

To my daughter Faith. She likes cricket, but for all the wrong reasons. Maybe she will enjoy the book just the same.

ACKNOWLEDGMENTS

A number of acknowledgments are in order. First to Mr Robin Marlar for his very kind foreword, and to Mr Dexter himself for so courteously answering a questionnaire at a very busy moment. Then, for the photographs, to the *Brighton Evening Argus*, Mr Patrick Eagar, Sport and General, and Barnaby's Picture Library. To Mr David Frith for the painting on the cover. To the staff of the Newspaper Library at Colindale and to Mr Stephen Green, Curator of the MCC Library, for their help and unfailing courtesy. To Sandra Forty for her wise and skilful editorial assistance. And, finally, to my wife without whose patient shouldering of many burdens which properly fall to me I could never write anything.

Bibliography

Wisden's Cricketers' Almanack, 1951-1969
The Cricketer, Playfair Cricket Monthly, British and overseas newspapers.
John Arlott, *Cricket Journal, 1958, 1959, 1960, 1961*
John Arlott, *Fred*
Ian Peebles, *Fight for the Ashes, 1958-59*
Jack Fingleton, *Four Chukkas to Australia*
Ron Roberts, *Fight for the Ashes, 1961*
Alan Ross, *Australia 63*
E W Swanton, *The Ashes in Suspense; the Test Matches of 1962-63*
Denzil Batchelor, *The Test Matches of 1964*
E W Swanton, *West Indies Revisited*
Charles Fortune, *MCC in South Africa, 1964-65*
Ted Dexter, *Ted Dexter Declares*
Colin Cowdrey, *MCC The autobiography of a cricketer*
Ralph Barker, *The Cricketing Family Edrich*
Geoffrey Boycott, *Boycott – the autobiography*
Ron Roberts, *The Cricketer's Bedtime Book*
Alan Gibson, *The Cricket Captains of England*
B J Wakley, *Classic Centuries*
D O Neely and others, *Men in White*
Christopher Martin-Jenkins, *Complete Who's Who of Test Cricketers*
W H Frindall, *Wisden Book of Test Cricket*
The Radleian, 1950-53

CONTENTS

In the 1965 Test against New Zealand, Dexter cuts a ball from
F J Cameron. *S & G Press Agency*

FOREWORD

Ted Dexter is one of the most glamorous figures associated with English cricket during the second half of the 20th Century. Handsome and articulate, he has cut a larger than life figure ever since he burst into the national consciousness as a Cambridge undergraduate more abundantly endowed with natural sporting ability than any teenager since C B Fry. His all round prowess as a cricketer was complemented by his outstanding ability as a golfer. More than that, he was intrigued by the wider world of adventure.

Born in Italy, married to an internationally famous model, he was never restricted by the essential Britishness of his student upbringing. Dexter epitomised style as a batsman scorching Test Match outfields with his bunch fist driving, as a golfer outdriving hitters among his golfing contemporaries, as a follower of racing, whether horses or dogs, whether as a light aircraft pilot, island hopping from Britain to Australia, or as a driver of fast cars and bikes. Involved in the world of fashion he and Susan, his wife, were among the pioneers of 'his' and 'hers' on the fashion scene. With the passing of years this attribute remains. Dexter can still cause a stir.

Nicknames seldom lie, and 'Lord Ted' was abundantly appropriate for him, not because of its snobbish connotations, which in his case were manifestly unfair, but because the aristocratic label correctly identified him among the best. Since his playing days Dexter, always a student of the games he played or was interested in, has become that rare bird a coach with an instant ability to analyse faults and the total conviction and understanding with which to put them right. When he became Chairman of the England Committee in the Spring of 1989 he told everyone that his whole life had served as a preparation for this position, then the most important position in English cricket. And he was right.

The poor results of that summer will have been a great sadness to him and a reminder that in any walk of life the main achievers are those who make correct judgements about others and lay down operating relationships which work.

Derek Lodge's study concerns itself not with Dexter the selector but Dexter the player, and most intriguingly, Dexter the Captain. There is no one better equipped to shine a light on cricketing careers by a study of the facts than Derek Lodge. Aficionados of his brilliant Statistical Notes in the Cricket Society Bulletin will be delighted that he has turned his attention for the first time to one of the major figures in the contemporary game.

Robin Marlar
Captain of Sussex 1955-59

Dexter batting for Sussex against Middlesex at Lords. *S & G Press Agency*

1 'Lord Edward'

Ted Dexter was undoubtedly one of the most majestically exciting cricketers of the sixties. He could electrify spectators and opposition alike with his sheer presence at the wicket. Yet his international career was all too short and his figures, while admirable, are not remarkable. Other titles in this series about great Test cricketers deal with batsmen who, in their time, have held such records as the highest aggregate in Test cricket, the most Test centuries made by an Englishman, or the most made against Australia, and so on – the list is as long as statistical analysis will allow. But in the record books no such distinctions are attached to the name of Ted Dexter: how, then, does he come to find himself in such exalted company?

The answer is not far to seek. Not only is he now at the very heart of England's cricket affairs, but he also dominated the scene some twenty-five years ago, in the 1960s. Younger readers will doubtless want to know about the many achievements of his earlier career, and older readers will, I hope, be glad to be reminded of his sterling deeds and to recall the excitement they felt when they were lucky enough to watch him at the crease or in the field.

Dexter attracted particular attention because he was not only a superbly attractive batsman but also a striking personality, or he was presented as one, which isn't quite the same thing. Very early in his career, round about 1959, an enterprising journalist coined the nickname of Lord Edward for him. In an age when instant nicknames are even more the rage, this has been abbreviated to Lord Ted. I haven't asked him whether he likes or approves of the tag, but I would suspect that he does not. It was originally a comment on his commanding batting style and occasional aloofness on the field, but it came to be believed that he assumed an arrogant, go-to-blazes style in personal relationships. I think he was maligned in this; he could be abstracted when considering a problem or decision and in that cocoon, could ignore a friend or acquaintance – but most of us are guilty of that, at some time or another.

Throughout his career and after it, he has made and kept many friends in the cricket world and nobody who was arrogant or, for example, unappreciative of the pressures on professional cricketers, would have

1

managed that. He is discussed in very many autobiographies of the period, but very few players are in any way critical of his manner; even Colin Cowdrey, whom he certainly overtook in the race for the permanent England captaincy, likes and admires him. In short, he may sometimes have been a difficult communicator, but it stemmed from deep thought, and not from any inner sense of superiority. If we are talking about aloof England captains, we can all name our own fancy in the hauteur stakes – Jardine? Maclaren? Lord Harris? even Hammond? – but Dexter isn't anywhere near that particular league. His nickname is comprehensible in terms of the kind of *player* he was, but if it is taken as a comment on the *man*, it says at once less and more, than the truth. Certainly the coiner of the name did Dexter no favour.

Ted Dexter rose to the top very quickly and dramatically. In July 1959 Peter May suddenly fell ill in the middle of a series against India, in which he had already made a chanceless century. He was rushed to hospital and had to undergo a serious operation. Optimists hoped that he would be back as good as new for the West Indies tour in December of that year, but pessimists feared that the end of an era had been reached. With good reason they wondered how soon England would be able to find a replacement as masterful and as reliable. When May was declared fit enough to take part in the tour it looked as though the optimists had won the day, but unhappily he fell ill once again in mid-series. He played only four more Tests for England two years later, in India in 1961.

The immediate replacement in the middle order was Mike Smith, an admirable batsman but not a commanding one at Test level. In that same Test, the fourth of the summer, the twenty-four year old Sussex player Ted Dexter was called to the England side to occupy the all-rounder's slot at No 6. His previous season had been far from auspicious. He had not been chosen as a member of the party to go to Australia, and when he was flown out to replace an injured player his performance was a failure. The only bright spot was a century against New Zealand at the end of the tour, but he was still regarded as a doubtful risk at Test level and some judges felt that he was lucky to be re-selected ahead of Brian Close.

The all-rounder's place in the England side had for ten years been admirably filled by Trevor Bailey, and many people thought that he would be asked to return to the side when all the available young hopefuls had been tried and found wanting. He was, after all, only 36 years old and still playing well. Dexter was a very surprising choice as his successor for many reasons: their styles could hardly have been more different. Dexter had the reputation of being something of a dasher, whereas Bailey's batting was totally reliable. As a bowler Dexter would try anything once, but Bailey was remembered as the man who had salvaged many a Test with accurate leg-theory, giving the batsman nothing at all to hit.

2

A few Test matches can make a vast difference to a reputation. By the time Dexter had played in four more – two in England and two in the West Indies – he was established as England's leading batsman and had started his climb in the batting order. No 3 was now his normal position, except when tactics indicated otherwise or when he needed to recover after a long spell of bowling. After another two years he was England's captain. It was a most dramatic rise: the only pity was that his time at the top was so short. He held his place as the leading batsman from January 1960 to June 1965, but in that time he made such an impact that those who were lucky enough to see him in action will certainly never forget him.

What kind of batsman was he? He was essentially a correct orthodox stroke-player, who did not play with his bat too far away from the front pad as some free batsmen do. He had a sound defence and, other than in the most exceptional circumstances, he always looked for ways of getting on top of the bowling and to do this would put added power and zest into his driving. He commanded all the strokes and hit the ball very hard indeed. He was well-built, kept himself extremely fit and punched his full weight behind every shot. His innings at Lord's in 1963, where he scored 70 against the formidable West Indies, was typical. The faster Hall and Griffith bowled against him the harder he drove them, and he was only finally dismissed lbw to Sobers as he played one of his rare defensive strokes. He had no particular *bête noire* among the many bowlers who confronted him. McKenzie and Benaud took Dexter's wicket more often than others, but they had the lion's share of the bowling against him. Benaud always fancied his chances, but the records show that between the two of them honours were more or less even.

Writing in 1960, while Dexter was still maturing, but after he had achieved his first real success on the tour of the West Indies, John Arlott summed him up:

Dexter's nickname of 'Lord Edward' is not inept. He has an imperious bearing and he bats with a lordly prodigality. Today, from a high upstanding stance, he drove – particularly through mid-on – with immense force. His front-of-the-wicket strokes – and they constitute most of his heavy fire-power – are a blend of timing and considerable strength, embellished with a final, wristy whip . . . In defence, he played with commendable straightness and hardly ever failed in his selection of the ball to strike and the one to stop, though some of his defensive strokes were hard enough to jar the fieldsmen's hands.

As a bowler, Dexter could hardly be described as a tight, remorseless attacker and it has to be admitted that he occasionally gave batsmen something to hit. He was a deceptively good bowler, always prepared to try something new and could generate unexpected pace from the pitch. He was a batsman who bowled rather than a complete all-rounder, but he

3

counted many first-class batsmen among his victims. Of the 66 wickets he took in Test matches, only ten were those of genuine tail-enders, which is perhaps another way of saying that captains – including Dexter himself – prefer to attack the tail with fast bowlers. At the outset of his career he had the reputation of being rather casual in the field. There were malicious stories about his habit of practising golf strokes when he thought no-one was looking, not unlike those about Armstrong taking surreptitious looks at a newspaper in the long field. But as his career developed all this changed, and by the time he was chosen to become England's captain Dexter was a dedicated and tigerish fielder, with a throw of deadly pace and accuracy.

2 The making of a cricketer

Almost all great cricketers have in their youth devoted hours of practice to the game or to some form of exercise which can be related to the game. It doesn't seem to matter very much how that practice time was spent, the important feature is the development of co-ordination of eye-hand-bat, but the nature of the upbringing may determine the *type* of player which emerges.

Bradman spent hours of solitary practice throwing a golf-ball at a paling and hitting the rebound and he developed into a fantastic natural striker of the ball. Hobbs was brought up on the cricket ground where his father was the groundsman, watching older players being coached, and he became one of the most correct of players, but with super-added genius which set him apart. May, Cowdrey and Jardine had conventional prep school and public school coaching and developed into conventional, stylish players. Most of the great West Indians learnt to play on the rough roads or in the sandy beaches, in games where you batted until you were out, and gave the bat up to the boy who had got you out. They grew up as acquisitive natural players, good on any sort of wicket – and of course they had usually learned to bowl a bit! These are generalisations and there are always exceptions, but early experience does mould the man.

Ted Dexter was the son of a businessman who joined the RAF on the outbreak of war in 1939. Consequently Ted moved with his family a lot, attending prep schools in Ulster, Wales, Scotland and England. Some of these had cricket facilities, some had not, but he began to get a feeling for the game at Norfolk House, Beaconsfield, where he says that he was already an attacking batsman. But a particularly formative influence was his close relationship with his elder brother John, himself to become an accomplished cricketer. Like brothers everywhere they fought and competed every day and young Ted developed into an assertive, combative games player who never admitted defeat, any more than he had ever admitted defeat in his battles with John.

When Ted arrived at Radley College, John was already there and on his way up the cricketing ladder, which must have helped to bring his brother into the limelight – had he needed any help. Ted made his way to join him

5

in the first eleven in 1950, at the age of fifteen. He himself says that he got there when he was fourteen, but the College records don't show this, and fifteen is early enough in all conscience, given the usual public school convention of keeping cocky youngsters in their place.

Radley had had a very good side for some years and were one of the best school sides in the country. They had a very strong fixture list, playing against some notable schools as well as several Oxford colleges and powerful clubs such as the Free Foresters and the Butterflies, who generally brought down good sides. It was an important part of Dexter's cricketing education to confront ex-Test players such as G O B Allen and H D Read. In 1950, he scored 51 against the Free Foresters, who had made a good declaration, but saw the College win by 6 wickets in what must have been a good day to watch, 523 runs being scored. Dexter also made 73 against Stowe, who were comprehensively beaten, and he finished third in the batting averages, on 31.19 and took 26 wickets. John Dexter took 23 wickets, with a slightly better average than Ted's, but he was somewhat less successful as a batsman, being evidently a born No 11.

In 1951 Ted Dexter was fourth in the batting averages – an indication of the strength of the batting, for he batted very well throughout the season for an average of 29.90, and he was second to John in the bowling averages taking 26 wickets at 18.88, as compared with John's 54 at 13.54. Ted scored 94 against the Free Foresters and 55 in a monstrous total of 367 for 9 against Sherborne. He was described in *The Radleian* as 'an astonishingly powerful and mature player for a boy of just sixteen' and the writer makes the point that he lost his wicket in several games when going for quick runs before a declaration.

1952 was another good year for Radley and for Dexter. The school won eight matches and drew seven. Dexter as he matured physically was becoming a really powerful and dominating batsman. He scored 581 runs at an average of 83.00 and headed Radley's batting, and he took 28 wickets, although he had to miss several games because of a knee injury and could not always bowl when he did play. He made several fine scores; 142 not out against Radley Rangers, 114 not out against Christ Church, Oxford, 54 not out against MCC, 51 against the Free Foresters. *The Radleian* summed him up as 'A tremendously powerful and graceful striker of the ball who had a wonderful season.' Radley had now lost only one match against another school since 1947.

Dexter and A C Walton (who went on to play for Oxford and Middlesex) both played at Lord's for the Southern Schools against the Rest and for the Public Schools XI against the Combined Services. Dexter scored 44, 8 and 43, and E M Wellings, writing in *Wisden* described the two Radley players as the most mature batsmen in the game. Dexter's power and maturity were the attributes singled out by most observers and

6

indeed, in the team photograph of that year he looks a lot more than his seventeen years, broad-shouldered and assured.

He was school cricket captain in 1953, his last year and under him the team maintained its good record, although three matches were lost, the College remained undefeated in inter-school matches with decisive wins over Westminster, Bradfield and St Edward's, Oxford. Dexter was top of both batting and bowling averages, with 873 runs at an average of 79.36 and 47 wickets at 13.48. He made runs against almost everybody: 132 not out against Westminster, 147 against Bradfield, 151 against the Berkshire Gentlemen, and five fifties. Against St Edward's, looking for a declaration, he scored 71 in 21 scoring strokes even hitting one six that carried for 110 yards. Radley scored throughout the season at 77.7 runs per hour.

Dexter was unsuccessful in the Lord's matches this year, getting out for 3,23,2 and 0. Wellings thought that he suffered from impulsiveness, and got out before allowing himself a preliminary look at the ball; but he saw this as a fault on the right side, and hoped that the boy would learn discretion without sacrificing his strokes. Easier said than done, but as far as anybody has managed it, Dexter did.

He now went off to do his National Service, before going up to Cambridge. Here again he didn't approach life in the same way as others, spending most of his time in Malaya, so that instead of getting that easy introduction to first-class cricket with the Combined Services team which other national servicemen enjoyed, he spent his time in regimental cricket or playing for one state against another, as well as doing some real soldiering, hunting for terrorists. He says that he was pretty bored most of the time, like many another amateur soldier and he went up to Cambridge in the autumn of 1955 eager to get on with the rest of his life.

He was thus out of the mainstream of cricket for two seasons at a vital stage of his development; contemporaries such as Peter Richardson and John Murray were playing for the Combined Services team as well as getting the occasional game for their counties. It left Dexter with some leeway to make up, though he could of course argue that he was learning rather more about life than those in a more sheltered environment.

3 An uncertain beginning

Dexter has admitted that he really wasn't very interested in playing cricket at Cambridge and credits his brother for putting up with this lackadaisical nonsense – he just put him down for the Freshmen's nets without consulting him! If this is true, John Dexter, himself a very good cricketer, deserves the thanks of cricket lovers all over the world, but somehow I think that Ted would have found his way into the Cambridge side sooner or later. Be that as it may, he stood out at the nets as a natural talent, was picked for the Freshmen's match and scored 120 without getting out. So he found himself in the university side and making his first-class debut in April 1956.

At this time the older universities, particularly Cambridge, were a regular source of top-flight batsmen. The pitch at Fenner's was a very good one and since 1946 Sheppard, May, Doggart, Bailey, Insole, Dewes and Subba Row had all emerged there. Not all managed as much as they promised when faced with formidable bowling on less favourable pitches, but they had their chance to be noticed. It would be no bad thing for Dexter when he did make the England side, to find several of his predecessors in the team. Because university cricket was so strong, the counties always took a strong side to both Cambridge and Oxford. Dexter's first three games happened to be against Surrey the reigning county champions, Yorkshire and Lancashire, and they fielded between them no fewer than ten Test bowlers who would submit his developing technique to a rigorous examination.

Dexter came in for Cambridge at No 3 but Peter Loader was always quick to spot a high backlift and slipped one under Dexter's guard before he had troubled the scorer. When the university batted again 198 behind, Dexter had to struggle against Loader, Laker and Lock, but it was Eric Bedser who finally got him after he had made a sturdy 44. The cricket professors were impressed, even though Cambridge were still well beaten.

In the next match Yorkshire batted pretty unimpressively and were 197 for 9 before Trueman and Cowan saved their faces by adding 54 for the last wicket. This time Dexter survived the early onslaught from Trueman and he and O'Brien took the score to 78 for 1 before he fell to Appleyard. The

8

rest of the batsmen did little, but Yorkshire were surprisingly negative in their second innings and the university managed a pretty creditable draw. This time Close got Dexter for another duck, again getting past the backlift. Nevertheless he was doing as well as a freshman could expect against this sort of bowling and he was clearly in for an extended run. He failed in both innings against Lancashire but by now he at least had the consolation of being dismissed by five different Test bowlers!

In the fourth game against Sussex, he got yet another duck in the first innings but in the second he came good by scoring a splendid 118 with two sixes, a five and eleven fours. From this moment on he became one of the players who caught the eye wherever he played. By the end of the season *Wisden* described him as 'an attractive, forceful player'.

After his impressive hundred against Sussex, Robin Marlar the county captain, inquired after his county qualification and intentions. Dexter, having no sort of qualification for any county, cheerfully agreed to play for Sussex – only to change his mind as far as 1956 was concerned when he went on a cricket tour of Denmark and met an attractive young lady in Copenhagen. He cried off – giving plenty of notice – but all oblivious as he later admitted of the implications for the county of this rather nineteenth century behaviour. Sussex were prepared to overlook it; they knew a great talent when they saw one. Dexter's first class season then was confined to his fourteen games for Cambridge.

Dexter began the 1957 season as secretary of the Cambridge side and its chief batting hope. Again the first match was against Surrey with their full Test-class attack. This time Dexter was dismissed by Alec Bedser and Lock for 11 and 7. Surrey won with some ease, as did Yorkshire in the next game, Trueman taking 11 for 75. Close got Dexter out in each innings. I enlarge on these early games to show just what university teams were up against in the fifties, and why a prolific university batsman was automatically considered as a Test prospect to a much greater extent than he would be today.

Essex visited Fenner's next and Dexter made a splendidly aggressive 100 not out in an innings total of 174 for 6 to set up a declaration. He followed this with some consistent batting and came across the West Indies for the first time, scoring 46 and 37. Then came his finest innings so far, when he scored a hundred before lunch against Lancashire and went on to make 185 in four hours. By the end of the Fenner's part of the programme, he had scored 816 runs and was beginning to be identified as a stylish, dashing batsman.

On tour Dexter was marginally less successful, but he made 60 against the MCC at Lord's and came to the university match with confidence. Sadly, he only made 7 but he had shown enough promise to be picked for the Gentlemen where he turned in a sensational bowling performance.

Until now he had bowled very little and had in fact taken only 18 first class wickets. Here May put him on as first change on a lifting wicket and he surprised himself and everybody else by taking 5 for 8 in 5 overs. Compton, captaining the Players in his last season as a professional, declared at the extraordinary score of 46 for 9 and the Gentlemen went for quick runs in the second innings. Dexter was out for 13 in each innings, but again he bowled well in the Players' second innings, dismissing Compton for the second time. The Players were relieved to get away with a draw.

This performance brought Dexter right into the limelight and close to Test selection. England were one up in a very interesting series against the West Indies and Trevor Bailey, who was the all-rounder of the side and had been its mainstay for five years, was injured. The selectors asked Dexter to make himself available as one of the twelve, and one can only imagine his feelings when he got the invitation on the very day that he sustained an ankle injury. He had no choice but to decline, it would have been folly to have played when only half fit, but he must have wondered if he'd ever get another chance.

Even if he had been present as one of the twelve at Leeds, Dexter would probably have been the one left out. The middle order batsmen, May, Graveney and Cowdrey were all having a great series and David Sheppard had been invited as the No 6 and would hardly have been made twelfth man. If Dexter had been picked, he would probably have got a wicket or two, as the match was played on a very green wicket and Loader got the only post-war hat-trick by an Englishman.

Dexter played in three matches for Sussex in 1957 without setting the Arun on fire. Only two other games that year are worthy of note. He played for MCC in the Lancashire centenary match and had the pleasure of seeing a fine innings of 76 from Sir Leonard Hutton, returning to first-class cricket after two years absence. Dexter himself made 22 and 61, but the match was ruined by bad weather. He was picked again for the Gentlemen at Scarborough and made an attractive 88 against a powerful attack. His selection for these two games shows that he was in everybody's mind as a cricketer who was both promising and a crowd-pleaser. A player to watch, in every sense.

During the following winter, Dexter made considerable progress as a golfer, and although he has always maintained that he never contemplated making golf his career, it was at this time that he began to acquire the playboy image that has never been entirely put behind him. He also met Susan, his future wife, at this time and the fact that she modelled clothes didn't escape the newspaper correspondents who, then as now, preferred an angle to a technical appreciation of a cricketer. Dexter was now, not only a cricketer of note but a 'personality' – for better or worse.

Dexter captained Cambridge in 1958. He had only two outstanding players, himself and Ossie Wheatley, a hard-working, accurate fast-medium bowler who was to become a popular captain of Glamorgan. *Wisden* is rather sniffy about Cambridge's season, describing it as 'disappointing' in that only three of the 18 first-class matches were won.

Dexter himself had a good university season. He had a great match against Lancashire, scoring 92 and 109 not out and made two other centuries against Sussex and D R Jardine's XI. He encountered the touring New Zealanders early on, when Cambridge did disastrously badly. 14 runs ahead on the first innings, they were put out for 46 by Blair and MacGibbon, and lost by 10 wickets.

The weather was the dominant theme of the 1958 season; the Test wickets were atrocious and twenty three championship matches reached no decision on the first innings. The universities were fortunate in that they had enough time to finish their match, but it was often interrupted. Cambridge made only 161 for 7 in 80 overs on the first day and Dexter boldly declared overnight. Oxford made a good start but collapsed against Hurd, who was strongly supported by Wheatley and by Dexter himself. Cambridge went in again, 19 behind, and this time batted much more entertainingly. Green and Cook made seventies, but Dexter's 58 made in 43 minutes, was acclaimed as the innings of the match. He was able to declare again and he himself was the most successful bowler, taking 4 for 14, all of them leading batsmen. Thus, he ended his university career with a most satisfying win.

Dexter was now a natural choice for the Gentlemen and Players match (in which he failed) and for the fourth Test. England were already three up in the series and in the happy position of being able to treat this game, in part, as a trial match to help the selectors pick a team for Australia. Dexter was one of the three new caps, and in retrospect it seems odd that he was not picked for the touring team. The team was to be announced on the Sunday and the weather took a hand to keep Dexter out. New Zealand batted well into the second day; they were slow but understandably so. In six innings so far their highest score had been 137, and they were taking what advantage they could of a slow, easy wicket. England were 192 for 2 at the close on the Friday and Dexter may have allowed himself to think that he would get in on the Saturday with England in a strong position and be able to play a spectacular innings to influence the selectors.

It was not to be; only 12 overs could be bowled on Saturday and the selectors had to pick the tour side without having a look at him. They left him out, and many people were appalled at the passing over of one whom they saw as a player of unmistakable class. RC Robertson-Glasgow had this to say about the selectors:

But a child of six, who'd played one season's cricket on the lawn with his mother, could surely have seen Dexter's genius. I've seen him some four times in all so far, and if ever a man shouted from the crease England class, maybe world class, it is Dexter. And these blind idiots, treble-bandaged moles leave him at home. He is a possible Trumper or Macartney . . . Ye Gods!

Stirring stuff, and indeed, Dexter was one of the most striking players to appear for a long time. But from the selectors' point of view Dexter had played very little county cricket and there were many examples of university players such as Doggart and Dewes who had not carried their brilliance into Test cricket. Seven batsmen were picked for the tour. There could be no argument about the merits of May, Cowdrey and Graveney. Richardson and Milton were selected as openers and Dexter was not in contention for their places. The other two were Watson and Subba Row. In 1958, they were second and third in the national averages, each with an average of 46, against Dexter's 35, much of it achieved at Fenner's. Averages are not everything, but surely have some significance if only as a form guide.

Dexter had now to consider his career outside cricket. A friend of his father's had a job in mind for him with some insurance brokers in London, but aware that Dexter was listed as a possible replacement if a batsman was injured in Australia he didn't 'place' him in London initially but employed him in his own business in Paris, to acquire business experience. Unwittingly, he thus fostered the Dexter legend. Out in Australia Subba Row fractured his wrist and Dexter was sent for. It made a marvellous story that the glamour boy, who just happened to be on the point of getting engaged to a model, was living it up in Paris when the call came. The fact that he was working for his living there hardly mattered, or at least it didn't get in the way of a good headline.

Poor Dexter had a most disastrous journey to Australia contending with fogs, engine trouble and a form of laryngitis and arrived, some five days after leaving Paris, exhausted and well-nigh speechless. By this time the England team had staggered round the State circuit, encountering doubtful bowling actions everywhere except against Queensland, where Ray Lindwall still reigned. England only occasionally showed glimpses of the form that had won them the last four home series. At the moment that Dexter landed they were stumbling to a defeat in the first Test, in which they had given one of the dreariest batting exhibitions of a particularly dreary epoch. It would be difficult for him to bat worse than that, one thought, but he would be expected to be bright and breezy from the word Go, and there was of course the problem of quick acclimatisation.

Acclimatisation was to prove difficult. Firstly there was the expected change in conditions – hard wickets, dazzling light and so on. Secondly, Dexter was not a regular member of the county circuit – that intimate club

12

to which all professionals belong and which makes slotting into a touring team so much easier. Dexter has written of the difficulties he encountered when appointed twelfth man for the second and fourth Tests on this tour; any junior pro, he says, would have had more idea than he had about the routine tasks to be performed at the intervals to make life easier for the team. It is not surprising if some of the players resented the insouciant attitude of this semi-aristocrat who had had a much better press than most of them – they couldn't have known that there was an uncertain youngster beneath that brash exterior. Finally, this was the year of the throwers in Australia and Dexter had to get used to the idea that almost everywhere he went there would be quick, unpredictable bowlers.

His first games were in Tasmania, and here at least he could feel at home; if any grounds in Australia look typically English, they are the cool and grassy arenas of Hobart and Launceston. Dexter and May had a lively little stand against an attack of medium-pacers, and Dexter must have been quite satisfied with his 38. Play was rained off and the party went on to Launceston to play a Combined XI. The usual reinforcements included only one bowler, Philpott, but Dexter failed to cash in on the opportunity for practice. Then on to Adelaide where he encountered his first throwers, two fast-medium bowlers named Trethewey and Hitchcox, instantly nicknamed Trethrowey and Pitchcox by the tourists. Even the partial Adelaide crowd acknowledged that these two actions were more than doubtful and Dexter fell to Hitchcox in the middle of an ugly little collapse on the first day. Fortunately, South Australia batted even worse than the visitors and a pretty dull match was very nearly won. Dexter's first five innings in Australia had produced only 89 runs and he was clearly not ready for the next Test at Melbourne.

That Test was to prove another disaster. Davidson sent back three batsmen in the third over of the match and although Bailey, May and Cowdrey fought back, England were bowled out for 259, nothing like enough on a good wicket. Australia made an excellent start, Harvey being at the top of his form. He and O'Neill were together at 255 for 2 and Australia must have had visions of a score of 600, but Statham and Loader had never given up and now brought about a collapse. The two established batsmen were out and Simpson and Benaud failed to score.

255 for 2 had become 262 for 6 and England seemed to be back in the match, the more so when there was no true recovery and Australia were out for 308 quite early on the fourth day. However, all England's fears about Meckiff, the most formidable of the 'doubtful' bowlers, were now fulfilled. He destroyed England in a couple of hours, taking 6 for 38. England were put out for 87, no batsman even reaching 20, and Australia won a surprisingly easy victory by 8 wickets. Watson and Richardson had looked particularly vulnerable – it was time for desperate remedies.

Although Dexter was no better prepared than before the Melbourne Test – the third Test immediately following on the second – he came into the side, together with Milton. It would be a pretty testing baptism of fire.

In England, Dexter had never played before a bigger crowd than 10,000 or so in the Old Trafford Test and now here he was going out to bat on the vast Sydney Oval with England at 97 for 4. The crowd on the Hill were audibly wondering whether he had any more to offer than the rest of the Poms who, it must be said, hadn't covered themselves with glory. Bailey and May had fallen to Meckiff and Slater, two of the doubtful bowlers who were causing England so much trouble, and Graveney had just been caught by Harvey off Benaud. The Australian captain, quite rightly, had no mercy on the newcomer and hedged him about with four close fielders. Dexter, trying not to prod a simple catch to one of these, applied his pads to an off-break and was caught in front, for 1. This was not an auspicious start and he was made to look worse by the next man in. Roy Swetman, the tiny wicket-keeper, playing in his first Test, applied himself boldly though with a little luck and made 41. Cowdrey, Lock and Trueman each made a few and England struggled to 219, made in 82 eight-ball overs. It wasn't a good score, but it was a good deal better than had seemed likely and Dexter was very aware that he had failed to distinguish himself.

The second day of the match was virtually washed out and England were all out late in the evening leaving Australia to bat out three overs. By the third day, May decided that whether or not the pitch had anything for the spinners, it certainly had nothing to offer the faster men and he brought Laker on. He was rewarded for this boldness, when Laker dismissed both Burke and Harvey very cheaply, but McDonald stayed, though not without a few misadventures against Laker. The tempo, as in the earlier matches, was uninspiring and the score was only 67 for 2 at the mid-afternoon break. When McDonald fell to Lock, this rate was accelerated by O'Neill and Favell who without taking complete command, neglected no scoring opportunity and 184 for 3 at the close was a healthy position for Australia.

On the fourth day May started with his two spinners who soon bagged both the overnight batsmen and, for good measure, Benaud, who took a most intemperate swing at Laker and was bowled. Given that his side were still 11 behind and would have to bat last, this was a real blunder, but his faith in the length of batting in the line-up was justified. Mackay and Davidson put on 115 for the seventh wicket and effectively made the game safe for Australia. May eventually turned to Trueman and Bailey and the fast man had Mackay with a yorker. Back came the spinners to finish things off, and Australia were all out for 357. They were 138 ahead and with just over two days to go, quite safe from defeat.

England however, were by no means safe. Luckily Meckiff the destroyer at Melbourne, had to go off with a heel injury very early on the fifth day. Bailey and Milton made England's best start of the series, but this was hardly difficult – the best opening partnership so far had been 28! They had only just passed this milestone when Milton fell to Benaud and Bailey soon followed him, caught by the substitute Bobby Simpson. At 37 for 2 England were back at the bottom of the hill and Graveney soon followed, lbw to a full toss. Everything that could go wrong for England on this tour did go wrong. However relief was at hand. Without the brooding shadow of Meckiff over them, May and Cowdrey produced the best English batting of the whole series. They were hardly in dominating form, but they cleared arrears almost without incident and, to the stupefaction of the crowd, the press, and possibly the batsmen, Benaud immediately went on to the defensive, introducing Mackay and Davidson with run-saving fields. Looking at the way England had batted so far in the series, his reaction seemed excessive. Benaud later explained that being two up, he saw no reason to let England back into the game – but May and Cowdrey had just played through a session of one and three-quarter hours in which they made 92 runs, hardly a runaway assault. The day ended with England 178 for 3, just 40 runs ahead.

On the last day Benaud apparently had a change of mind, or perhaps heart; he went back on to the attack, but England were unable to capitalise, making only 53 in the morning session. Soon after lunch May was bowled by Burke, yet another dubious bowler, in fact the worst of the lot. Nobody seems to have been in any doubt that Jimmy Burke threw every ball, but generally speaking he was so innocuous that nobody bothered to make a fuss about him until the more general furore began. In his current form Dexter was hardly likely to take the bull by the horns and he made no attempt to do so. He batted for 33 balls, made three good drives, but as soon as Benaud returned he had him caught at the wicket off a ball that both popped and turned. It had been a pretty inauspicious debut – 12 runs in two attempts – but he had done no worse than some others of greater experience.

May was never in a position to make a really challenging declaration, so he let the innings run on until Cowdrey arrived at his hundred, made in 362 minutes. Australia were left with 150 to make in 110 minutes. The openers went cheaply to Laker, and Australia made no further attempt at the target, which was hardly surprising – May could always have closed the game down with his faster men. This was England's best performance of the series, but it was hardly inspiring; there would have to be changes and it was difficult to see Dexter keeping his place.

This was Dexter's first encounter with Benaud and their paths were to cross twice more before Benaud retired. The cricketing public were fascinated by their personal duel, as the hard-hitting Dexter tried to master the leg-spinner who for his part, while having a very healthy respect for Dexter's batting, reckoned that Dexter always gave him a chance to get him out. The duel reached its climax when they were opposed as captains, but the two got on very well personally and their encounters never failed to provide top-class entertainment, at least until their final meeting.

May and the selectors gave Dexter every opportunity to find his form before the fourth Test at Adelaide, playing him against both Victoria and New South Wales, but he made only 47 for twice out, while Watson made a solid hundred against Victoria and regained his place. May himself made a very fine hundred against NSW and there were signs that the English batsmen were coming to terms with the conditions. The biggest cloud on the horizon was yet another new Australian bowler, the gigantic Rorke. He was – if possible – even more worrying than Meckiff, being another who bowled with a bent arm, plus he also dragged a very long way over the bowling crease, so that he was delivering from about 18 yards. He took 4 for 57 in the NSW match and the English batsmen were entitled to be apprehensive about what Rorke might do in the Test. He replaced the injured Meckiff and the great Ray Lindwall was recalled in place of Slater.

England's chances suffered a blow when Laker, the best of the bowlers in the first three Tests, reported unfit on the morning of the match. Lock, the only other spinner in the original party had taken only five wickets. May gambled when he won the toss and put Australia in hoping for a little early life in the wicket. He didn't get it, although he nearly got McDonald's wicket, Statham shaving the off-stump very early on. It was the last chance the bowlers had until five o'clock, though the umpire turned down a very confident appeal against Burke. Australia were 200 for 1 at the interval and the Ashes were on their way back to them.

This is Dexter's story, which gives us an excellent excuse not to dwell on this rather depressing match. Australia went on to 476, batting well into the third day and all England's fears of Rorke were justified. Overstepping by quite a long way, he tore the middle out of the England batting, leaving Benaud to make short work of the tail, until Statham came in at No 11 and played a fine forcing innings of 36. Nevertheless England found themselves following on 236 behind, and although Richardson and Watson gave them their best start of the series, and May and Graveney made fifties, this was nowhere near enough and Australia won easily by 10 wickets. Dexter again was twelfth man, and by his own account, had not carried out his duties with much conviction. He must have been feeling somewhat out of things at this stage, having joined a side which was doing badly and able to do nothing to help.

Nevertheless Dexter got a place in the final Melbourne Test, but only because England had suffered a succession of accidents: Milton was so badly injured that he played no more on the tour, Evans injured a finger and was out of commission, Statham and Loader were injured in a car crash up-country, not critically but still seriously enough to keep them out of this game and the New Zealand leg of the tour, and as if this wasn't enough, Watson broke down while bowling in the nets. May was reduced to twelve fit players. The selectors took a final gamble by omitting Lock who had taken just 15 wickets in four Tests, at an average of 75, and gave Mortimore his first Test chance. With Meckiff fit again Australia picked five bowlers – they were going all out for a win.

This time Benaud put England in and became the first captain to win an Ashes Test after doing so since Douglas, nearly half a century earlier. Bailey and May were out with 13 on the board and soon enough, Dexter was walking in at 109 for 4. He was out first ball, playing with a decidedly crooked bat at a ball that was leaving him. He was disconcerted, one imagines, when Mortimore, the other reserve but selected for his bowling, made a sensible and confident 44. In time Mortimore was to set Dexter's feet, or more accurately his bat, on the right path but the moment had not yet come. England were all out for 205 and deep in trouble yet again. Trueman and Tyson attacked with spirit and had Australia at 83 for 3, but then Mackay turned on one of his most obdurate performances, supporting McDonald in a partnership of 71 that took a lot of life and fire out of the bowlers. On the third morning both the heroes and Davidson were quickly dismissed, but Benaud and Grout ensured a good lead for Australia, hooking the fast men in a way that was beyond the England batsmen. Australia totalled 351, and England went in again with one last chance to save their reputations, if not the match.

Alas, it was not to be. At the start of the innings Ray Lindwall's tally of Test wickets equalled that of Clarrie Grimmett – 216 – and he was naturally anxious to take the lead. It only took a short time, he beat and bowled Bailey with his fourth ball and followed this by having May taken in the slips. 12 for 2. Richardson and Cowdrey batted out the day and started most positively next morning only to be parted by an unfortunate and controversial run-out. There was undoubtedly a misunderstanding, but Cowdrey appeared to have beaten a swift throw from O'Neill. The umpire thought otherwise and this, the last disputed decision of a series where they had been all too frequent, really ended English hopes of making a game of it. Cowdrey had been batting very well and Richardson seemed dispirited by his departure. He himself was lbw, sweeping at Benaud and the unhappy Dexter had to come in, on a pair, at 105 for 4, two balls before lunch. Things could hardly have been worse for him.

17

He survived those two balls and got off the mark afterwards with two overthrows. This was his only piece of good fortune for he was soon out, once again chasing an off-side ball and once again doing so with a crooked bat – he had made only 6. Even Ian Peebles, the kindliest of critics, commented that 'it was apparent that he has still some way to go technically to live long in this torrid atmosphere.' Graveney was England's last real hope, and he batted well enough for a while before falling to Davidson's outswinger. At the very end Trueman swung the bat with Yorkshire vigour and imagination hitting Davidson for 14 in one over and making 36 in all, but England were all out for 214 and Australia soon knocked off the runs required. McDonald, easily the batsman of the series, was undefeated with 51 and finished with 519 runs.

The Australian tour was an intensely disappointing series for Dexter personally and for those who believed in him – and they were many.

Dexter's initial exclusion from the party had been fiercely criticised and the call for him was hailed by some as providential – now we should see what the true Corinthian approach would do – that sort of thing. On the other hand, there were those who believed that the slow climb up the mountain was the only way to success, that untutored brilliance would never succeed. If one were writing a novel about the series, Dexter's apparent failure would be presented in terms of his failure to relate to his worthy professional colleagues. He would be shown reading Keats or doing the *Times* crossword, instead of taking advice from the peasants he despised. In fact, that was precisely how he was often portrayed by the more sensational papers, but as I have tried to show, it isn't at all how it was. He was no arrogant young Cantab, but a worried young cricketer who at this very early stage lacked the experience and technique to take charge of the series and shake it up. He may even have wondered whether his Test career was over before it had properly begun.

	Innings	N.O.	H.S.	Runs	Average	100	50
1958/59 (A)	4	—	11	18	4.50	—	—
To date	5	—	52	70	14.00	—	1

Happily the tide turned for Dexter even before he left Australia for New Zealand. It is greatly to his credit – and incidentally gives the lie to the chatter about his failure to get on with his team-mates – that, in the two days between the end of the fifth Test, and the party's moving on to New Zealand, he was working away in the nets when John Mortimore asked him why he was batting with the face of his bat open. Startled, Dexter replied that he was doing no such thing, but Mortimore showed him; he turned the bat minutely in his hands and his timing returned. It was as simple as that.

Dexter could hardly wait to get to the wicket in New Zealand. He wasn't helped by having to open the innings against Otago and he duly failed, but in the Christchurch Test it all came right. On a wicket that helped the bowlers throughout, England lost early wickets and when Dexter went in at 126 for 4 at No 6 it seemed a repeat of the Australian story. May, a little out of touch himself, was able to settle Dexter at the wicket and then he was away. Each batsman stayed with him for a while and Trueman and Lock saw him to his century, the eighth and ninth wicket stands producing 81 and 62 runs. Dexter hit twenty-four fours in his 141, and batted for four and a quarter hours. He had arrived.

New Zealand were shot out by Tony Lock – and, at about this time, showed him a film which lined *him* up with those Australian throwers – and England moved on to Basin Reserve. Here, Dexter enjoyed the extraordinary luxury of coming in to bat at 410 for 4 but he failed to cash in and, in fact, failed in each of his last three innings on the tour, the third of these being in the rain-ruined second Test at Auckland. It didn't seem to matter; he had proved to himself that he could score runs in a Test, and thus established his position for the rest of his all too short career. He did, incidentally, take his first three Test wickets in this second Test. The first, for the record, was J W Guy.

	Innings	N.O.	H.S.	Runs	Average	100	50
1958/59 (NZ)	2	—	141	142	71.00	1	—
To date	7	—	141	212	30.18	1	—

4 The selectors take a chance

After such a traumatic Australasian tour it was hardly surprising that Dexter took a little while to settle in to the 1959 season. He had impressed enough to be selected for the MCC against the touring Indians in the traditional first trial for the prospective Test series. He did well coming in at 192 for 3, he hammered a two hour century before the declaration, but it wasn't quite enough to get him into the Test team.

The selectors were in experimental mood, picking three new men: Taylor, Horton and Greenhough and recalling Barrington who hadn't played in a Test since 1955. They also made it clear that they thought neither Bailey nor Dexter fully fit for a five day Test. In fact both played for their counties during the Test match, but neither was able to bowl very much and it should be remembered that Dexter was considered very much an all-rounder at this stage of his career. Bailey was clearly coming to the end of his marvellous Test career, so the vacancy was there if Dexter could make good his claim.

The Indian team was not a strong one and the new England side won the first three Tests very comfortably although Horton, the all-rounder in the first two games, did nothing sensational, leaving Dexter with not unreasonable hopes of selection. Close came in at No 6 for the third Test but had little chance to shine as England were already 379 for 4. Meanwhile Dexter had a fine run in July with successive innings of 54, 117 and 91 all not out, and 92, and in the process forcing himself on the attention of the selectors. He was picked for the Test, but before that he played for the Gentlemen at Lords without distinguishing himself so that the pressure was really on him to show what he could do in the Old Trafford Test.

John Arlott's contemporary journal represents a widely held view of Dexter at the time. Arlott begins by saying that it is difficult to see that England's best eleven, picked for a hypothetical Test against Australia, could leave out Bailey, or for that matter Evans, who had just been left out in favour of Swetman. He goes on to discuss the preference of Dexter 'a spectacular but not yet proven batsman' to Close 'who may consider himself unfortunate to be left out. In the third Test he batted better than

20

was necessary, bowled better than anyone had a right to expect, and fielded well enough; since then he has made a century against the Gentlemen. It is very perplexing'. Perhaps Arlott was striving *not* to be dazzled by 'Lord Edward' with his brilliance and promise, but he is reflecting a very general contemporary view of Dexter as a 'Fenner's batsman' yet to prove himself in county cricket. Views which were soon to change.

Peter May reported sick before the fourth Test at Manchester against the Indians, and went into hospital for the operation which was to cause him so much trouble over the next two years. Cowdrey, who was originally left out to make room for Smith, took over the captaincy and started well by winning the toss. Parkhouse failed but Pullar, who looked as safe as the Bank of England, made 131 and Cowdrey 67 and at the end of the first day England were 304 for 3 and Dexter had not yet come in. It began to look as though this would not be his chance to impress, for by the time he came in they would be going for quick runs. However the side for the tour of the West Indies was not to be announced until after the fifth Test and he should get another opportunity.

On the second day Smith and Barrington took the score to 371 before Smith was out. Dexter was faced with three spinners, the leg-break bowlers Gupte and Borde, plus Nadkarni a very tight left-armer, and both *Wisden* and Arlott are in no doubt that he struggled. Arlott says that he 'clung desperately to the forward defensive lunge' and made 13 runs of 'less than his usual quality'. These 13 runs took him nearly an hour, which does sound pretty un-Dexter like. Arlott attributes this to the fact that he had yet to learn to submit to the grinding disciplines of county batting and therefore of Test batting. He says too that 'his judgement of flight and spin are unimpressive for one so clearly gifted'.

Maybe, but we must take account of the stresses of the occasion – Dexter had come in with his side well placed, but he was also playing to establish himself in the England side. Might he not have decided that this was the moment to show that he *could* submit himself to the grinding discipline? Actually there was plenty of time and the weather was perfect. Dexter finally went for 13 to Surendranath having had no sustained opportunity to show that he could master the spinners. The later batsman lashed out and England were all out for 490.

The rest of the match belongs more to Cowdrey's story than to Dexter's. India collapsed to 127 for 6 at the end of the second day. Cowdrey announced before the third day began that he would not enforce the follow-on if he had the opportunity to do so. This was logical enough as it would give the selectors an extended look at their experimental side and the holiday crowds would have more entertainment – and the decision having been taken it was sensible to announce it in advance to bring in a large Saturday crowd. But this was a diplomatic blunder as it made the Indians feel that they were being patronised, as well as being used merely as batting and bowling practice for the coming West Indies tour and understandably it put them on their mettle. India were all out for 208 and when England batted again they bowled tightly to defensive fields and set out to make England work for every run, so that when Dexter came in promoted to No 3 he was still very much on trial.

The situation put Dexter under very real pressure; he needed to make runs but he also had to make them attractively, furthermore the crowd were more than a little restive and he had a reputation for bright play to sustain. He struggled to get going and looked careworn as he did so. At the other end Parkhouse at least looked relaxed, managing to play something like his natural game. At tea England had scored at only 45 an hour, a desperately slow rate. After the break Parkhouse got out and Cowdrey and Smith whose places were not in doubt, played more freely and got out also. Then Dexter at last began to open up and play his strokes. He didn't last long but he saved a little face with a determined 45.

Barrington had nothing to lose by throwing the bat and did just that for the liveliest innings of the day. Towards the end of play Illingworth and Swetman were taking runs off every ball and Cowdrey was able to declare on 256 for 8 – a massive 547 ahead. It had been a rather absurd day's cricket, 346 runs had been scored, a wholly satisfactory figure, but the wrong people had scored them.

India batted much better in the second innings and came quite close to saving the game, Baig, a twenty-year-old Oxford freshman, made a fine brave century after being knocked out by a fast ball from Rhodes. Dexter had a good spell of bowling, eventually dismissing Baig (112) with a brilliant pick-up and throw.

Dexter had not had a bad match, but his place in the touring team was still in doubt unless the selectors took a bold decision and played him for his potential. There was a case to be made for this and an almost equally strong one for giving him another year to mature. However his name was on the selector's list of twenty-nine players who were asked to state whether they were available in the winter, but for Dexter ultimate selection would depend on how well he played in the next few weeks. The selectors had emphasised that the list was not an exclusive one and that others might play themselves into the party; in fact nobody did. As so often happens in cricket the evidence was inconclusive. Between the fourth and fifth Tests, he played four games for Sussex, and his performances were: 0,10, 0,38, 127, 7,112.

In all probability, the decisive days were August 8 and 10, when he bowled out the top half of the Lancashire order and then made a robust 112 to set up a big win against a strong county side. He would possibly have made his way back into the England side if he had failed then, but for the moment it was this performance that set his foot on the ladder.

Nevertheless when Dexter was picked for the last Test at the Oval, he still appeared to be on trial. India who were without Umrigar and Manjrekar, their two best batsmen, never got going and were all out for 140. Dexter bowled really well, in several short spells, and took 2 for 24 in 16 overs and could have got more. He had gone part of the way towards satisfying the selectors, although bowling under West Indian skies would be a very different matter. He was unlucky when England batted. Two wickets fell cheaply and Subba Row and Smith embarked on a long and rather tedious stand. Then a short shower enlivened the wicket; Subba Row got out, and Dexter and Barrington were both out before they were in, so to speak. Dexter was caught at the wicket off Surendranth for a duck, the ball coming quickly off the pitch. The later batsmen who were not depending on their batting to win selection, then made quick runs off Gupte in particular, all of which didn't put Dexter in too good a light.

These were difficult times for Dexter, leading to awkward decisions for the selectors, as India were dismissed cheaply and Dexter got no second chance to shine. Over the whole series Barrington, Cowdrey, Pullar and Smith had batted well and Dexter had had little opportunity. May would be picked if fit, and the batting line-up would be a strong one, with or without Dexter. However the selectors were willing to gamble on him and when the side was announced, Dexter was in. Bailey withdrew for business reasons, but it is probable that the selectors would have gone for Dexter anyway. They had now given him several chances and were obviously backing him as a player of pedigree. Whether they would continue to do so if he didn't excel in the West Indies was another matter.

	Innings	N.O.	H.S.	Runs	Average	100	50
1959	3	—	45	58	19.33	—	—
To date	10	—	141	270	27.00	1	1

5 'I take back all I have said'

Dexter had a nasty scare before the West Indies tour began when he contracted jaundice, and for a long time it was touch and go whether he would be fit, but he recovered just in time. On the voyage out, Peter May took him to one side and told him that he would almost certainly be playing in the first Test; there are too few preliminary matches in a West Indies tour for the team to be settled by elimination and it made sense to determine the Test side in advance, but it was thoughtful and generous of May to tell Dexter so early. Not many captains would have done so and those who liked to criticise May when he was chairman of the selectors, for his inability to communicate with the players, will be pleased to know that he was such a sympathetic leader.

A tour of the West Indies has never been an easy ride. The islands, and Guyana too, produce more cricketers to the acre than anywhere else in the world – not excluding Yorkshire! Touring sides are apt to encounter an unknown player whose natural talent enables him to score a rapid hundred or take five cheap wickets. Along with their enthusiasm and natural ability, their cricket now was tempered by what one can best describe as a robust professionalism. The grounds were small by Test Match standards, so that the players were overlooked by the spirited and well-informed crowds, commenting volubly on every aspect of the play, augmented by hundreds more perching in every tree just outside the fence. The pitches were very fast, polished till the players' reflections could be seen, but in those days, very true and predictable. The fast bowling was very fast, but for the most part not aimed at the head or body – but there would certainly be the odd flier. Batting would be a challenging business.

The MCC party had something to live down. Len Hutton's tour, six years earlier, had been a stormy business complete with a full-scale riot, a lot of visible dissent from the MCC players when decisions didn't go their way and some very hostile partisanship from the pressmen of both countries. Since then, the West Indies had been well beaten by both Australia and England, but there were signs that they were recovering their form. It would be a difficult series to win and perhaps an even more difficult one to conduct with grace and dignity.

24

The tour began with an easy win over the Windward Islands, in which Dexter didn't play. Then a heavy defeat by ten wickets at the hands of Barbados, no great surprise, since Barbados were as usual very strong, and the MCC side not yet acclimatised. MCC did get full marks for sportsmanship by playing on in the rain towards the end. Dexter's contribution was unsensational. He scored 33 and 26, and took 1 wicket for 105 but he was still selected for the Test.

England were to have rather less than their share of good luck in this series; the first misfortune was that Statham fell during those wet closing overs of the Barbados match and was too lame to play in the Test. England may have considered using Dexter as an opening partner for Trueman and packing the batting, but took the orthodox decision and played Moss, the reserve fast bowler. Illingworth and Allen completed the attack.

When England batted, Hall and Watson put everything into the attack, whistling quite a few bouncers around the ears of Pullar and Cowdrey, who resisted everything and coped very well with Ramadhin when he came on. The little spinner was by no means the threat he had been six years earlier, the long stand by May and Cowdrey at Edgbaston in 1957 had taught English batsmen to play him as an off-spinner. Watson came back and had Cowdrey caught close in by Sobers, but Barrington, England's new No 3, batted sensibly and well, while Pullar continued on his placid way. They had put on over a hundred when Pullar was run out, perhaps backing up a little slowly, and when May failed England were 162 for 3 and in some trouble on a beautiful wicket. Smith was a poor starter against fast bowling, but he survived a few near things and England were 188 for 3 at the end of the day.

Smith and Barrington began cautiously on the second day, happy to find the wicket distinctly slower. But when Ramadhin came on, Smith set about him with some enthusiasm, once even sweeping him for six. The game was beginning to go England's way when Barrington reached his hundred, but Smith got out at 251 and Dexter came in, five minutes before lunch.

The game was still nicely poised. England badly needed a score from Dexter. If he went cheaply, they would be hard put to it to reach 400 and on such an easy pitch, the West Indies would probably sail past that, and put England under pressure. The innings was also a vital one for Dexter personally – it was one of the critical moments of his career. A failure or two and Subba Row would replace him and it might be a long time before he got another chance. But the wicket was a beauty, the bowling at least halfway to being mastered, and if he *could* make a hundred . . .

Dexter was outwardly unmoved and put a shortish ball away through the covers for four, before going to lunch. His resolution was further tested after the interval. At 291, Barrington was given out, caught down the leg-side; he was taken aback by the decision and certainly the English correspondents felt that he had been well inside the ball. However, he was out and Illingworth soon followed him. At 303 for 6, things were serious. Swetman the No 8 was an unorthodox, bold batsman, not over-concerned with the textbook. In this innings, he had some luck, but battled away using his feet well, while Dexter settled down and played a succession of fine strokes, placing the ball through mid-wicket and cracking it past cover in his most opulent style.

E W Swanton commented that he reminded older watchers of Walter Hammond and, coming from him, there could be no greater compliment. When the new ball was taken, Dexter really cut loose, smashing one ball so hard through mid-off that it rebounded off the pickets more than half-way back to the bowler, and steering a flier from Watson over the slips' heads for four. When the partnership had added 123 runs and he was on 99, Dexter saw Swetman caught at the wicket, but this in no way disconcerted him. He struck one more four off Hall before the close, to complete what the *Cricketer* correspondent saw as 'a very fine century'. The last three batsmen supported him for a further hour in the morning, while he went on in the same commanding vein, taking out his bat for 136 in a total of 482.

This one majestic innings transformed Dexter's career. He was seen, henceforth, as the great white hope of English batting, and this had its effect on his confidence and his play. The English press really went to town. Brian Chapman wrote 'He has come to stay' and Charles Bray always an honest critic, even if sometimes a harsh one, went further:

I take back all I have said. On this performance, he is a really fine batsman.

In summing up the first day of the innings, Mr Swanton wrote:

He has always looked a good player against speed, and when the new ball came this evening he played a series of strokes of a power that among current batsmen even May could hardly have equalled.

If this doesn't sound breathlessly complimentary, we should remember that Swanton has always been among the more measured critics, and that May was generally regarded then, as he still is, as the very best English batsman since the war.

Some people were afraid that all this high praise might go to Dexter's head, but there is absolutely no evidence that it ever did – his feet remained firmly on the ground. The greater danger was that too much would now be expected of him, as happened to both May and Cowdrey before him, Botham and Gower after him – but it all made a welcome change from some sharp and sometimes unfair criticism in the past.

Meanwhile, the West Indies had a match to save, and they did so most efficiently after a poor start when McMorris managed to get himself run out off a no-ball. They were 102 for 3 when Barrington, of all people, had Hunte caught at the wicket. The fact that Barrington was bowling at all is an indication that England were well on top, but there could be no more calming influence in a crisis than Frank Worrell, and he and Sobers now batted for *two days* less an hour lost to rain, to take the score to 501 before Sobers was out. Worrell was by now desperately tired, and he had struggled for two hours for only 10 runs more when Alexander declared.

Nobody could know it at the time, but Worrell was surely already suffering from the early stages of leukaemia that was to claim him at the tragically young age of 42. Dexter had a lot of bowling in this innings, and got 2 wickets for 15 runs though he was perhaps fortunate to be on in the final stages when the batsmen were hitting out. He bowled 37.4 overs, the most he ever bowled in an innings, and conceded 85 runs. He had had a hard match, but had now established himself in the England team.

The team now moved on to Trinidad and beat the island team twice before the Test. The first win was a lucky one, Trinidad made a generous declaration after being well ahead on the first innings and Dexter helped the win by scoring a rapid 69. In this first match, a young slow left arm spinner called Charran Singh did well getting 5 for 57, and he was duly brought into the Test team. Statham was fit again, and England played their strongest side. The unlucky Subba Row had batted well against Trinidad, but had no chance of being included because both Dexter and Smith had batted well in the first Test.

England won the toss again, and once again Hall and Watson launched a fierce attack. England by lunch were 57 for 3, and things looked very bad indeed. Dexter was promoted above Smith, and together with Barrington met fire with fire. Dexter, in particular, brought off a succession of the most brilliant strokes into the V between mid-wicket and extra-cover, forcing Alexander to drop his fielders back to save the fours, so that the batsmen were able to push quietly for singles. It was a classic example of seizing the initiative from rampant bowlers, and Barrington was very nearly as assertive as Dexter.

By tea-time, they had added 113 in 35 overs, a tremendous rate in a crisis, and the balance of the game had swung to England, where it stayed. Soon after tea, Dexter played a relaxed drive at Singh and was caught and bowled for 77, scored in 157 minutes, but he had done his job. Smith had to face the new ball, but his vulnerability against the fast stuff was not on view, and he scored a placid unspectacular hundred in some five hours. Barrington also scored a hundred, voicing his displeasure at some short bowling from Watson, who was unofficially warned by the umpire, as was

Hall. England made 382, 306 coming from Barrington, Dexter and Smith, and it was enough.

When the West Indies batted, Trueman and Statham also served up plenty of bouncers, but were generally straighter and livelier than Hall and Watson, and reduced the home team to 45 for 5, an appalling performance on a very good wicket. There was no recovering from this. Butcher and Alexander made a very slow stand and during this period frustration built up in the crowd which was to lead to trouble. The West Indian spectator is apt to think that if you are in batting trouble, the remedy is to hit out, not to graft your way out. Butcher and Alexander fell, after a very slow stand, and at 98, the local hero, Charran Singh, was run out by a sharp throw from Dexter. There is absolutely no doubt that he was out by a yard, but for some reason, the crowd erupted at this decision. It may have been because their own Trinidad man was out or possibly because there had been heavy betting about whether the total would reach a hundred. Certainly, the crowd were packed dangerously tight and a number had taken a drink or two. Whatever the reasons, the bottles began to fly and the crowd soon spilled on to the pitch. Play was abandoned for the day and it was agreed that time should be added on the succeeding days. The match went on and there was no further disturbance.

The fourth day was an odd one. The West Indies were quickly finished off for 112, and May decided to bat again. He had plenty of time and the wicket could only get worse, it was the logical decision, but the batsmen allowed themselves to be tied down when quick runs were needed; wickets fell when they tried to hit their way out of trouble and Dexter found himself coming in at 97 for 3. He got a nasty ball from Hall, which moved off the seam and was bowled for nought. In the context of the match it meant little, but a quick fifty from him would have made good watching. England tobogganed to 133 for 7, 403 ahead and the West Indies may have had a glimmer of hope, but Illingworth and Trueman took charge. They knocked Singh off and played the new ball with assurance. May was able to declare at 230 for 9, asking the West Indies to make 501 to win or more probably, to bat for ten hours to save the game.

On the fifth day, the West Indies batted soundly and carefully, and May relied chiefly on his three spinners, though neither Illingworth nor Barrington took a wicket. He was criticised for making no use of Dexter and, indeed, with the batsmen looking secure if slow (Barrington bowled 18 overs for 15 runs) he should perhaps have tried everything. On the final day, Trueman soon had Sobers, and he and Statham went through the middle order. Kanhai and Alexander made a late stand and May at last put Dexter on. He bowled a full-toss and Kanhai unbelievably holed out at mid-wicket. Dexter rubbed it in by having Ramadhin lbw first ball. For the first time in his Test career, he was on a hat-trick, but Singh survived the

28

next ball and batted well enough for an hour until Barrington finished off the innings and the match.

England were now one up and the lead would take some clawing back. All the England bowlers had played their full part, except Illingworth, who had been bowling with an injured finger, and all the batsmen, except for May and Cowdrey, had shown good form. More importantly, the crowd troubles had been overcome, thanks in large part to the manifestly good relations between the teams.

The tourists went on to Jamaica, where May at last made a hundred, sharing in a spectacular stand of 155 in about two hours with Dexter who scored 75. Worrell was unable to play in the third Test which weakened the West Indian bowling but as things turned out this didn't matter. May won the toss for the third time and England batted on what looked to be an even better pitch than the first two. In photographs taken during this match, it is possible to detect clear reflections of the players on the pitch, and this is one of the significant differences between matches played outside England at that time and the Tests of the eighties; the bounce was even, not excessive, whereas today the batsman can never be sure whether the ball will fly at his ribs or at his head, a point ignored by those old-timers who are scornful about the use of helmets.

Hall and Watson could do little but dig it in and at first it seemed that the batsmen would survive the early onslaught but Pullar and Barrington fell, one to an outswinger and one to a flier. Then May got a real popper and Hunte dived from short-leg to take a dazzling catch. Dexter thus came in at 68 for 3 and played a most uncharacteristic game, if one were to believe all those stories about his unthinking and cavalier approach. He put his head down and played, as he was generally able to do in a crisis, and things were looking a little better when, just after tea, Hall produced another fine ball which just 'took off'. Dexter slashed, Alexander also took off and took a superb catch off a stroke which would probably have cleared first slip, if it had got that far.

Dexter had gone for 25. An exhilarated Hall now yorked Smith first ball. The next eighty minutes were fraught with danger, physical and moral. At one end Hall and then Watson, turned on the most intimidating bowling of a pretty lively series, at the other, Ramadhin teased and tormented. In all it was an excellent working-out of the theory that contrast often imposes a greater strain on the batsmen than concentrated assault. However, Cowdrey and Illingworth were equal to the demands made on them. Cowdrey batted better as his innings progressed, valiantly supported by Illingworth, Trueman and Allen. At last he was out for 114 made in nearly seven hours, the first 42 having come in about half that time. It had been a slow, but priceless innings and England's 277 was a score they would have settled for more than happily when Smith was out at 113 for 5.

Hunte fell early, Kanhai was run out, and the West Indies were 81 for 2 at the close. Dexter had bowled 6 overs for only 9 runs, a fine spell. Next day, Sobers bestrode the scene batting all day and scoring 125. No wicket fell on this third day, though McMorris was hit under the heart by Statham and had to retire, happily with no serious consequences. Dexter again bowled 6 overs, but this time he went for 29. It was the sort of thing that was apt to happen to anyone when Sobers was in form.

On the fourth day, England turned the game right round, dismissing West Indies for 353 after they had been 299 for 2. Dexter was not used, but all the other bowlers took wickets. Pullar and Cowdrey batted out the day for 65, and the game was back on an even keel with the odds on a draw.

On the fifth morning, Cowdrey played some of the best cricket of his great career. It was one of those hours in which the batsman intuitively knows what is coming before the ball is bowled. Again and again, he was in position for the hook in plenty of time and he hit 76 runs including thirteen fours in the morning session. The batsmen then seemed to become aware that Cowdrey was on the brink of a remarkable feat. Only five batsmen have scored two centuries in a match for England, and here he was on 93. He began to poke about a little, as did Pullar trying to give him the strike. After a frustrating half-hour, Pullar was lbw pushing across the line and then Cowdrey tried to cut a ball from Scarlett that was too close to his body and was caught behind for 97. It was later said that he had gloved one ball that was signalled as four leg-byes, so that he had in fact made two hundreds, but whether he would have reached the hundred if those four runs had been credited to him and on the board, can only be conjectured.

It was now England's turn to fall apart, very much as the West Indies had done on the previous day. Barrington and May were very tentative against the spinners, and when Barrington was out to Solomon, the third of the spinners to be tried, Dexter came in and didn't look very much better. He hit one four and was beginning to settle when the new ball was taken. In Watson's first over, he played an elegant late cut for four, thick-edged another four past third slip, jabbed down on a shooter and then had his leg stump torpedoed by another. It had been a momentous over and Dexter was a little unlucky. He had only made 16 and had not had much of a match. May played his biggest innings of the series, scoring 45, but nobody else got many, and England were all out for 305, leaving the West Indies to score 230 at about a run a minute. It was nicely poised, but if Allen and Statham had not added 25 for the last wicket, and used up some forty minutes, the home team would have had a relatively easy task and would probably have won.

30

As it was, McMorris was out at once, but Hunte and Kanhai began to go for the runs, Hunte being particularly sparkling, scoring 40 out of 48. When Trueman got through him, Sobers came in and batted brightly. The West Indies were up with the clock and looking good when Dexter made one of his timely interventions. Kanhai played a defensive push to him at cover, and apparently had no thought of running, but Sobers went, was sent back and saw Dexter keeping his head admirably, throw quickly and accurately to the bowler Statham, who easily ran Sobers out.

Thereafter, Kanhai was the only man who could win the game for his side until he was unfortunately seized with cramp just when he was going well. Unbelievably, the umpires were unsure of the law about claiming a runner, and referred the matter to May. Even more unbelievably, the normally courteous May refused. One can only assume that he himself was in such discomfort (he was about to withdraw from the tour, though nobody was aware of this at the time) that he was unable to think it through. Kanhai had a swing and was bowled and Alexander settled for the draw. It is fair to say that Kanhai would almost certainly not have been able to win the match on his own, and that May's refusal made no difference, but it is also fair to say that Sobers and Kanhai together might very well have pulled it off, and that Dexter's coolness under pressure had been decisive. He had been one of the best fielders throughout the tour and this set the seal on his performance.

Dexter scored a brilliant 107 with six sixes and nine fours in just ninety minutes against the Leeward Islands. But all else was overshadowed by the news that May's operation wound had opened up again, and had in fact been troubling him so badly for weeks that he would have to abandon the tour temporarily at least. This explained both his loss of form and his uncharacteristic behaviour during the Test and there was nothing but sympathy for him. England decided not to send for another player – Parks was available and on the spot coaching in Trinidad if wanted. Cowdrey took over the captaincy and Subba Row came into the side. He deserved the promotion, but it would put more pressure on Dexter for he and Barrington were now perceived as the leading middle-order batsmen.

Cowdrey proved as lucky with the toss as May had been and he started in the same solid batting form as he had displayed at Kingston. Solid was the word, for he and Pullar went slowly against some indifferent bowling and English watchers hoped that they were not putting too much pressure on Dexter and the later batsmen. However, England were one up and time was on their side as was the weather, 75 minutes being lost at the outset. It was almost teatime before Pullar got out with the score on 73. Barrington was suffering from a virus and Subba Row, not Dexter, came in next, a clear indication of Cowdrey's intentions. He batted pleasantly till he fell to Sobers, and Cowdrey and Barrington saw out the day, though Barrington suffered a nasty crack on the elbow.

Cowdrey got the faintest of touches against Hall and was out at once on the second day and Dexter, yet again, was batting in a crisis, at 152 for 3. He came close to playing on, but otherwise looked very safe and was soon handling the fast bowlers with a confidence that bordered on contempt. He straight-drove both Hall and Watson, and almost took cover's leg off with a square cut. At the other end, however, things were going badly wrong. Barrington had looked increasingly uncomfortable and finally had to go off for attention to his elbow, and Smith, Illingworth and Swetman all fell for virtually nothing. Well as Dexter was playing, the score went to 175 for 6. It was left to Allen who had batted admirably throughout the tour, to stay with Dexter until well beyond lunch. Dexter was taking fours all around the wicket and a recovery was under way when still seeking to dominate the bowling, he went for a hook off Hall, fractionally misjudged it and was brilliantly taken at square-leg by Hunte for 39. It had been as good an innings as he had played on the tour, but he had been virtually compelled to go on attacking and it had not quite come off. Barrington came back, but was very uncomfortable. He stayed while Allen went to his first Test fifty and England finally reached 295, better than it might have been but barely adequate on these wickets and with the West Indian batsmen.

But the West Indies batted no better, the third day was spoiled by rain, and England's over-rate on the fourth was miserably slow, by the standards of the day. Only Sobers, who was close to his best form, batted well, but never quite enough to run away with the game. Walcott, who had been recalled with the idea of boosting the scoring rate, failed to get a start and at the end of the fourth day they were 332 for 4. A draw was inevitable.

On the fifth day Worrell and Sobers were out immediately and with them went any faint hope of a big West Indian score and an English panic. The later batsmen made a few and Alexander declared at 402 for 8, but it was all too late. Dexter had had only 5 overs which had cost 20 runs. He had not been at his best, and Cowdrey, trying to contain the batsmen could not afford him. England went in with some eight hours to play. The openers made a good start, but Cowdrey was stumped at 40. He had previously taken the interesting decision to bat Dexter at No 3, Subba Row and Barrington were both nursing injuries, and the move was a logical one, but it is worth noting that from now on Dexter was the acknowledged England No 3, except when Barrington was in prime form. Both of them, totally dissimilar as they were, preferred the third place and the batting generally had a more positive look when they batted higher. Certainly Dexter, forceful as he was, never needed to be protected.

32

In this match Dexter opened discreetly against the spinners and when Hall came back he treated him with such contempt that, by the end of the day, Alexander had recourse to his two veterans, Walcott and Worrell, a clear indication that Dexter had mastered the attack. In fairness, it must be said that Watson, Hall's fast bowling partner was injured, and that any fast bowler looks better if he is bowling in harness. In the morning Dexter played a patient waiting game, batting in the most canny fashion against Worrell, Singh and Scarlett and making only 30 before lunch. This slow build-up was an indication that he was totally confident of his ability to assemble a big innings and well aware that he was the man to steer England to safety.

When Hall took the new ball after lunch, Dexter flicked a really fast half-volley to leg for four and immediately Hall's head drooped and he knew that he was mastered. The tough experienced Worrell bowled very tightly for half an hour or so until Dexter drove him through the covers, and he too seemed to know that for this day at least, he had met his master. Subba Row joined in the revels and together they took the score to the safety of 258 for 2. When he had reached his hundred with a terrific straight drive to the screen, Dexter seemed likely to cut loose altogether but he fell to a miraculous catch by Worrell off a drive that appeared to be going first bounce to the boundary. The bowler was Walcott, so the two West Indian veterans had the satisfaction of removing this new threat. It was a fitting end to a fine innings of 110, not one of Dexter's fastest but exactly what was required.

Mr Swanton, at the end of the match, summed up Dexter's overall performance in measured terms:

From the first innings one saw him play in Barbados, it seemed that Dexter was bound to make a great many runs on this tour. He was playing so very straight, his judgement of length was so certain and, of course, the power of his strokes was prodigious.

A glowing tribute, and in marked contrast to the comments passed by some people (not Swanton) only one year earlier. The wheel turns rapidly in cricket.

Subba Row completed his hundred before the close which came at 334 for 8; England had saved the game with honour and some distinction, and could do no worse than share the series. However, they now suffered a double blow. May had been hanging on, hoping against hope for a recovery, but he had to acknowledge defeat and went home; in fact, he missed the whole of the 1960 season too. Brian Statham had also to go home. His young son was very ill indeed, and after a most worrying time, he had no alternative but to ask for his release, which could not, of course, be refused. This brought in Moss, a great trier, as he had shown in

Bridgetown but less penetrative than Statham, giving the West Indies the chance to run away with things.

Meanwhile, Swetman had been keeping a little untidily and hadn't been in the runs since his excellent innings in the first Test. The MCC management decided that the time had come to call on Parks; this seemed a little hard on Andrew, who had done nothing wrong, but there was everything to be said for lengthening the batting line-up, as May's illness had changed everything. Parks scored a hundred against Berbice in the only match played between the fourth and fifth Tests. It was a faintly ludicrous affair on a very easy wicket, on which the first seven MCC batsmen all made fifties, but it did give Parks, who made 183, useful practice in the middle.

Cowdrey won the toss, yet again, and he himself batted as elegantly and as powerfully as at Kingston. Pullar was out early and Dexter came in to lead the way in a vigorous attack on the bowling. Cowdrey was content to give him his head, and he batted without error, hitting four after four in the morning session. In the afternoon Cowdrey got going and Dexter took a breather while the captain handled the fast bowlers with skilful timing and grace. Ramadhin was brought on to arrest the flow of runs, but Dexter was his master on the day, coming down the wicket to drive him to the sight-screen. The score at tea was 179 for 1, and it seemed that England might make almost any score, but this series wasn't like that. Dexter developed a mild cramp after tea which first slowed him down and then led him into error against Sobers as his concentration wavered. He tried to lift a googly over mid-on, but miscued and was taken by the bowler, Sobers then got Cowdrey to prop at one, only to be caught by Alexander diving in front of him – a superb catch. Dexter had made 76, and Cowdrey 119.

England now fell away yet again, and 210 for 1 became 393 all out, with only Barrington (89) and Parks (43) making substantial scores. When the West Indies batted, Hunte hooked at Trueman, missed and was hit on the head. He had to retire and Alexander decided to come in himself, a curious decision when the need was for quick runs. McMorris, never a lucky batsman, was run out when Trueman deflected an Alexander drive on to the stumps and the West Indies were off to a sticky start.

The clouds opened on the third day and two hours' play was lost; moreover, England maintained a slow over-rate. Cowdrey was in no doubt about the objective and, as before, he was reluctant to use Dexter's bowling very much. However, when Hunte duly plastered, returned and embarked on a late stand with Ramadhin, Cowdrey called on Dexter, who very soon had the little man caught at slip and followed this by sitting Hall on his backside, as the players put it, by serving him up a bouncer. This caused both Hall and the crowd immense amusement and, incidentally, demonstrated Dexter's increasing confidence. It showed that he didn't

34

fear retaliation, and he was ready to show that he didn't treat Test matches with undue solemnity, but perhaps he would not have risked this if he had not already played a couple of really solid innings to demonstrate his commitment.

England went in again 55 ahead, after Alexander had declared with 8 wickets down and they tumbled into trouble. Hall despite a badly strained side, opened the bowling at half-pace, and Cowdrey, to the horror of the English camp, placed a slow half-volley straight into short-leg's hands. This occurred with some 4 overs to go on the fourth day and for once Dexter was protected by a night-watchman. Allen was the obvious choice and was able to bat for an hour on the fifth morning, and when he was run out, Dexter joined Pullar for his last innings of the series. He batted quite beautifully, hitting Ramadhin for fours on both sides of the wicket, and 'pasted' Worrell through the covers 'as hard as even he has hit a ball on this tour' to quote Mr Swanton. But Dexter lost Pullar, Subba and Barrington while all this was happening and then he himself was run out while on 47 when Hunte recovered from a misfield and threw the wicket down with unerring accuracy. Dexter was not often at fault between the wickets but with the score at 148 for 6, this looked like being a calamitously expensive mistake.

Now the selectors' move in recruiting Parks was justified, for he came in and played with the utmost confidence. He and Smith went quietly along until the new ball was due, and a short shower fell just at that moment. Alexander had to gamble on the new ball, even though Hall was unfit and the shine would soon be wiped off. But Smith and Parks hit it to all parts of the ground, virtually saving the match by nightfall. On the last day, there was a sharp little argument about the timing of a declaration. Walter Robins, the England manager, was a consistent advocate of brighter cricket and wanted Cowdrey to make a declaration which would at least give the West Indies the ghost of a chance. However Cowdrey, with the full support of his team, took the view that they had battled for twenty-nine days to reach the point where they were about to become the first England side to return victorious from the West Indies, and he was not going to throw the other side a lifeline which they didn't deserve.

Dexter whole-heartedly supports this decision in his autobiography, but Robins never really forgave Cowdrey. Cowdrey finally declared when Parks had got his 100 and Smith had managed to get himself out to Hunte, of all people. The match ended in anti-climax, with Worrell and Sobers batting breezily against the joke bowlers and Pullar taking his only Test wicket.

It had been a great series and Dexter who had gone out as a rising star in some people's eyes, a lucky young man in the eyes of others, returned as England's leading middle-order batsman. He topped the averages very comfortably and from now on was expected to lead the way. It was not yet apparent that Barrington was also going to dominate the bowlers in his own very individual style.

	Innings	N.O.	H.S.	Runs	Average	100	50
1959/60	9	1	136	526	65.75	2	2
To date	19	1	141	796	44.22	3	3

6 In a minor key

Dexter began the 1960 season in tremendous form though he had every excuse not to. He had just finished a really strenuous tour and his first county championship match began just one month after the end of the fifth Test. To add further pressure he was now the captain of Sussex at the age of twenty-five after only one full season of county cricket. It was a lot to ask, and several of the West Indies party did start poorly – indeed Barrington was so out of touch that he was left out of the side for the first Test at Birmingham.

Dexter's scores in the first four county matches were: 23, 93, 18, 133, 96, 76, 4, 151 not out, totalling 594 by May 13 at an average of 85. He seemed to have an excellent chance of completing his thousand runs before the end of May, but he had a poor match for the MCC against the South African touring team, getting only 9 and 2 and there was no fixture in which he could play in the three days immediately following that match. He completed his thousand on June 6 when he made another hundred (105) against Middlesex. He was undoubtedly in great form.

The South Africans had been having a trying time; they encountered some anti-apartheid demonstrations, but these had not yet become a major issue. More critically in strictly cricketing terms, they had picked Geoffrey Griffin, a twenty year old fast bowler, who had been no-balled for throwing in two domestic matches some eighteen months earlier. After the events in Australia this was an insensitive and risky selection and it inevitably led to trouble. After getting through three matches without being called, Griffin fell foul of the umpires in the MCC match, the most exposed occasion possible short of a Test. When the tourists played at Nottingham he was called several times for throwing and also for dragging his foot. The tour managers were in real difficulty. They had only two genuinely fast men, Griffin and Adcock, and they could hardly afford to leave him out. They packed Griffin off to Alf Gover's cricket school to work on his action and then picked him for the Test with their hearts in their mouths. England picked Walker and Barber, both all-rounders, instead of Barrington and the injured Allen.

Among the great fascinations of cricket are the individual duels within the context of the team struggle. In this 1960 series the cricket world was on the edge of its seat waiting to see whether Dexter, the enterprising and classical stroke-maker, could get on top of Tayfield and Goddard, respectively the game's best off-spinner (now that Laker had gone) and the meanest defensive bowler on the international scene. Other bowlers, notably the genuinely fast Adcock joined in the battle, but it was the attempt to hit the unhittable bowlers that was the prime focus of interest.

A side in trouble can usually be sure that its captain will lose the toss, and McGlew lost this one. Adcock got Cowdrey early and Dexter came in. He was now the established No 3 at least until May returned and great things were expected of him. He started well, looking for and getting runs even off Trevor Goddard. Griffin meanwhile was concentrating on bowling correctly and by bowling well within himself he avoided being no-balled, but he was no threat either. Dexter scored quite freely off all the bowlers before lunch, but then the picture changed.

Dexter was having to play very positively to get the upper hand against Tayfield. However the bowler won their first round by tying Dexter down completely until the batsman got a little impatient and played too soon at a slower ball and was bowled for 52. Pullar was already out to Goddard and the score was 100 for 3. England had to mount a recovery operation and did so, but it wasn't very exciting. Smith and Subba Row were sound enough players, but not conspicuously attractive ones. They batted out the day to finish at 175 for 3 off 98 overs. Smith fell early on the second day and although Parks seemed determined to get on with things he, like Dexter, had to take account of the realities of the situation, namely that Tayfield, Adcock and Goddard were all bowling accurately and well. He scored only 35 in two hours and none of the later batsmen could make better progress. England were all out for 292 and it was South Africa's turn to show if they could do better.

Trueman and Statham had the first 3 wickets down for 40 and South Africa were in all sorts of trouble. The last two experienced batsmen, McLean and Waite, came together. The former played one or two fine strokes but then he lofted a hook off Trueman and was marvellously caught by Statham with a running catch off a ball coming over his shoulder – the most difficult kind of all. South Africa were 114 for 5 at the close with Waite and O'Linn hanging on by their eyebrows. They struggled on between the showers on the Saturday, but Illingworth put in a fine tight spell and got them all out for 186, leaving England with a comfortable lead.

Pullar had broken a bone in his arm in the first innings and was to bat only if required. England started with their reserve opener Subba Row and Cowdrey who was out for a duck. Dexter came in and immediately began to bat forcefully, hitting Goddard in a way that few batsmen ever managed. He hooked him for four and took two more superb boundaries through the off-side off his back foot. He was obviously determined to get on top of this tight accurate attack, but all too soon for the enraptured spectators he got another riser from Adcock and gloved it into his wicket and he was out for 26 spectacular runs. He may have been attacking a little too early, for Subba Row and Parks were quickly out and England were 74 for 4, with Pullar unlikely to make much of a contribution.

The crisis was overcome by the usual sturdy performance from the England tail, enlivened by some fluent hitting from Trueman and Statham. Trueman in particular let fly, taking 16 in an over off Tayfield and they had added 45 before Trueman swung once too often. Statham had a swish at Tayfield while Walker propped at the other end. Pullar did come in to bat although it seemed unnecessary with England 300 ahead, particularly so when Statham gave his wicket away in an attempt to protect Pullar from further injury. Statham, Trueman and Illingworth then ate their way through the South African batting. Only McLean and Waite got past twenty and England won by exactly 100 runs. Dexter had bowled 6 overs for 4 runs.

Griffin had not been no-balled during the Test but he was called again in the Hampshire match and the crisis was resurrected and unresolved. Barrington came back for Pullar and Moss replaced Barber to make up a 'Lords' attack' of four seamers including Dexter. Once again Cowdrey failed when England batted and Dexter came in at 7 for 1. Almost at once Griffin was no-balled by umpire Lee twice in succession, his next ball, delivered pretty circumspectly, was hammered through the covers by Dexter. The young man was on the rack.

The players were off and on the field all afternoon as the light came and went, but Dexter played a succession of fine strokes, undisturbed by the interruptions and the intermittent calling of Griffin. When he got out, it was in an attempt to get on top of Adcock, on the day the best-looking of the bowlers. Dexter tried to drive him and was picked up at second slip by McLean, for 56. Barrington and Subba Row played out time and then went on for another hour on the second day.

The cricket was dull and the chief interest lay in the continued scrutiny of Griffin's action. From time to time umpire Lee would call him, but few spectators were able to detect any difference between the deliveries which were called and those which were not. It looked as though the umpires had discussed the point and decided to make their views known to the South African captain without calling every ball, as they probably felt entitled to do. Adcock took two wickets with the new ball, but when he tired, Smith began to play more fluently against the slower bowlers and was on the verge of his century when Griffin had him caught behind.

This had been the last ball of an over. Walker hit two sixes and a single off the next over, and was bowled by Griffin off the first ball of his next over, so that Griffin was now on a hat-trick, though few people on the ground actually realised it. Trueman, the next man in, certainly wasn't aware of it and aimed a haymaker at the next ball, which bowled him. Griffin had his hat-trick, in what was to be his last Test.

Cowdrey declared at the overnight score of 362 for 8. The weather continued overcast, favouring the talented England seamers, whom most of the South Africans lacked the experience and class to deal with. Trueman, who had had a very hard match at the Oval earlier in the week, wasn't quite at his best, but Statham bowled a wonderful spell of 12-5-36-5 in the morning session, and South Africa were shot out for 152. Cowdrey may have hesitated before asking them to follow on, but his bowlers would be able to rest on Sunday and time might not be on his side with so much rain about. He put them in again and Statham bowled McGlew before rain drove them all off at five o'clock.

On the Monday Statham was again in glorious form and a rested Trueman looked more like himself. Once again wickets fell steadily and the innings and the match ended soon after lunch. Dexter hadn't got on in the first innings, but this time he bowled 4 overs and took 2 wickets. There followed a sad episode. It was at that time the custom to stage an exhibition match if a Test ended early on either the third or the fourth day, and it was this exhibition which effectively ended Griffin's career. He was now bowling at umpire Lee's end, which meant that it was Syd Buller's task to judge his action. He took a stern and uncompromising view of his duty and he clearly believed that Griffin's basic action was a throw. He scrutinised his first two deliveries with care and then called the next three and was clearly ready to call every one thereafter. McGlew was in a dilemma about even getting the over finished, but Griffin finished it bowling underarm and didn't bowl again on the tour, although he played in a number of county games as a batsman. He had everyone's sympathy.

All the furore over Griffin had obscured the fact that England had won two pretty comfortable victories over a strongish South African side. In due course they would be looking for a team to take on the Australians next year, and looking in particular for a spin attack. But the priority was to make sure of the series.

Dexter had a poor match in the third Test at Trent Bridge. Cowdrey won the eighth England toss in succession and together with Subba Row he made the best start of the series so far. Adcock beat the bat more than once, but as he tired the batsmen looked happier, till Tayfield came on and bowled Subba with his arm-ball. Once again the stage was set for a battle between Dexter and Tayfield, but it wasn't to be, as Adcock immediately bowled Dexter for 3 straight after lunch. It still seemed that England

40

would make a good score; the wicket was benign and Barrington began in good form, but he lost Cowdrey and Smith to Goddard, and Parks ran himself out in rather casual fashion. Thereafter, it was up to the all-rounders to give Barrington what support they could. The score struggled to 287, better than had seemed probable, but not enough.

It turned out to be more than enough. Trueman took two quick wickets, Goddard was run out, and Statham came very close to a hat-trick when after he had dismissed McLean and Wesley with consecutive balls, Fellows-Smith very nearly played the next one into his wicket. Trueman then scythed through the tail and South Africa were all out for 88, their lowest score in England since 1924. The follow-on figure in those days was 150 and Cowdrey put them in again. South Africa lost three wickets that night and another match looked like ending early.

On the third day, McGlew and O'Linn saw the openers Trueman and Statham off, and suddenly looked completely at ease against the rest of the attack. The transformation was positively dramatic, but alas, the stand ended equally dramatically, when they went for a quick single and McGlew collided, quite accidentally, with Moss the bowler, and was run out. Cowdrey would clearly have liked to withdraw the appeal, but it couldn't be done, the appeal had been made in good faith, and the obstruction had not been wilful. McGlew had to go and although O'Linn fought most valiantly for 98, and Waite, batting with a dislocated finger, made a very brave 60, they were all out for 247, and England required only 49 to win. There was half an hour to go, and some people thought that they should go for the runs that night just in case it rained for the next two days, but Cowdrey declined to take any risk. It is interesting that the advocates of adventure all thought that Cowdrey should take Dexter in with him.

Some hours were lost on Monday morning, and Cowdrey must have had some anxious moments, but the skies cleared by three o'clock and they were able to take the field. Cowdrey got out with the scores level and Dexter had to come in. He watched Adcock bowl a maiden to Subba Row, then himself mishooked a catch and was out for a duck. This made no difference to the match, or to anybody's opinion of Dexter. England were now three up, despite May's absence and with no major contribution from Cowdrey or Dexter. They were manifestly the stronger side, but they were also having most of the luck.

The first two days at Old Trafford were washed out, but England's luck continued when Cowdrey won the toss again and decided to bat. South Africa had a lot to do to win in three days and retrieve their reputation. This time Pullar and Subba Row opened to give Cowdrey more freedom to play his strokes at No 4. Pullar was out early and yet again Dexter had to establish the innings before he could cut loose. However he wasted very little time on embarking on what was to become one of those brilliant cameo innings which is remembered with nostalgia and regret.

Dexter started with firm but in no way extravagant strokes, but when Tayfield came on he set about him as though he had decided that this was the day when he was going to win their personal duel. He hit him for three fours and a six in the space of two overs and the long anticipated confrontation was getting really dramatic. The contemporary comments of John Arlott and EW Swanton are fascinating insights into the professional critical view of Dexter. First Arlott:

There is about Dexter's cricket a quality which smacks of the Regency. When he hits the ball, there is no question of checking the stroke sufficiently to change it if necessary; once he has committed himself he goes right through with the full swing to the end.

Then Swanton:

. . . he began against Tayfield with two controlled short-arm hooks. When Tayfield responded with a fuller length, Dexter made a series of drives of which Hammond would have been proud. From one, mid-off unashamedly removed his hand.

Dexter was compared with Hammond more often than was any other post-war batsman. They shared a graceful power and a general unwillingness to be tied down. Compton also had the same qualities, but he had that touch of unorthodoxy that set him apart. Of the more modern players, Botham is more impetuous, and Gatting rather less 'over' the ball, though in his treatment of the spinners he sometimes recalls Hammond.

Yet again the Tayfield-Dexter duel was brought to an end when another bowler intervened; Pothecary brought Dexter down with a good length ball which did just enough to beat his forward stroke. He was applauded in as though he had made a hundred, not 38, and Cowdrey took over the attacking role. He hit Adcock for two beautiful fours, hooked at the next and was caught off his glove. It just wasn't the stroke-player's day, but neither was it anyone else's. Adcock and Goddard, who had the remarkable figures of 24-16-26-3, wrapped up the innings for 260. Only Barrington reliable as ever, held them up with a sensible 76.

260 was a vulnerable score but the South Africans were a pretty vulnerable batting side, and Trueman and Statham now sliced into them yet again. In no time at all they were 62 for 4, and even the follow-on could not be ruled out. Roy McLean had had four successive failures, but he now played South Africa's best innings of the summer. At his finest, as now, he could bat like an angel. He hit Allen for a succession of brilliant fours and

42

when Dexter came on, he played him with the same ease. O'Linn, a patient batsman, joined him in a stand of 102 of which O'Linn made only 14, and they steered South Africa out of trouble. In what was now a three day match there was little chance of a result once the follow-on had been avoided. McLean made 109, and the total reached 229, only 31 behind England.

Subba Row had broken his thumb trying to bring off a catch in the slips, and Cowdrey had to open once again. He lost Pullar early and this brought Dexter in. The only chance of a finish was for these two to score off everything and for Cowdrey to declare at lunchtime, but Cowdrey, just after hitting Adcock for an effortless six, played down the wrong line to him and was bowled. Dexter and Illingworth played out the day, but both were out early on the last morning. Dexter driving Pothecary to cover, on 22 found McLean who took a really excellent catch inches from the ground. Padgett, playing in his first Test, failed and just for a moment England at 71 for 5 were in trouble but Barrington, even though he was lame and batting with a runner, was equal to the challenge and made a fighting 35. Cowdrey understandably played it very safe since he knew that Statham was under the weather and would not be at his best if he could bowl at all. South Africa were set to make 185 in 105 minutes and the game ended in a quiet draw.

Dexter was not having a very good series and he must have enjoyed even more the bank holiday match against Middlesex when he produced one of his finest all-round performances. He scored 157 in an innings characterised by *Wisden* as 'sound yet attractive', and when Middlesex were batting to save the game, he took 7 for 24 in 18 overs, statistically his best bowling performance.

At the Oval Cowdrey yet again won the toss, but his batsmen totally failed to take advantage of it. Cowdrey himself was out early and Dexter made a most cautious start. For once, he seemed to be setting out his stall for a big innings, but this diligent approach seldom paid off for him. He saw Pullar, Barrington and Mike Smith get out and finally collected a very good break-back ball from Adcock which bowled him for 28. England were in trouble, this time they couldn't get out of it and they were all out for 155.

The innings lasted into the second day due to time being lost to rain and bad light, but conditions improved and several of the South Africans played better than at any other time during the series. The attack looked for a time to be short of inspiration, but Dexter came on and bowled an excellent spell. He moved the ball both ways in the air and achieved pace off the pitch. It was one of those days when he really did look like the answer to England's need of an all rounder, and his contribution to the containment of South Africa in this match was certainly very important.

But for a variety of reasons he never subsequently became the integral part of the attack that Trevor Bailey had been, perhaps it was unreasonable to expect it. He tied the batsmen down on this second day and then dismissed Fellows-Smith and McLean with successive balls – both off-cutters – and once again he was on a hat-trick, which Waite only averted by scrambling the ball away off the edge. Dexter did get Waite out in the end, but not until he had made 77 and the score was 252 for 5. England should really have got the South Africans out for a score of 300 or so, but a lot of catches went down and Tayfield and McKinnon had an invaluable late stand by which time all the bowlers were thoroughly tired. South Africa eventually made 419 and England for the first time were in danger of losing the match.

The fourth day was almost unreal. Over the previous few years, England supporters had become used to some pretty dreary Test cricket, especially when England were behind. However Cowdrey was in one of those golden moods which sometimes visited him, and he and Pullar rolled back the years and made 290 in opulent pre-war style, Cowdrey scoring 88 before lunch. Dexter might have been expected to make something of this situation – an easy wicket, tired bowlers and plenty of batting to come – but he seemed to be bewildered by the opportunity, or by Tayfield, and made only an uncomfortable 16 in an hour before Tayfield bowled him through the gate. Their promised duel had never really come to life, but the bowler had had the last laugh. The game rather died on its feet after Dexter was out and England were 380 for 4 at the close, only 116 ahead and unable to take risks. On the last day, the later batsmen scraped together enough runs to enable Cowdrey to declare and set the improbable target of 216 in three hours, but the rain came and ruined what might, just possibly, have been a good finish.

It had been an interesting series though not a wildly exciting one. Several South Africans had been shown to be past their best and England hadn't, perhaps, done enough rebuilding. Dexter had had a moderate series. He had often looked like taking charge and playing a big fast innings, but somehow it hadn't happened. He was however now the established No 3 and there were intriguing possibilities about his bowling.

	Innings	N.O.	H.S.	Runs	Average	100	50
1960	9	—	56	241	26.77	—	2
To date	28	1	141	1037	38.40	3	5

7 To the very brink of triumph

England didn't tour abroad in the winter of 1960-1, although there was an interesting B tour to New Zealand, in which eleven past or future England players took part. Cricket lovers around the world were enthralled by a superbly exciting series in Australia, where the West Indies although losing three games to one made countless friends by their enterprising play and good sportsmanship. The effect on England and Dexter was twofold; the Tests between England and Australia in 1961, and more particularly when England next toured in 1962-3, had a lot to live up to in terms of attractive play. Dexter was expected to lead the way in this – he was indisputably the handsomest batsman of the new English generation, a considerable burden for anyone to bear.

Unfortunately Dexter made none too good a start to the new season. He was carrying a knee injury and only played in five Sussex matches before the first Test at Edgbaston. The only game in which he achieved any sort of success was the bank holiday fixture at Lord's, when he scored 47 and 65. Dexter was obviously in the selectors' mind as a future England captain when they asked him to lead the MCC against Australia at the end of May, but he had to refuse on account of his injury; Colin Cowdrey took on the job. However, in spite of his lack of county success, Dexter was picked for the Test subject only to his fitness – and John Edrich was asked to understudy in case Dexter had to drop out.

The Australians had an unfortunate start to their tour with rain following them around the country. The opening match at Worcester was reduced to brief snatches of play between showers and their second match at Derby was virtually washed out. The first day of the Yorkshire match was lost to rain and the next two played on a pudding of a pitch. At last the Australians' luck changed when they beat Lancashire in glorious sunshine with both Harvey and Burge making hundreds. Then at the Oval the touring camp was immensely encouraged by a very fine innings from Bill Lawry. Lawry was a tall left-hander who had never played Test cricket, but had been included on the tour party on the strength of his consistent batting for Victoria. Against Surrey he made 165 in a total of 341 for 7 and it was apparent that Australia had a new star. Lawry justified this optimism by establishing himself as the foundation stone of Australian batting for the next ten years. He made another hundred against Cambridge and a third in the MCC match, which the Australians won with ease after a very positive declaration from Benaud.

In all of their later pre-Test matches the tourists were only in danger of defeat once, in the Sussex match, which immediately preceeded the first Test. In this O'Neill had to retire with an injured knee sustained during the Sussex first innings and without his batting they needed 9 runs to win with only 1 wicket to fall when time was called. For the Australians only one question mark remained; Benaud was suffering from a shoulder injury and although he would play in the first Test, he was nowhere nearly fully fit and might not be able to bowl a full ration of overs. O'Neill eventually reported fit and the Australians were able to line up their strongest team for the Test – the same that had defeated the West Indies, plus Lawry. They would take a lot of beating!

England were able to choose from all the most talented players in the country with the vital exception of Peter May, who had played in most of Surrey's matches but was doubtful of his fitness for a five day game. He scored 153 against Somerset on the day before the Test and could clearly hope to be fit for the second Test at Lords. The England batting was Pullar, Subba Row, Dexter (or Edrich), Cowdrey (the captain), plus Barrington and Mike Smith in for May. Trueman and Statham were still the best opening bowlers in the country and at Edgbaston they would be supported by the off-spinners Allen and Illingworth, though on another ground a third seamer would have been played, particularly as Dexter (if he played) would not be up to much bowling. The only new cap was John Murray, the Middlesex wicket-keeper.

Although the weather had been fine for some weeks, it was very overcast on the first day. Cowdrey must have thought about taking the field when he won the toss, but he reasoned that the wicket would only get worse and with two spinners in the side he would rather be bowling than batting on the fifth day.

The wicket looked to be slow and even paced when Pullar and Subba Row started, but the players were soon off the field as the first shower fell. When play resumed, the shower appeared to have enlivened the pitch. There was no-one better than Alan Davidson at exploiting the least bit of help such as this and he created uncertainty in Pullar's mind and then bowled him with what looked very like a half-volley. Dexter came in at 36 for 1, an awkward moment. He made a good start with a cracking hook for 4 off Davidson and a handsome stroke through the covers off Mackay – it was all too good to be true. Mackay got one to pop and Dexter, trying to keep it down, only managed to deflect it to Davidson at short-leg. He was out for 10. Mackay, a medium-paced 'wobbler' had found a wicket to suit him and he troubled everyone. Subba Row and Cowdrey survived with difficulty until lunch, but then it rained again. There was a brief spell of play after lunch and then another shower causing the pitch to get crankier all the time.

Cowdrey was out in the next spasm of play to Misson and then Mackay took three wickets in four balls – the feat is as rare as the hat-trick in Test cricket and his victims were a distinguished group: Barrington, Smith and Subba Row. More importantly, he had broken the back of the England innings. England at 122 for 6 had Illingworth and Murray at the crease and were in the deepest trouble.

This was no easy moment for Murray to make his first Test appearance, but he was an accomplished batsman who would play some fine innings for England. He and Illingworth settled in and saw off Davidson who was having a poor day. Benaud came on next; he was reluctant to do much bowling because of his injury, but he now did the trick and got rid of both batsmen. Trueman and Allen were left to bat out the day, the former hitting a thumping six off the tiring Mackay, who didn't often have such a long stint.

The next day the clouds were much higher and there was every prospect of an uninterrupted day on a good batting wicket. Australia were well placed and things looked even better for them when Allen was soon run out and Trueman holed out off Benaud. England were all out for 195, Benaud had wound the innings up efficiently, but Mackay with 4 for 57 had taken the important wickets.

Australia's new opening pair, Lawry and McDonald made a sound start until Statham had McDonald feeling for one and caught at gully. Lawry took no risks and was looking every inch a Test batsman, as indeed he was to do throughout his career. He had progressed to 57 without problems when he edged a ball from Illingworth, which may possibly have pitched in a footmark, and gave Murray his first Test catch. O'Neill joined Harvey and an already satisfactory scoring rate now got quite out of hand. They were Australia's finest attacking batsmen, running well between the wickets, alternating rapid singles and thumping fours till Cowdrey could scarcely set a field.

O'Neill's knee had clearly mended very quickly, unfortunately the same couldn't be said of Dexter's. He was doing a good job in the covers, but the particular strain of bowling was too much of a hazard and he was only able to bowl five overs. This gave Cowdrey a further problem in that his only other bowler was Barrington, and he dared not risk him against two fine batsmen in full flow. Australia scored 149 between lunch and tea, positive cricket indeed. It is fair to say though that England bowled forty overs in the two hours, something which would not happen today when a side was being hammered.

Virtue was rewarded after tea when Statham had O'Neill playing on, for 82, and although Harvey went on to make a magnificent hundred (his fifth against England) both he and Burge fell to Allen before the close when Australia were 359 for 5, made in 330 minutes.

Saturday was much like the first day with play being interrupted by frequent showers. England's bowlers, understandably weary after their marathon, made much less of the conditions than had Mackay. Cowdrey predictably set very defensive fields from the outset. Davidson fell pretty early, but Mackay was again at the centre of the action, scoring 64 in his own highly individual style. He would never make the coaching manuals, but he could be the most irritatingly effective batsman against anything but the best of the spinners and he nudged and nurdled away against the quicker men. He easily outscored Simpson and saw Benaud play a typically aggressive knock of 36 before declaring at 516 for 9.

England now had an awkward fifty minutes to face before the close of play, right at the beginning of their long climb to wipe off a deficit of 321. Australia's total was their highest in England since 1934 when they made 701 at the Oval, but why had Benaud not declared earlier? He probably estimated that because the light was poor an appeal would have been successful sooner or later had he sent England in to bat. As it happened, yet another shower brought the players off after just two uneventful overs.

By Monday the pitch had recovered, but the clouds were still low and English supporters feared another fraught day. However the pitch was very dead indeed and Misson and Davidson found no early life. Simpson came on as first change which suggested that Benaud was still carrying his shoulder injury, unless he was waiting for Dexter. Subba Row led the batting, accumulating runs off his legs and scoring deceptively fast – his 50 came in a hundred minutes, not a bad rate in the circumstances. At 93 Pullar was caught off Misson down the leg side and Dexter entered the arena with England still 228 behind.

Dexter's situation was anything but comfortable; not only were England still facing a tremendous uphill slog – not the kind of game he liked to play – but against Australia, his less than inspiring record read: Innings 5, Not out 0, Runs 28, Average 5.6. His record in Tests at home was relatively poor too, 361 runs in 14 innings at an average of 25.7. Spectators in England still had to be convinced of his talent.

Whatever Dexter had done against the West Indies, the Australians were fairly sure that they had him worked out, and they attacked with confidence. Benaud immediately brought himself on, but Subba Row wisely kept the strike until lunchtime. After lunch Benaud beat Dexter twice, appealing confidently but unsuccessfully when a top-spinner got through. Dexter was dropped by Mackay off Davidson and altogether was looking uncomfortable when the rain came down again, at 106 for 1. The first few overs of the fifth day would be interesting and possibly decisive.

Tuesday dawned fine and England supporters may well have taken this to be another sign that Providence was a good Australian. Mackay and Davidson opened the bowling, though Benaud must have been tempted to take the ball himself and have a go at Dexter before he settled in, but he had to see whether there was any juice in the pitch for the seamers. There wasn't. Mackay began with a close set field, but bowled a half-volley and a long hop in his first over, both of which were hit by Dexter for four with elegant disdainful strokes. Benaud then removed Mackay from the firing line and came on himself, but he also went for two fours in an over. Davidson was the next to feel the weight of Dexter's bat, and in 29 minutes Dexter scored 29 runs. The tide was certainly turning, even if there was still a lot to do.

Aware that the match was still there to be saved, Dexter played with caution once Benaud struck a length but none of the other bowlers troubled him. He saw Subba Row to his hundred and competed his own fifty, before Benaud took the new ball. Misson at once bowled Subba Row, the score being then 202, and Cowdrey looked very uncomfortable. Fortunately for England, Dexter was playing with the utmost confidence, even if he was scoring more slowly, but hearts were in mouths when Cowdrey played a ball from Mackay on to his foot and then into his wicket. At 239 for 3 England were 82 behind and few Englishmen had much appetite for lunch.

Back at the wicket after lunch Dexter and Barrington looked very solid. They took no liberties against Mackay, but Misson bowled a rather loose over which was worth 10 to Dexter – three cracking strokes, all round the wicket – and took him on to 95. Just before three o'clock, Dexter completed his first hundred against Australia with his seventeenth four. It had taken him 219 minutes, very good going in an uphill fight and had certainly revised Australian opinion. Benaud made a valiant attempt to bowl, but he was obviously in great pain and gave himself only two overs. England drew level with Australia at 3.45pm and secured the draw. There couldn't be a declaration – there simply wasn't time to bowl the Australians out.

At tea England were 339 for 3, just 18 ahead, and then at last Dexter felt that he could let himself go. In the final fifteen minutes of his innings he scored 32, before being stumped as he went a long way down the pitch to Simpson. He had scored 180 in 344 minutes, hitting 31 fours. It had been a masterly performance in which he had been very solid, never allowing the initiative to pass to the bowlers, and in the process he had totally altered the 'feel' of the series. England now had a batsman who was capable of

49

taking the game to the enemy and if May or Cowdrey could find their best form, anything might happen.

The last time England had beaten Australia at Lord's was as far back as 1934, when Verity found a wicket to suit him, and the previous victory had been in 1896! The omens were not favourable, but in 1961 the Australians had their own troubles. Benaud played in neither of the county matches between the first and second Tests and would clearly be no more than half-fit, if he could play at all.

England seemed likely to have everybody fit and more or less in form. The selectors provisionally picked May – he had a calf injury now, but it was not thought to be serious – but meanwhile it seemed sensible for Cowdrey to captain the side. May replaced Smith and Lock came in for Allen, which presented a more balanced attack. Benaud was fit to bat, but not bowl and he decided not to play so Harvey took over as captain. The critical decision proved to be the inclusion of Graham McKenzie, a young fast bowler of immense promise, coming into the side for his first Test.

Cowdrey won the toss, the twelfth time in succession that an England captain had done so. The day was dry but overcast. Cowdrey had no hesitation in batting on what looked a perfectly good wicket. But he was in for a rude shock. Every few years, a mysterious ridge appears at Lord's and nothing the groundsmen can do can prevent it and nobody can explain it – and this was one of the years. Every so often something odd happened when the ball was bowled towards the Nursery end, and Australia had four seam bowlers to exploit it. Davidson, a bowler of ripe experience, McKenzie and Misson, both younger men able to whip down all-sorts with immense enthusiasm, and Mackay wobbling the ball about to produce movement off the seam when the faster men could not.

Harvey opened with McKenzie – a gesture of confidence in him – but although the young man beat the bat once or twice, it was Davidson who made the break, bowling Pullar on the forward stroke when the score was only 26. Dexter was soon fending down a couple of lifters and was then hit over the heart by a third. Batting was going to be no fun at all in this match. Dexter mis-hit a hook and was dropped, at which point he seemed to make up his mind to take his runs while he could, as he was bound to get the unplayable ball sooner or later. For a batsman of his type, it was a rational decision. Subba Row, more of a grafter, had made his way to 48 and was looking secure, when he tried to work Mackay on the leg-side and was clearly lbw. Then Dexter fell. He tried to play Misson off his legs with a good firm stroke to mid-wicket, but the ball seemed to 'stop' on him, and he couldn't keep it down. McKenzie took a pretty comfortable catch at ankle height.

At lunch England were 87 for 3 of which Dexter had scored 27. Dexter might have been more sternly criticised than he was for playing a firm attacking stroke in the last over before lunch, but his fall was swallowed up in the general collapse which followed. McKenzie and Davidson simply blew away the middle order and in no time at all, England were 167 for 9. Trueman and Statham then took advantage of the somewhat peculiar courtesy of the day which spared fast bowlers any short-pitched bowling. This was a convention owing more to the fear of retaliation than to chivalry, for the slow bowlers didn't escape. They added 39 before Davidson bowled Trueman, to finish with 5 for 42. It had all worked out very much as at Edgbaston, and the crowd sat back to see if Australia could score 500 again. It looked unlikely, on the wicket.

As it turned out it took a superb innings from Lawry to put Australia on top. Conditions remained the same throughout the match, violent, unpredictable bounce with the barest movement off the seam which was just enough to worry everybody except Lawry. He watched McDonald and Simpson go on the first evening. The wicket was no better next day. The ball was doing everything, in the air and off the pitch, lifting, shooting and moving literally off the seam and Trueman and Statham may even have done too much with it, so that the batsmen were, to coin a phrase, not good enough to get a touch. It made frustrating but exciting watching for England supporters as the time ticked by and runs accumulated. Simply by staying together for the first hour until the bowlers tired, Lawry and Harvey would have gone half-way towards winning the match, but they also scored fifty invaluable runs, enough to prove decisive.

Cowdrey's tactics were obvious. The so-called ridge was at the Nursery end, and he would therefore bowl Trueman and Statham in short spells from the Pavilion end. Dexter would bowl from the Nursery end; there was life there too and if he was collared the spinners could do a containing job. So Dexter was on half-an-hour after the start, bowling steadily and well but without beating the bat. When Trueman came back after the first hour, he got rid of Harvey by giving him two shortish ones on his legs followed by an off-stump lifter at which he flinched, ever so slightly, and was caught at slip. In came O'Neill, but Dexter struck a great blow for his side by bowling him for 1, with an inswinger. Burge edged Trueman just out of short-leg's reach – it was the critical moment of the innings. Burge, like Lawry, was a real fighter and together they battled on, beaten outside the off-stump, edging to third man, hooking anything short, but never once dropping their guard. When Lock came on, he tied them down while never looking like getting them out, and when Burge was out top-edging a hook, Australia were only 23 runs behind, Lawry was in sight of a great, match-winning hundred and the England fast bowlers were weary men.

Lawry reached his hundred and was generously applauded by a knowledgable crowd before he battled on with no lapse in concentration. Mackay no mean No 8, was now with him and obstructing the bowlers in

51

his own inimitable style; he looked the most inelegant of players, but this only made him more frustrating to bowl at. Finally, Dexter got Lawry out trying to drive and instead edging to Murray. He had made 130 in six hours and had almost certainly won the match for Australia. Lawry was cheered from the field by friend and foe alike, but the innings was very far from over. Dexter got Grout out at once, and with three wickets taken at the less difficult end, had done a fine job for his side. But by now the fast men had shot their bolt, and Mackay and McKenzie had helped themselves to 48 by the end of the day when the score was 286 for 8. Next day, Misson, a remarkably talented last man, helped Mackay to add 49 for the last wicket. The last two wickets had cost 102 runs giving Australia a match-winning lead of 134.

Dexter was very unlucky when England batted again. Coming in when Subba Row was caught at the wicket for 8, he began with power and elegance, hitting two glorious fours off Davidson, but McKenzie then attacked him with some short-pitched bowling. This was legitimate enough, particularly so since Dexter had tested *him* with a few bouncers the night before, in defiance of the fast-bowlers convention. Dexter was never much of a one for these slightly hypocritical rules and he would not have been resentful of McKenzie's trying him out with a few bouncers, but he tried to hook one, and felt it strike his pad and fall, ever so gently, on to his wicket when he was on 17. Unlucky for England, but it was the crucial wicket. Only Pullar and Barrington made any real showing against Davidson and McKenzie, and England were all out for 202, not a really bad score on this wicket, but put cruelly in perspective by Lawry's magnificent batting and McKenzie's excellent figures of 29-13-37-5.

The game wasn't quite over. Australia only needed 69, but in the certain knowledge that they wouldn't be bowling for long, Trueman and Statham gave it all they had. They took 4 wickets for 19, two apiece, and with the score at 31 with the last ball before lunch, Burge was all but caught by Lock at square-leg, the ball escaping the fieldsman's grasp when his hand touched the ground. Even if Burge had been caught, Australia could still have squeaked home, but it would have been excitingly close. As it was Australia won by 5 wickets. They had outplayed England at all points, and it left a slightly sour taste in the mouth when a horde of surveyors took the field before all the spectators had left the ground. It looked very much as if the England authorities were seeking to blame the pitch for the defeat, which may have been good for team morale, but was a poor piece of public relations.

The selectors refused to panic and persevered with the same batsmen, who ought to be used to the Australian attack by now. They made just one bowling change, recalling Allen for Illingworth; but another change was forced upon them when Statham was injured. Here, they sprung a surprise, picking the forty year old Les Jackson of Derbyshire. He had played in just one Test, twelve years earlier although his county record was superb and he could be relied upon to do a good job. May now resumed the captaincy and Benaud was just fit enough to play for Australia.

The pitch at Leeds had a bare and sandy look, contrasting ominously with the green of the outfield. It rather looked as though the England spinners would take centre stage and Benaud's fitness would be severely tested. Now, at last, May lost the toss, just when winning it was all-important, and Australia batted first.

To begin with, the fast bowlers didn't come quickly on to the bat and when Allen came on, he got little turn. Scoring was slow but safe. Perhaps the wicket would turn out better than it looked, but Lawry was clearly unhappy with it. He miscued against Lock, made a few wild hits, and was finally lbw to Lock, seemingly in two minds about having another hit. Harvey looked much happier, driving both the spinners for four, but after lunch, McDonald, having reached a hard-won fifty, tried to give Lock the charge and was stumped. O'Neill batted soundly with Harvey and the score climbed to 187 for 2. Australia were in a strong position on a pitch that could only get worse.

Suddenly and dramatically the game changed. May took the new ball, largely because he hoped that once the shine was off it would give his spinners more purchase and bounce. He didn't hope for much from the faster men, but he got a pleasant surprise. O'Neill edged Trueman to Cowdrey at slip, and Harvey glanced him to leg-slip where Lock made a fine catch. Out of the blue the bowling looked full of menace and Trueman and Jackson simply ran through the Australians. Only Davidson who finished with 22 not out, got into double figures, and Australia were all out for 237. Subba Row and Pullar safely played out the last fifteen minutes, although Davidson bowled two frightening lifters. It remained to be seen whether the England batsmen would cope any better, or whether the 180 runs made by the top half of the Australian order would be decisive in a low-scoring match.

Davidson and McKenzie continued to get a lot of movement on the second day, but once Pullar and Subba Row realised that the way to survive was to get on the back foot and nudge, they looked much safer. Benaud, still unable to put everything into his bowling, couldn't get much turn, and like May he relied on his quick bowlers. When Subba Row fell to Davidson, May sent Cowdrey in. This was a sound move on a pitch that called for solidity rather than panache; it should not be seen as a reflection on Dexter, and he didn't take it as one.

The tension increased when Davidson cut his pace and looked for the maximum amount of movement, but Pullar and Cowdrey kept the score moving with some good running between the wickets. The highspot came when Cowdrey took 14 in an over off Simpson and batting very well indeed, brought up his 50 in 102 minutes. Pullar played on to Benaud at 145 when he was on 53. May started edgily, and Benaud brought himself on to increase the pressure. Scoring was slow and the crowd were restive, but to the connoisseur this was the critical period of the game, and perhaps of the rubber. Cricket is a subtle, sophisticated game and we cannot look for perpetual excitement. As the old Yorkshire player said, according to Neville Cardus 'Public needs educating up to it.'

Benaud took the new ball and Davidson immediately caught May off his own bowling, off one which stopped a little. England were 190 for 3, just three runs more than Australia had been at the same point in their innings, and there could so easily be another collapse. Dexter, once again, came in to a crisis. He tried at first, to hammer his way through but after a couple of close calls off drives that he couldn't keep down he soon settled for the nudging game that the others had played, demonstrating, not for the first time, that he was a cricketer of patience and acumen. 'Lord Edward' was by no means the reckless hitter that the popular press loved to portray.

One man who did live up to his popular image was Colin Cowdrey. He always reckoned to 'walk' if he knew he was out, and now, on 93, he got a very faint deflection down the leg-side and was walking on his way almost before Grout had completed the catch, a fine piece of sportsmanship, whatever may be one's view of the batsman's right to let the umpire decide. Barrington came in and swept Benaud for four to give England the lead just before the close. With six wickets in hand, England were in a good but not impregnable, position.

Next day Australia fought back in typical fashion. Davidson, now bowling round the wicket like an orthodox English-type spinner, kept Dexter and Barrington defending desperately, and only one run had come in half an hour when he had Barrington caught by Simpson at slip. Dexter tried to get on top, hit one four and was then bowled through the gate, by Davidson. He had made only 28 in well over two hours, but the difficulties had been there for all to see. Trueman fell at once having hit a 4 off his second ball and holed out off the third, and England were 252 for 7 and needing runs to compensate for having to bat last. The runs came from Lock, a somewhat unlikely batting hero, though he was to be a hero again in 1963. He now had a real swing at Benaud and took 30 runs off him in three overs. England finished with 299, 62 ahead. The lead was useful, but nowhere near decisive.

Jackson removed McDonald, and Lawry and Harvey came together in a partnership which for a time looked like bringing Australia well into the game. They didn't find the going easy and Trueman beat them outside the off-stump from time to time, but they kept on taking enough singles to prevent May staking everything on attack. They had nearly cleared the deficit when May tried Allen, who immediately had Lawry caught by Murray. O'Neill was troubled by Allen but gave no actual chance, and Harvey was batting superbly, getting right down the pitch to kill the spin.

May changed his method of attack again by bringing Trueman back. Harvey went for a drive, but the ball held up a little and he lifted it to Dexter who held the catch. Allen bowled Burge for a duck, and Trueman finding that there was now something in the wicket shortened his run and bowled off-cutters with devastating effect. Four more wickets fell to him, for no runs at all. O'Neill, Simpson, Benaud and Mackay were all beaten by vicious turn. It was reminiscent of Laker's domination of the Australians in 1956, although Trueman was a very different kind of bowler and just a little more demonstrative about his success!

Australia were all out for 120, Trueman taking 6 for 30. England needed only 59 to win and had time to get them on the third day. They got them for two wickets and Dexter didn't have to bat. For once Dexter had made little real contribution to an England win; he had played an uncharacteristic innings, had taken one catch and hadn't bowled. It could be said that it was hardly his sort of wicket, or his sort of match.

England continued to tinker with the bowling; Statham was fit again and replaced Jackson, but then Flavell of Worcestershire, who was having a good season, was brought in as a third seamer, in place of Lock. Jackson, who had taken four good wickets at Leeds, was more than a little unlucky to be left out. Then Cowdrey fell ill with tonsillitis and Close was invited to Manchester as cover for him. Cowdrey was clearly unfit on match day, and Close came in – it was a fateful mishap.

Benaud won the toss again and although the Old Trafford wicket was on the green side, he batted, calculating that if Australia didn't make a score on the first day, the disadvantage would be outweighed by England's having to bat last. Well, that's how it turned out, but he was lucky, in that England made crucial mistakes. Lawry was Australia's star; he lost Simpson and Harvey cheaply, and then poor O'Neill had a most unpleasant time. Flavell hit him on the body three times in one over and Statham also struck him. He was in some distress and was physically sick at the wicket but, rightly or wrongly, he soldiered on until Trueman bounced one at him and, trying to avoid it, he kicked his wicket down.

Dexter was on by now as the fourth seamer, as May sought to exploit every bit of greenness in the pitch, but Lawry and Burge were proof against all that the bowlers could do, and Burge was trying to counter-attack when he was bowled. Then the rain came leaving Australia poorly placed overnight at 124 for 4. Lawry on 64, was their only hope, if they were to make a score, but he fell to Statham early on the second day and the innings folded. Dexter was lucky, perhaps, to pick up three cheap wickets. May had put him on early, holding Trueman back for the new ball, but Dexter rattled Davidson, Benaud and Grout out in a lively spell, and the new ball was not required. He had taken 3 for 16 in forty balls.

For the fourth time in the series, the side batting first had failed; the wicket was getting easier, and England would surely now make a big score to overtake the Australian total of 190 and win the match. Benaud had no choice but to attack, and Davidson at once had Subba Row caught at slip. Dexter had been out of form in the county matches played since the Leeds Test and if Cowdrey had been playing he would doubtless have batted next, but Dexter had to face the music. He began by playing and missing a couple of times against Davidson, who was firing away in inspired form. Pullar looked pretty safe at the other end but after lunch, Dexter had found his form, hitting one perfect square drive off Davidson. It didn't last; he mistimed a hook off Mackay and was put down by O'Neill, of all people at mid-on and then hooked again at McKenzie and was safely taken by Davidson for 16. It had not been an impressive display, but, miserably out of touch, he had tried to hit his way out of trouble. This is an Australian or West Indian reaction to difficulty, rather than an English one, but Dexter always seemed to be more of a West Indian type of player, going for his strokes and hitting the ball on the up. It was immensely exciting when it came off, but of course he was vulnerable to criticism when it didn't. It was now left for the rest of the batsmen to build the innings.

May soon settled and batted as well as at any time since his illness. He overtook Pullar, who had allowed himself to get bogged down, and reached his 50 in 106 minutes. English supporters started to relax and Australia were beginning to look weary and fretful as Pullar regained his fluency and the hundred partnership came up. At once, Pullar was bowled by a full-toss from Davidson – he was probably unable to believe his eyes. Close came in against Australia for the first time in ten years and played out the day calmly, while May began to play with forceful charm, ending on 90, out of 187 for 3.

England were only three runs behind, and should really have gone on to a very big score, but this Australian side was full of fight and resource and when the new ball was taken early on the Saturday, Davidson struck, having May caught at slip by way of Grout's glove. At the same score, Close was lbw to McKenzie, and Barrington and Murray were left to retrieve a pretty difficult situation. They couldn't be blamed for making rather heavy weather of it, but the great thing was that they stayed and stayed, and hit the bad ball when it came along. Murray was even bold enough to loft Mackay for a straight four and at lunch England were 264 for 5 and moving towards a secure position. After lunch, Mackay had Murray caught, but Allen, in good batting form at this time, made a brave

56

if edgy start, while Barrington took most of Davidson and handled him well. The pavilion critics were inclined to grumble at the rate of progress, but the 300 came up in seven hours or so, which we should think acceptable, if not very exciting, today. In the context of the match of course it was perfectly all right, for time was on England's side. Allen was out before tea when England were 361 for 7 and getting on top.

At this point, we encounter a strange incident, worth dwelling on a little as it illustrates the particular pressures on England captains and players at this time. This was always going to be a year in which the spirit in which the game was played was as important as the result; everybody had been very disturbed about the funereal pace of the 1958-9 series, and the Australia-West Indies duel had set a new agenda. One of the most fervent advocates of brighter and more positive cricket was Walter Robins, who had tried to persuade Cowdrey into a quixotic declaration at Port-of-Spain. Dexter tells in his book how Robins now came into the dressing-room at Old Trafford and insisted that it was time for England to go for quick runs. It wasn't time, England needed a bigger lead and, in any event, Robins had no authority to make any such demand. He wasn't a selector at all – and nobody but the chairman had any right to suggest a change of tactics to the captain. Because of his own vigorous play and his forceful image Dexter was to come under this sort of pressure, generally more subtly expressed, throughout his Test career, and it is interesting that, in commenting on the Robins incident, he is clearly of the view that the intervention was ill-timed and in his own words, 'unforgivable'.

Whether because of Mr Robins or not, the batsmen did have a hit after tea, and the last 3 wickets fell for just 6 runs. Australia 177 behind, still had a glimmer of hope, when they should have been shut out of the match. Simpson and Lawry survived the day, though Lawry gave a couple of chances, and on the Monday they struggled to 113 before Simpson was out. Harvey was dropped twice, one of the chances being off Dexter's bowling, before Dexter had him caught at the wicket, but by now Australia were only two runs behind and prospering.

From this moment on, the match swung wildly from one side to the other and back again, with England always seeming to be just ahead, until they faltered before Benaud's final assault. Lawry reached his hundred, a fine fighting effort which had lasted four and a half hours, and was out without adding to his score. May took the new ball to attack Burge, but although he and O'Neill had some bad moments, they scored fast against the bowling of Trueman and Statham. Dexter came back and defeated Burge and Booth; he probably bowled as well in this match as he ever did in a Test. Between these dismissals Statham had O'Neill caught for a courageous 67, in which he was hit several times, as he had been in the first innings, but never flinched. Australia were 296 for 6, only 119 ahead, and it seemed that England had the match won, but Mackay and Davidson were the right men for a crisis and they kept the bowlers out till the close.

The final day was one of the most exciting in Test history and for England a desperately disappointing one. Allen began by getting rid of Mackay, Benaud and Grout without a run being scored off him. Australia were 157 ahead, with only the inexperienced McKenzie to bat. Davidson, however, was still very much there and he hit a couple of fours off Close and then, taking his courage in both hands, took 20 off Allen in a single over – two fours and two sixes. May's nerve faltered at this – who can blame him? – and he whisked Allen off, reasoning that Davidson would not score as fast off Trueman and Statham, and that it only needed one straight fast ball to get rid of McKenzie. But the youngster proved equal to every challenge and they put on 98 together before Flavell bowled McKenzie for a most worthy 32. Davidson was left not out on 77. He never did make a Test hundred, but this was an innings that deserved to be ranked alongside all the hundreds ever made.

England needed 256 in 230 minutes and for once the runs-time equation had worked out perfectly. Not many people were betting on England though – 250 takes a lot of getting in the fourth innings of a Test. Somebody would have to play a big, fast innings – it wouldn't be achieved with thirties and forties. Any one of several England players might do it, but somehow Dexter was thought the most likely one. Pullar and Subba Row scored 40 at a run a minute, and when Pullar was out, the stage was set for Dexter. True, he was out of form, but this was the kind of challenge to bring the best out of him.

He got away at once with two crashing off-drives for four from Davidson, and it was good to see him singling out the most dangerous adversary and going for him. Subba Row was encouraged to go for Davidson too, and although he gave a half-chance to Benaud at short-leg, he also pulled Davidson twice to the mid-wicket boundary. Benaud was relying heavily on Davidson, and he seemed to have kept him on too long when they took 16 off the last two overs of a fourteen-over spell.

At the other end, Benaud himself was plugging away conceding few runs and troubling Subba Row with balls which turned quickly out of the rough, but not apparently bothering Dexter at all. McKenzie replaced Davidson and Dexter hit him for 11 runs in his first over as well as sending down two wides. Benaud took McKenzie off and to general surprise brought on Simpson, who was meat and drink to Dexter. He went for five fours in four overs and Benaud turned to Mackay again but it seemed now that every bowler came alike to Dexter and that he was going to steer England to a comfortable win. He hit Mackay for a towering six to long-on and England at 150 for 1, were practically home.

Benaud, though, was a man who never acknowledged defeat. At this stage he had taken 5 for 310 in the series – incidentally, he had scored 3 runs in his last 4 innings – but he kept himself on. He really had no choice, his other bowlers having all been knocked off. He tried going round the wicket to make the very most of the rough and now at the last possible moment, he was rewarded for his steadfastness and professionalism. He tied Dexter down with five balls which dropped on the off-stump and went away, and then he bowled the fateful ball. It turned and lifted just a little more. Dexter went for the square-cut, top-edged and was easily caught by Grout. He was roared home by an ecstatic crowd, who must have been convinced that England had won the match. He had made 76 in eighty-four minutes, with 14 fours and a six. England wanted only 106, at a run a minute.

Instead of pausing to take stock – and there was plenty of time to do so – the England batsmen dashed at the task in a thoroughly uncontrolled and undisciplined way; perhaps the Robins influence again? May swept at a big leg-break from Benaud, forgot to leave his back leg in place and was bowled round his legs. Close played a series of horrifying sweeps at balls pitching outside the off-stump and holed out. Barrington looked sounder than his two predecessors, but lost Subba Row in the last over before tea. He dug in after the break, but the game had slipped away for the last time. Murray was taken at slip and Barrington fell lbw to Mackay. This looked to be a marginal decision, but in all honesty it didn't matter – the match was settled. Appropriately, Davidson was brought back in time to take the last wicket, for the victory would have been impossible if he had not played that fighting innings, but it was Benaud's flair and inspiring leadership that had won Australia the Test.

Brian Close was heavily punished for his eccentric little innings, but he was to come back again and again. May decided to bow out of Test cricket from this day; it is fascinating to speculate what would have happened if he had made that tiny adjustment of his foot and England had won the match. He might have gone on, if he had regained the Ashes in 1961, he would have come under great pressure to defend them in 1962-3, and not only his career but those of Cowdrey and Dexter at least would have been changed, very possibly for the better. Who can say?

For the moment it remained for Englishmen to congratulate Benaud and to decide how to win the final Test and so share the honours of the series. Cowdrey was fit enough to return and the selectors went for two spinners, as they generally did at the Oval in those days. Lock was recalled, but surprisingly Trueman, not Flavell, made way for him. There appears no logic in this. Flavell was the older man, but had much less Test experience. It seemed that Trueman was being punished because Benaud had been able to spin the ball out of his footmarks. As in the matter of the post-match surveying operation at Lord's, extraneous factors were being blamed for a defeat inflicted by better cricketers and better cricket. It was all rather sad.

Dexter continued to make little of his opportunities in county cricket, but of course his Test place was secure for years to come. With Cowdrey in the side again, May would be able to drop Dexter down the order, hoping for an attacking innings from him. For the fifth and final Test at the Oval May won the toss and batted, and for the fifth time in the series the side batting first made a hash of it. It was unbelievable.

Three wickets went down in no time at all, though it may not have seemed that way to Cowdrey, who batted twenty minutes for no runs at all; he was in one of his broody phases and never looked like getting off the mark. Dexter came in at 20 for 3 and he and May tried to hit their way out of trouble. They scored 32 in half an hour, both hitting boundaries all around the ground. They were only too aware that the series was lost and felt there was little to do but entertain, but those who applauded loudest were the first to condemn Dexter when he went for a cut and was caught at the wicket while on 24. It was ever thus – play your strokes, but don't get out – it's an easier game played from the pavilion.

Barrington and May dug in after lunch but May, playing as it turned out in his last Test, skied the ball to cover when he had made 71, and the innings closed at 256 early on the second day. Australia could have been expected to relax now that they had won the Ashes, but although Lawry and Harvey went early, O'Neill still had a point to prove. By his own standards he had had a pretty moderate series and had yet to score a hundred against England.

This was the ideal opportunity and O'Neill now scored the fastest hundred of the series with a succession of brilliant strokes in under three hours. When he was out, Burge carried on with the hitting and he too reached his hundred early on the third day. This was his first Test hundred in his twenty-first Test, a telling comment on Australian selection policy. Australians have usually been prepared to persevere with a batsman of obvious class even when the hundreds don't come and it pays off. Burge made three more hundreds in his next twenty-one Tests. In more recent times, we have seen the pattern repeated, when the Australian selectors stayed with Steve Waugh as he went for twenty-six Tests without a hundred, to be rewarded when he scored two big hundreds in the first two Tests of the 1989 summer and effectively won a series for them. English selectors with many more players to pick from, are far more inclined to chop and change, and don't put a team together in the same effective way. When Dexter himself became the chairman of selectors, he made it clear that he would want to build a side on a more permanent basis, but was

60

cruelly frustrated by some very indifferent batting from the chosen few, and by the South African affair. That's show-business.

Burge went on to the huge score of 181 before getting out having a slog at Allen, and Australia on 494 had built a lead of 238. In the second innings Dexter batted at No 3 and this time he certainly got out through a lapse in concentration. He hooked a long-hop from Mackay, failed to keep it down and found the one man on the leg-side who caught it gratefully. He hadn't even put a run on the board. He returned to the pavilion in a stony silence for it had not been a wise or well-executed stroke at a time when England only had a draw to play for. The critics had already forgotten his wonderful innings at Old Trafford, it seemed, but then as now there was little gratitude in cricket. It was this kind of stroke that earned Dexter the reputation of a carefree and careless batsman, but it should be said that he didn't often get out in an irresponsible way and had as good a defence as any of his contemporaries. It was all a question of public image.

Play was interrupted by rain shortly after Dexter got out and when they started again May set about Mackay aggressively. Throughout the series, the England batsmen felt that Mackay was getting away with it, that he was a very ordinary bowler who ought to be hittable, and here was May trying yet again to prove it. But Mackay had the last laugh as the captain lofted a catch behind the bowler. Mackay now got Cowdrey out and had taken all four wickets. To add to England's troubles, Subba Row who was batting calmly and well, had strained a muscle and was in need of a runner. Under the usual convention this had to be a player who had already batted. Cowdrey was under the weather – he hadn't fielded in the Australian innings – and it would not be expected that the captain would take the job on, and the choice was between Dexter and Pullar. Dexter volunteered cheerfully for the thankless task, which earned him some bonus points from any who were still inclined to see him as a dilettante. Not that this would have influenced him in any way, he was and remains a thoroughly good-natured man whose instinct is to help and not to pass by – but this was not always appreciated by those who deal in black and white.

Dexter had plenty of work to do, for Subba Row batted on for a long time playing a patient, match-saving innings. Barrington stayed with him until the end of the fourth day and on into the fifth as Subba Row completed his hundred on the last morning. Interestingly he only played against Australia in this one series and so had made centuries in his first Ashes Test and also in his last. The statisticians were quick to unearth the fact that the last player to do this had been Maurice Leyland, another fighting left-hander. Subba Row batted on into the afternoon, until he tried to hit Benaud against the spin and lofted a catch. England were only 24 ahead when he got out, but the bowling was looking threadbare and Barrington and then Murray saved the game with ease.

In all it had been an odd series, the side batting second always establishing an advantage, which was only clawed back at Old Trafford. England had had their chances to win both the lost matches, but against that, had had the worst of the two draws. They had been beaten by the more positive side. Dexter had had a very mixed series. He had played two unforgettable innings, but like his colleagues, had too often failed in the first innings, and helped hand the advantage to Australia.

To express this in figures:

First innings: 10, 27, 28, 16, 24   105 runs, average 21.00
Second innings: 180, 17, 76, 0   273 runs, average 68.25

Some critics took this as evidence that his concentration faltered; if it were so, he had overcome it by the next series against Australia.

	Innings	N.O.	H.S.	Runs	Average	100	50
1961	9	—	180	378	42.00	1	1
To date	37	1	180	1415	39.30	4	6

England were to tour India and Pakistan that winter. May had said that he wouldn't be touring again, which amounted to a retirement from Test cricket. Dexter was invited to captain the side and accepted. It wasn't going to be easy, the schedule was a daunting one, with eight Tests spread over almost five months and there were certain to be a number of newcomers to Test cricket in the side. Dexter, still a relatively inexperienced captain, would need all the luck that was going if he was to win more Tests than he lost.

8 Touring captain

The MCC tour of the sub-continent of India was always going to be a difficult one. Most captains would prefer to begin by leading the side at home and learning the ropes there – to begin in India and Pakistan and with a weakened side was asking a lot of Dexter. To make matters worse, the programme was a very odd one; because India accepted an invitation to go to the West Indies *after* they had arranged the details of the MCC visit, the Indian section of the tour had to be sandwiched between two halves of the Pakistan series, a uniquely difficult task for the touring party and one which should never have been agreed to.

May and Subba Row had announced their partial retirement and full retirement, respectively and at least six other players – Cowdrey, Edrich, Flavell, Statham, Close and Trueman – had turned down the opportunity to take part. Dexter therefore had a half-strength side, but in the circumstances the selectors did a good job. Three batsmen already established in the full Test side – Dexter, Barrington and Pullar – were joined by M J K Smith, Parfitt, Russell and the recalled Peter Richardson. Barber and Knight were the all-rounders, Millman and Murray the wicket-keepers. The bowling was the weakest link. Lock and Allen were experienced spinners, but the pacemen, White of Hampshire, D R Smith of Gloucestershire and A Brown of Kent, would all be making Test debuts on some unpromising wickets. Not surprisingly, they didn't achieve very much, and none of them played in Tests after this tour.

Dexter had the immediate problem of determining his side for the first Test at Lahore, which was to be the third match of the tour. He tried out all the bowlers, but England's chances suffered a real blow when Lock, the likeliest of the bowlers, was injured and had to miss the Test. This meant that Barber would be carrying a heavy load as the second spinner and, to make matters worse, Imtiaz won the toss, and England had to bat last.

White took a couple of early wickets, but that was too good to last and Dexter was soon faced with a problem. His fast bowlers couldn't get much out of the pitch and he needed to conserve the energies of his spinners Allen and Barber. Everybody was rather patronising about Dexter's captaincy on this tour, but here he showed imagination, putting on Eric

Russell, the Middlesex batsman who had bowled only two overs for Middlesex in the 1961 championship season. Russell rewarded Dexter's confidence, bowling 19 overs at a steady medium pace and conceding only 25 runs, enabling Allen and Barber to get the rest they needed.

Nevertheless, Pakistan reached 315 for 3 and Dexter must have wondered where his next wicket was coming from until Burki played a careless stroke, Mushtaq ran himself out, and suddenly England had two fresh men to bowl at. Dexter immediately went on to the attack bringing on Barber the senior leg-spinner and crowding the batsmen. In no time the score was 387 for 9 at which point Pakistan declared. Not much evidence here of unimaginative leadership from Dexter.

England, like Pakistan, lost two quick wickets and like Pakistan, they recovered. Barrington and Smith put on 192 and Dexter came in at the unexpectedly good score of 213 for 3; he played a consolidating innings looking for a big lead, but was unlucky enough to tread on his wicket when he was on 20 while playing an attacking stroke. England collapsed and were all out 7 runs behind, but Dexter was in no way dismayed. He and Brown took 3 wickets cheaply and then he attacked again, crowding the batsmen as they struggled against Allen and Barber. Pakistan slid to 148 for 9 and then the last-wicket pair, Afaq Hussain and Haseeb Ahsan put on 52 to make a match of it. Haseeb, who was pretty lucky on this occasion, was to cross England's path again, as Pakistan's manager in the troubled 1980s.

England had now to make 208 in the fourth innings; it was not going to be easy, as there were only 250 minutes to go, and there was always the possibility of an unscheduled interruption of one kind or another. 2 wickets went down for 17, and 3 for 86, but Dexter's nerve was more than equal to the occasion. He played a commanding innings well supported by Barber, not then the attacking batsman he was to become. Dexter was soon driving the ball hard on both sides of the wicket and compelling Imtiaz to drop his fielders back, leaving plenty of room for the short singles. Dexter and Barber added 101 in 85 minutes and the match was won with deceptive ease. It was a good start to Dexter's time as captain; it is worth noting that England have played seventeen Tests in Pakistan since that day and have yet to win again.

This tour was conducted at a tremendous pace and, although there were only sixteen days between the end of the Lahore Test, and the first day of the first Test against India at Bombay, they contained three matches and a lot of travelling. The tour moved to India and would really be judged by England's success or failure there. England had managed to draw the previous series in India, but it was never easy to defeat India on their own wickets and although they were, so to speak, between teams, they had some formidable batsmen. MCC had to play three other matches and do a lot of travelling between the end of the Lahore Test and the first day of the first Test in Bombay, hardly the ideal sort of preparation. Most of the batsmen struck form except Dexter himself, but his turn would come. It was apparent that Dexter would have to rely very heavily on Allen and Lock, his two main spinners, to take the wickets for him. Everything seemed to point to a high-scoring series.

Dexter won the toss at Bombay and everything went well from the start. Pullar and Richardson made 159 for the first wicket and the score was 228 for 3 when Dexter joined Barrington. Realising that a really big score was needed he didn't try to thrash the bowling around but took his runs where he could scoring 85 in 185 minutes before he was bowled by Salim Durani. This was Durani's first Test wicket, but he was to play a significant part in the series. Barrington went serenely on to 151 with little support from the other batsmen and Dexter declared at 500 for 8, the first time England had topped 500 since 1957. He had to bowl India out twice if he was to win and the wicket was a very easy one. On the third day, England got through 100 overs, a good and positive piece of cricket in the heat, but although India made only 213 in the five and a half hours, they lost only 4 wickets. Durani and Borde, who had each bowled 30 overs in the England innings, were well established in a match-saving partnership at the end of the day. Next day, they went on to make 315, and although Lock took some cheap wickets towards the end of the innings, India were all out for 390, only 110 behind. Dexter's first attempt to wrest a win out of the Indian side and the conditions had clearly failed.

England went briskly for runs in their second innings, scoring 184 for 5 at more than 3 an over, an unusually high rate on these slow wickets. But India were never going to respond to Dexter's challenging declaration which set them to make 297 in 245 minutes and the only relief from a measured plod came when Dexter put on his joke bowlers after tea. These were remarkably successful against some relaxed batting, Smith taking his only Test wicket and Richardson two of his three. England had had the best of the draw and they had deserved to, having played most of the positive cricket.

England had a fright in the second Test at Kanpur, but escaped thanks in large part to some positive batting from Dexter and others. It almost seemed that India had picked too many all-rounders and half-bowlers, but they each made their contribution. Contractor won the toss and India batted really solidly, Dexter setting defensive fields from the outset. Umrigar, who generally batted much better in India than in England, made a very solid hundred, although he was dropped twice off Lock. India made 467 for 8 before Contractor declared early on the third day – it was that sort of match. Dexter gave himself a very long bowl sending down 31 overs and taking 2 for 84.

India had recalled Subhash Gupte, their little leg-spinner, and he usually got some response out of even the most unpromising wicket. He did so this time, taking 5 for 90. Dexter was out for 2, and England at one time were really looking down the barrel at 162 for 8, but Lock, always likely to make a few when those above him failed, joined Barber in a piece of cheerfully agreeable batting. They added 81 for the ninth wicket (Barber 69 not out, Lock 49) and England got to 244, not by any means enough to save the follow-on – but encouraging.

Pullar led the way in the second innings and England were 200 for 1 at the end of the fourth day, with Pullar past his hundred. On the last day, Pullar and Smith fell quickly, but Dexter was more than equal to the crisis, and he and Barrington put on 206 at more than a run a minute as the bowlers tired. Dexter was still not out on 126 at the end of the match, when England on 497 for 5, had comfortably saved the game. The critics of Dexter's captaincy might have said that he should at some point have declared, but there was really no moment when he could sensibly have done so. England were only 274 ahead at the close and a teatime declaration must have left India to score about 170 in two hours – probably not time enough to get the runs and certainly not time enough to bowl them out, whatever happened. Dexter's captaincy so far was meeting every test.

Between the second and third Tests, MCC actually encountered a pitch that took a little spin and bowled North Zone out twice for a comfortable win. But it was back to normal at Delhi, where India batted first on the flattest of wickets. Jaisimha, who had been one of India's two most consistent batsmen so far with 56, 51 and 70, now scored his first hundred and Manjrekar, the other leading batsman (68, 84, 96) went to 189 not out. However the other batsmen failed to back them and India made 466 against an attack well managed by Dexter, the three spinners, Lock, Allen and Barber, bowling 112 overs between them. Allen returned the excellent figures of 47-18-87-4. England had no qualms about matching this effort on this wicket, and had made 256 for 3 when rain washed out the last two days, a loss regretted only by Barrington and Dexter who were left not out with 113 and 45 respectively.

Barrington had now scored hundreds in four consecutive Tests and Dexter must have been worried about what would happen when he ran out of form, as everybody does, sooner or later (well, everybody except Bradman, who was an exception to every rule) or fell ill, as English players do in India. It was the unlucky Pullar who now fell ill for the second time on the tour, and he had to be replaced by Russell. Murray had already had to go home suffering from varicose veins and Millman replaced him. Altogether, it was the low point of the tour, and there were four Tests still to be played. India were in the middle of one of their periodic disciplinary arguments and left out Kripal Singh and Gupte.

The wicket at Delhi looked like taking spin and Gupte's omission might have been critical, but here we come to two important figures in the series – Borde and Durani. These two are sometimes forgotten when Indian cricket history is discussed, but they were considerable players at this time. Chandra Borde was a free, assured batsman who scored over 3000 runs in Tests. He often found himself in the same teams as Gupte and tended therefore to get fewer opportunities to bowl than his tidy leg-spin deserved, but he was a much better bowler than a Test career average of 46 would suggest. Durani was a flighty slow left-arm bowler who was soon to be supplanted by Bedi, but before that he was to play the leading part in winning the last two Tests and the series.

The Calcutta toss was a good one to win, Contractor won it and India took the field and batted slowly on the first day, for 221 for 5. There was nothing in the wicket for the faster men and every possibility that it would break up later; slow play was the right tactic, and there wasn't a lot that Dexter could do about it. On the second day India accelerated, Dexter used Lock and Allen most of the time and they worked their way through the batting, but India totalled 380 in nine hours and the damage was done. England didn't begin too well, losing 3 wickets on the second evening and on the third day Dexter himself was the only one to show any sort of form. He scored 57 in good time, but he fell at last to Borde's quicker ball. England were all out for 212, Borde and Durani sharing 9 wickets.

Contractor didn't enforce the follow-on because time was on his side. Lock and Allen got his men into trouble however, and soon after the start of the fourth day, India were 119 for 5, only 287 ahead, and there was almost a prospect of what would be a most improbable victory. Borde, however, was a most useful man to be coming in at No 8, and he saw them through to 252, making the top score of 61. Dexter could do little but rely on Lock and Allen. They didn't let him down, taking 8 for 206 between them in 89 overs, but England had now to make an enormous 421 on a turning wicket. Dexter came in at 27 for 2 and played a fine fighting innings – the *Cricketer* correspondent described his stroke-play as 'superb and confident', and he hit eleven fours in his 62, but nobody else made fifty and the tail rather fell away. England were all out for 233 and could now only share the honours of the series.

The unfortunate Pullar went down, yet again, with dysentery, on the eve of the fifth and final Test at Madras. India, expecting a spinners' wicket, played four slow bowlers including Erapalli Prasanna, the first of their famous four spinners to be capped. Dexter was also pretty sure that the wicket would take spin – it was after all India's strength – but he only had three spinners to select, including Barber the all-rounder; and, of course, Contractor won the toss.

India had their best opening day so far in terms of the rate of scoring, but they lost 7 wickets in making 296, and it seemed that England still had a chance. Lock and Allen had bowled pretty tightly, but Barber had been a little expensive. Dexter had been bold enough to use Parfitt, a very occasional bowler – one more piece of evidence that he was using his imagination. On the second day, Engineer, batting at No 9, hit Knight for 16 in his first over and from then on there was little Dexter could do, though he did get Engineer out himself. India finished on 428 and England didn't bat very well. Dexter was again bowled by Borde for 2 and Smith was the only man to bat up to form, scoring 73. India, 147 ahead, really didn't bat very well either in their second innings, except for Manjrekar who scored 85. Lock took 6 wickets.

The wicket was now taking a great deal of spin and any Indian score would have sufficed. England never looked like making the 338 they were set and when Dexter fell again to Borde for 3, and they were 90 for 5, it seemed that they would be very comprehensively humiliated. Barrington fought hard as always, and all the later batsmen made a few, so that the final score was 209 – defeat, but not disgrace.

England had lost the series, but there was still a month to go. The side had now to return to Pakistan and begin again, only four days later to defend that slender 1-0 lead that they had almost forgotten about. It would be a severe test of Dexter's captaincy. He had to devise ways of getting Pakistan out on good wickets, or at least of preventing them from making big scores and getting England out, plus he had also to maintain morale in his own party. He managed it, and it was much to his credit.

He began boldly enough by leaving out all the specialist opening bowlers who would have got nothing out of the Dacca wicket, relying instead on his spinners to get the wickets. This meant that he himself would be opening the bowling with Knight – as so often no-one could doubt his energy and appetite for the fight – and it also meant that he could lengthen his batting line-up. Naturally Imtiaz won the toss again – this always seems to happen to sides when they are down – but England managed to get through 111 overs on the first day. This was good, sporting cricket from a side that was one up. Some might say that it wasn't business, but no lover of the game will condemn Dexter for that. Pakistan batted extremely slowly, making only 175 for 2 in those 111 overs, Hanif Mohammad making 64 not out. Hanif could be desperately difficult to get out, but sometimes, as in this game, he didn't play the right game for this side. On the second day, he went on at the same measured pace, to score 111, but after lunch, the other batsmen speeded up quite dramatically, Burki actually scoring 89 in the afternoon session. It was an amazing

68

contrast with the first day, and one does wonder if an earlier acceleration would have paid off. Lock, who bowled 73 overs in all and took 4 for 155, must have been totally exhausted by the end, but he still had work to do. Dexter himself bowled 28 overs for 34 runs, but he wasn't bowling during the grand assault.

England were left with a difficult hour's batting on the second day, but Pullar and Barber did really well to score 57 in that time, and they went on to 198 on the third day before Barber was out. Barrington and Pullar took the score to 333 for 1 before the end of the third day, and there seemed to be a historic score in the making, but poor Pullar was looking terribly tired. He had had three debilitating bouts of illness during the tour and was much weakened. He was soon out on the fourth day, and England collapsed, inexplicably, to some pretty innocuous-looking bowling. Dexter made only 12.

England were nevertheless 46 ahead, and in no sort of danger; but Pakistan were not at all inclined to look for a win. They made a good start and Dexter again used his joke bowlers, Richardson taking his third and last Test wicket, while Lock and Allen bowled little seamers. Pakistan became a little careless and suddenly they were 159 for 6 and Dexter was crowding the batsmen and Lock and Allen were bowling 'properly'. Was this clever captaincy on Dexter's part, lulling them into a sense of false security? It's impossible to say, but if Benaud or Brearley had been in charge, the collapse would no doubt have been ascribed to their genius. But the received wisdom was that Dexter was an unimaginative captain, and he got no credit. In any case, Hanif was still there and the momentary crisis passed. Hanif made his second hundred – he batted for 893 minutes in his two innings – and England were left to bat out the last hour or so. Lock had bowled 115 overs in the match and Allen 83, and there was another Test to be played at Karachi in a week's time.

The long march now caught up with Barrington, he was attacked by fibrositis, and couldn't play in this last Test. This was a serious blow to England's hopes of saving the series, for Barrington was distinctly the most reliable man to stay and score if the side got into trouble; moreover, Pullar was still weak after his illness. If Pakistan won the toss – as they did – there could be trouble in store. This time, the wicket didn't seem to be one that would help the spinners and White came back to open the bowling, but he pulled a muscle after bowling only 16 balls and Dexter was already a bowler short. His response was to put in a good spell himself in harness with Knight and Pakistan were reduced to 56 for 4. Once again, those who thought Dexter wasn't an inspirational leader must have been looking the other way.

Hanif was still there however – he was at this time probably the most difficult man to dismiss in world cricket – and he made 67 and helped Alim-ud-Din well on the way to his hundred. Pakistan were all out before the close for 253. It wasn't a good score and Pakistan weren't going to win from there. It had been a really good performance in the field from a side which lacked one of its strike bowlers. England were a little timid in their reply, making only 219 for 2 on the second day. Dexter was himself a little out of sorts and had to play himself back into form. On the third day, he looked much more like his old self and played all the bowlers with total confidence. He finished with a chanceless 205, his highest Test score and only double century of his Test career, hitting twenty-two fours. Parfitt supported him with 111, but the tail rather fell away, the last 4 wickets going down for 5 runs.

Nevertheless, England totalled 507, 254 ahead, and there was a chance of another win; but the wicket was getting slower all the time and there was always that man Hanif. This time, he batted for five hours for 89, which meant that in the last two Tests he had batted for approximately twenty-four hours, for 371 runs. Unfortunately he had been unexciting as well as slow and unlikely to lead to victories, but he had averted defeat. Pakistan were 404 for 8 at the end, and England left the arena without reluctance after such a very long campaign. Dexter had kept his side together, leading by example. He took the very last wicket, and finished with 3 for 86 in 32 overs.

It had been a very hard tour as everybody had expected. Only Parfitt of the newcomers had really distinguished himself and England had owed a lot to the older hands. Dexter was blamed, somewhat unfairly, for the failure to beat India, and he was to have to fight to retain the captaincy, but I find no evidence to suggest that he was responsible for the losses. He had managed his somewhat flimsy bowling as well as possible and had in particular nursed Lock and Allen, his chief weapons, to the end. It is fair to say that people in England didn't really appreciate at this time how difficult it was to beat India on Indian soil and in future England would make more of an effort to send the first team. Dexter had batted well indeed and he and Barrington had shown they would be the mainstays of England for a year or two to come.

	Innings	N.O.	H.S.	Runs	Average	100	50
v. India 1961/62	9	2	126	409	58.42	1	3
v. Pakistan 1961/62	4	1	205	303	101.00	1	1
To date	50	4	205	2127	46.22	6	10

9 Three gentlemen of England

From time to time the cricket establishment in England appears to be trying to create the atmosphere of a soap opera in its management of the game; this is no new phenomenon, having been observable since the heyday of Dr Grace. The plot is frequently thickened by the activities of the tabloid press and sometimes compounded by the serious papers. One of the most popular recurring themes is the selection of the England captain. The form, psyche, management ability and sex-life of potential candidates come under the microscope and many players have found it a bruising experience. Not only are they thoroughly worked over by the media, but they are frequently exploited, even betrayed, by the selectors and committees working, they believe, in the interests of the game. The 1962 instalment of the recurring drama is an important part of the Dexter story.

At the beginning of 1962 Peter May had declared himself unavailable for future tours so it was clear that it would make no sense to pick him against the 1962 Pakistani tourists. England needed to establish a captain for the winter tour of Australia and he would have to cut his teeth, so to speak, on Pakistan. May, then, would not captain against Pakistan and to pick him as a player would put the captain in an invidious position. Cowdrey had led the side during the absences of May following his operation and subsequent relapse and was seen as the man with the best right to the permanent succession. On the other hand, Dexter had led the side on a difficult tour of the Indian sub-continent when Cowdrey had declared himself unavailable. Opinions about Dexter's leadership had varied but it could certainly be argued that he deserved the chance to lead the full strength of England at home. The selectors thought so anyway, and appointed him for the first two Tests.

Dexter had had a wearing tour and this showed in the way he started the season, but in his sixth first class match he scored a hundred before lunch against the tourists finishing with 117 and took 6 wickets. He had come into form at the right time.

England effectively went into the first Test with the side that had played against the Australians, save that the experienced Graveney returned to replace May, Parfitt came in for Subba Row and Millman took over from Murray. Graveney had not played for England since the 1958-9 tour and had spent 1961 qualifying for Worcestershire. He had started the season in good form and his experience would be invaluable.

Dexter won the toss on a beautiful batting wicket. When Pullar got out at 31, he came in and played an innings which *Wisden* described as 'immaculate in style'. He and Cowdrey, in terrific form, put on 166 in 135 minutes before Dexter, going for a big hit off Intikhab, the pick of the bowlers, skied the ball to mid-off. He had made 72 including seven fours. Graveney came in and batted beautifully for 97 and Cowdrey scored 159; the Edgbaston crowd had enjoyed fine batting from the three handsomest batsmen in England. Dexter was able to declare at lunch on the second day at 544 for 5, and that sort of score hasn't often been made since by England in eight hours.

Pakistan were soon in trouble. Two wickets fell for 30, the brothers Hanif and Mushtaq Mohammad added 78 before the spinners struck with 3 quick wickets and the score at the close was 149 for 5. Next day, Dexter gave his two spinners a long bowl at the sixth wicket pair, Imtiaz and Wallis Mathias, before taking the new ball. Statham, in fact, bowled Wallis while still warming up with the old ball and 3 more wickets fell for 4 runs, before Intikhab and D'Souza, hitting out vigorously, added 40 for the tenth wicket. Naturally, Dexter asked Pakistan to follow on and this time they began rather better, Hanif and Ijaz making 60 for the first wicket. Allen then broke through and Pakistan were 158 for 4 by the close.

On the fourth day Dexter was able to take the new ball when he needed the breakthrough and Pakistan subsided gently to 274. There were a few hearty knocks at the end, but the innings win was never in doubt. It was generally agreed that Dexter had not had much to beat, but that he had conducted operations with calm and finesse.

For the second Test, England selected an unchanged side, but were then compelled to make two changes. Pullar and Statham were injured and replaced by two men making their first Test appearances; Stewart, the Surrey opener, who had been knocking on the door for some time, and Coldwell of Worcestershire, a reliable fast-medium bowler of the typically English kind, who was expected to do well at home, but might not be so effective on tour. Pakistan brought in Alim-ud-Din as a batsman, and substituted Farooq, another fast-medium man, for the leg-spinner Intikhab, a switch which didn't promise interesting watching, but was logical enough at Lord's where seamers usually prosper.

It was one of those days when the toss is described as a good one to lose – an overcast day and a green pitch. Burki won the toss and decided not to risk fielding first. By lunchtime, he knew that he had taken the greater risk in batting. The wicket and the heavy atmosphere had given every possible assistance to Trueman and Coldwell, who ripped the heart out of the batting. Pakistan were 76 for 6 at lunch, Trueman having taken his 200th Test wicket. Dexter's contribution had been to manage the field-setting well, to take a catch off Trueman, and to come on as first change and bowl Saeed Ahmed. There was no recovery after lunch and Pakistan were out for exactly 100, Trueman taking 6 for 31.

It looked a different game when England batted. Stewart looking nervous was slow and uncertain, but Cowdrey was assured and it was a surprise when he fell first, for 41 out of 59. Dexter came in and was at his very best. Ron Roberts, writing in *Playfair Cricket Monthly* followed E W Swanton in describing Dexter as 'the most exciting English batsman since the days of Walter Hammond' which may have been a little hard on Compton and May, but gives some idea of contemporary opinion. Dexter made 65 in 95 minutes, but when he was third out and Barrington fell without scoring, England were suddenly 168 for 4 and not totally secure. Graveney took over on the second day and scored a splendid chanceless 153 in just over four hours. He was now thoroughly re-established in the England middle order, and indeed the whole of the batting had a settled look. England scored 370 in all and when Pakistan slid to 77 for 4 against Coldwell, it looked as though the match would be over very early on Saturday.

However, there followed an odd incident which, for a time, seemed to put Dexter's chance of leading the side to Australia at risk. Dexter's own account of events is a little more dramatic than *Wisden's* but there is nothing unusual about *Wisden's* offering the truth, but not the whole truth. Towards the end of the second day, Burki and Nasim-ul-Ghani, both formidable batsmen, came together. They saw the day out and made a good start on the Saturday. The London crowd saw no reason why Lock, who had not got on at all in the first innings, should not have an opportunity and they said so. Dexter put him on and he was gratefully received by the batsmen. It was not Lock's wicket and they were more accustomed to spin than to speed. When Lock was hit so freely, Dexter should no doubt have taken him off, but he felt that the bowler was entitled to a long opportunity to think them out. It didn't happen and Dexter, who had not been in favour of Lock's selection in the first place, rather felt that he had been over-influenced by crowd pressures. When the batsmen left the field, still undefeated, at lunchtime, it was observed that Dexter failed to applaud them and there were those who chose to be offended by this.

Dexter was criticized as insensitive and ungracious. There was also a cynical interpretation of the incident. It had been announced that if play should end before 3.30 pm on the Saturday, an exhibition match would be arranged and it was no secret that the players were not fond of these bunfight matches, which often proved anti-climatic. Some observers thought that England were, literally, spinning things out so that they would not have to participate in an exhibition. The *Cricketer* correspondent suggested that, with no incentive to finish, England 'may have taken things a shade easily' but was at pains to say that this was subconscious and not deliberate. The end of it all was that England won comfortably before the close of play, but Cowdrey was made captain for the third Test at Leeds. There was no censure of Dexter and the general impression was that Cowdrey was to be given the chance to show what he could do; but there was just a little feeling in the air.

Meanwhile, a third candidate for the captaincy had emerged. David Sheppard had been in and out of the England side some years earlier and had led the team twice against Pakistan in 1954, and was a rival to Len Hutton for the captaincy in Australia. He was now ordained in the Church of England and most people assumed his Test career to be over, but he was due for a holiday and was persuaded to return to the Sussex side and to consider making himself available to tour Australia. It was no secret that Walter Robins, now the chairman of selectors, was seriously considering proposing him as captain. On the first day of the Lord's Test, Sheppard made a century against Oxford University for Sussex in his first game of the season, and the soap opera was well under way. Sheppard was not picked for the third Test, but continued to play himself quietly into form in county cricket, Dexter meanwhile played under Cowdrey's captaincy. Statham was fit again and replaced the injured Coldwell. Titmus replaced Lock, which was hardly surprising, and Murray came in as wicket-keeper. Pakistan also made changes and included Javed Akhtar, an off-spinner who had been sent for to reinforce the side, and was playing in the Test with no previous English experience, which was surely a mistake.

This time, Burki did put England in and things went very well for him at first, with England losing 6 wickets for 180. Munir Malik and Mahmood Hussain, both big men of no outstanding pace, did the damage, but as at Lord's, it was the combination of green pitch and heavy atmosphere that was really responsible. Stewart grafted skilfully and made 86 in four hours, but the senior batsmen all failed. Dexter scored 20 before Mahmood bowled him and there was a suggestion that he was reluctant to put his head down and play as Stewart was doing at the other end. The *Cricketer* correspondent commented, a trifle acidly, that he seemed to be interested mainly in hitting boundaries. Some ninety minutes were lost on the first day, and the score at the close was 194 for 6 with Parfitt and Murray together.

On the second day, conditions were much better for batting and the weaknesses in the Pakistan attack were exposed. Parfitt and Murray went on to 247 and then Allen and Parfitt added 99, followed by Trueman and

74

Statham who each played lively, hard-hitting innings. Burki was criticised for over-bowling Munir, who sent down 49 overs and took 5 for 128, but he had very little choice. Farooq was injured, Akhtar totally inexperienced in English conditions and Mahmood seemingly incapable of bowling at the wicket. Even Nasim-ul-Ghani, generally the tightest of bowlers, went for five runs an over.

428, after the score had stood at 180 for 6, was a huge and demoralising total and the batsmen, hampered by injuries to Hanif, Burki and Farooq, failed to conquer the pressure. In the first innings, Dexter produced a sharp and accurate spell to wind up the innings at 131, his analysis being 9.1-3-10-4, and he took another wicket in the second innings. All the England bowlers took wickets and Pakistan were out twice for a total of 311, 180 of the runs being scored by two men, Alim-ud-Din and Saeed. It was a most disappointing display.

Attention now switched to the captaincy and it was generally supposed that the matter would be settled, as it had been in 1950, by performances in the Gentlemen-Players match (the distinction between amateurs and professionals was officially abolished during the following winter and no more Gentlemen-Players matches were held). In passing it's worth mentioning that Dexter remained an amateur all his career and was never paid for his cricketing services for Sussex or England.

Sheppard had not made many runs after his first success at Oxford, but there was every reason to play him against the Players and thus give him one last chance to snatch the prize. Careful observers though had been impressed by Dexter's performance against Surrey a week before the Lord's game, while Sheppard got out for 4 and then struggled for 105 minutes for 24 in the second innings, Dexter produced the all-round performance of his life. He took 7 for 38 in Surrey's first innings, then scored 94 in 135 minutes when Sussex batted a second time, and finally when Surrey needed only 30 runs to win with seven wickets in hand, he took a wicket and made two close-in catches in the space of five balls. Surrey never recovered, and Sussex won. It was an example of genius and personality winning a lost match which must have impressed the selectors, although they made no announcement about the captaincy until after the Lord's match.

Cowdrey was appointed to captain the Gentlemen but was ill, so Dexter led in the vital game – or perhaps more correctly, the game that appeared to be vital. He and Sheppard both batted well on the opening day, Dexter making 55, but Sheppard going one better with a classic 112. The newspapers saw this as decisive and unanimously hailed Sheppard the next morning, only to be proved wrong by the appointment of Dexter on the same day.

My own view is that the selectors got it right. Remember that English cricket was rather under the spell of Richie Benaud at this time. He had led the side which massacred May's tourists in 1958-9 and had retained the Ashes in that sensational Old Trafford Test in 1961. Both as leg-spinner and as captain, Benaud was intimidating. Sheppard might have had the character to deal with him, but his batting form was suspect as the tour itself was to prove. Cowdrey was seen as too nice a chap to be faced with Benaud, which is probably the grossest of libels on both men, but that was how people saw it. Dexter was named as the man and had achieved the pinnacle, only four years after his Test debut. After the announcement, everybody lost interest in the Gentlemen-Players match which ended in an even draw. Trueman captaining the Players, made one of the biggest hits seen at Lord's for years, almost clearing the stand at the Nursery end.

The caravan moved on to Nottingham, where Dexter was reinstated as England captain. Cowdrey was still unfit and was replaced as an opener by Sheppard, who was still very much in contention for a player's place on the tour, Pullar came back to replace Stewart, Knight and Lock took over from Barrington and Allen. Pakistan had sent for their veteran bowler, Fazal Mahmood, who flew in just four days before the match. Burki had very bad luck on the first day. He won the toss on another very humid morning and put England in, but before play could start the rains came and washed out play for the day. The next morning conditions were much more favourable for batting, but the decision had been taken. Pullar went early and there followed a fascinating partnership. Sheppard struggled for a long time, but Dexter was in superb form from the start. His driving was described by one observer as almost awesome in its power. Sheppard slowly found his touch and was beginning to overhaul Dexter when they both got out in the eighties, Sheppard for 83 and Dexter for 85. This brought no relief to the bowlers as Graveney and Parfitt went on to make centuries. This was actually Parfitt's fifth hundred against the tourists, three in the Tests and two for Middlesex in the preceding game. The side to tour Australia was picking itself – or the batsmen were. The bowling was another matter.

Time was running against Dexter, however, and he was obliged to declare at lunch on the third scheduled day, with the score at 428 for 5. Fazal had bowled almost throughout, sending down 60 overs and taking 3 for 130. Pakistan were fighting with their backs to the wall from the start and were 127 for 6 by the close. More time was lost on the fourth day and although at one time Pakistan were 78 for 3, a stubborn unbeaten century by the nineteen year old Mushtaq saved the game, Pakistan being 7 runs on with 4 wickets in hand when the end came. Dexter had managed his bowling with skill, but it was asking a good deal of his ageing fast bowlers to expect them to bowl a side out twice in, effectively, two days.

England had won the series very decisively and were able to indulge in some experimental selection for the final Test at the Oval, even leaving out players whose presence was required by counties close to the head of the Championship table. Pullar was unfit, but Cowdrey was now fit again and able to replace him. Barrington came back for Graveney, Coldwell and Larter, a new cap, opened the bowling in place of Trueman and Statham. Allen and Illingworth were the spinners, for Titmus and Lock.

This time Dexter won the toss and batted on a true batsman's pitch. Cowdrey and Sheppard began at what we would now describe as a normal speed for the opening day of a Test, but was then considered 'sedate' by *Wisden* – 76 in two hours. However, they saw off the first energies of Pakistan's only two seam bowlers, Fazal and D'Souza, and thereafter it was plain sailing. Sheppard was out for 57, and then Cowdrey and Dexter simply dismantled the Pakistan attack, scoring 248 in 165 minutes. Cowdrey was second out at 365, having hit one six and twenty-three fours in his 182. England were 406 for 2 at the close, an awe-inspiring total.

Pakistan had gone into the match with a fairly ill-balanced attack for English conditions and once Fazal and D'Souza lost their early nip, there was very little for the batsmen to worry about. Burki seems to have managed the attack in a somewhat eccentric fashion. Throughout the innings, he and Saeed bowled one over apiece and Nasim bowled nine. Otherwise the bowling was shared by three men, the openers and Intikhab, who sent down 129 overs between them.

Dexter was out quite early on the second morning, doubtless to Burki's relief. He had hit five sixes and eighteen fours, and scored 172 in 228 minutes . His batting was rapturously acclaimed. The *Cricketer* described it neatly, as 'a combination of the debonair, the dashing and the deliberate' and *Playfair* said boldly that he was 'as good a batsman as there is in world cricket today' – high praise, when one thinks of Sobers and O'Neill.

Dexter declared rather early by today's standards, at 480 for 5 and set about the business of getting Pakistan out twice on a placid pitch. His chief strike bowler was Larter who, inexperienced as he was, had pace and great height. He struck in his second over, dismissing Ijaz Butt and thereafter Dexter used him in short spells. Imtiaz and Mushtaq added 82 for the second wicket, but once Larter had parted them only Hanif, coming in rather far down the order at No 6, made runs and Pakistan were all out for 183 early on the Saturday. They did rather better in the follow-on, Imtiaz and Mushtaq again having a long partnership, but England were able to nibble their way through the rest and won by 10 wickets early on the fourth day. Larter had taken 9 wickets for 145 in his first Test, and it seemed that England had found a new star. But he didn't play in England again until

1965 and was only intermittently successful on tour, but he remains one of the might-have-beens of Test history.

In all it had been a rather odd season for Dexter. He had led England very competently in four Tests and had survived the little hiccup at Lord's, but he cannot have been helped by the very public debate about the tour captaincy. He had now emerged as the major batsman in an impressive England line-up and the forthcoming series in Australia would turn on the struggle between him and Benaud, both in leadership terms and in terms of Dexter's ability to deal with the leg-spinner. A most intriguing series was in prospect.

	Innings	N.O.	H.S.	Runs	Average	100	50
1962	6	1	172	446	89.20	1	3
To date	56	5	205	2573	50.45	7	13

10 A disappointing finale

For once the England team for the 1962-3 tour was pretty well received by the critics. The team had more or less picked itself and the most doubtful decision was the inclusion of three off-spinners, Allen, Illingworth and Titmus. There was nobody to turn the ball away from the right-hander except for Barrington. He was essentially a batsman who bowled a little, rather than an all-rounder, though he did get through quite a few overs on the tour. Many people thought that Lock should have gone and this view was confirmed when he signed up with Western Australia and went on to have a pretty good season. The other bowlers were Statham and Trueman, great fast bowlers but now aged 32 and 31 respectively, Larter, Coldwell and Knight, the Essex all-rounder who bowled at a good round fast-medium pace and batted with assurance.

The England batting line-up was strong; Dexter himself, Barrington, Cowdrey, Graveney and Pullar all had solid achievements to their credit and Parfitt had shown real promise against Pakistan. The biggest doubt was Sheppard, who had done as well as anyone could have expected on his return, averaging 44 in first-class cricket in 1962, but he had looked more than a little tentative at times. The selectors were gambling on his undoubted class, by the end of the tour they could tell themselves that the gamble had paid off, but only just. The party was completed by Murray and A C Smith, two wicket-keepers who were both enterprising batsmen.

The greatest surprise was the appointment of the Duke of Norfolk, the Earl Marshal of England, as the manager. To this day nobody is quite sure whose idea this was, but the Duke did a first-class public relations job, taking the limelight off Dexter in the most helpful way. His assistant manager would clearly have to do a lot of work on the cricket and financial side and Alec Bedser was the ideal choice. A dedicated servant of English cricket and a good friend of Australia, he was one of the major factors in making it a thoroughly happy tour, and when the Duke had to return to Britain in the exercise of his official duties (among other things to supervise a very private rehearsal of Sir Winston Churchill's funeral) and S C Griffith the MCC secretary, took over, Bedser was able to manage the transition which might otherwise have presented a few difficulties. A

79

slightly awkward-looking arrangement in fact worked out perfectly well.

The most intriguing prospect this winter was the captaincy battle. Benaud was sure to be the Australian captain, after his success in 1961, and Dexter had been picked as the captain least likely to be overawed by him. Benaud was a formidable personality and a deep thinker about the game, and there were those who believed he would out-think Dexter at every point. It didn't quite work out like that, Dexter had ideas of his own and the eventual result – a 1-1 draw – probably represented a draw between the captains too. This duel was further enhanced because Benaud was his team's most consistently formidable bowler and Dexter with his forthright approach, was the batsman whose job would be to subdue the leg-spinner.

The tour began in the roller-coaster fashion that veteran followers of the game have come to expect. A good win over Western Australia, with Titmus and Larter making an excellent start and Dexter hitting an impressive 76, was followed by a disastrous defeat at the hands of a Combined XI. The trouble was that few of the MCC batsmen could cope with some lively fast bowling from McKenzie and Hoare, who took 17 wickets between them at a cost of only 206 runs. MCC had rather the better of a draw against South Australia, a not-out 137 from Titmus being a real bonus, and then made a massive 633 for 7 against a rather second-rate Australian XI attack at Melbourne. This was the highest MCC score in Australia since the Bodyline tour of 1932-3. Barrington was the leading scorer with 219 not out and Dexter scored 102 in 110 minutes, Knight also chipping in with a hundred. England came nowhere near winning this match, the Australian XI making 451 and 201 for 4, and this highlighted the difficulties facing Dexter if he was to force victory over Australia. He had to conserve the energies of his two veteran fast bowlers using his second-line fast attack which was manifestly less dangerous and the accurate but hardly penetrative spin attack. Worst of all, the catching was unreliable to put it kindly, and this was a particular weakness of Sheppard's. His batting technique was making up for some slowness of reaction, but he was so liable to error in the field that he was likely to go into each innings owing his captain a few runs.

The next match against New South Wales, by far the strongest State side, was a critical one – they had easily won the Sheffield Shield the preceding season and they were led by Benaud. MCC fielded very nearly their strongest side, omitting only Barrington of the Test certainties and they were slaughtered. Pullar, enjoying some luck, made 132 in the first innings, but nobody else made many. Dexter made 42 in as many minutes, without getting on top of Benaud. MCC were out for 348 and NSW scored 532 for 6, Simpson and O'Neill making handsome centuries and everybody making hay of the spinners. Trueman, ominously, had to go off

80

with lumbago, and this meant that Dexter had to bowl himself more than he might have liked. He too was very expensive, and when MCC batted again, he played a weary stroke at Benaud and was out for 5. Benaud went on to take 7 for 18 and MCC had lost a State match by an innings for the first time in the twentieth century. First blood to Benaud as captain and bowler.

Some team morale was restored in the Queensland match when the tourists made 581 for 6, Barrington again making a big hundred and four others, including Dexter, passing fifty. However, Queensland were not a strong bowling side and although they were reinforced by Wes Hall, the pitch was so slow that he could do little on it. One thing he did was to break his wicket-keeper's jaw, and Grout had to miss the first three Tests, which was an unexpected bit of good luck for England though not for Australia.

England had only two critical selection decisions to make for the first Test. Parfitt was preferred to Graveney as the No 6 batsman for his fine fielding which was needed to strengthen England's doubtful fielding. (In passing, it says much about the strength of the batting that it was the No 6 slot for which Graveney had to contend.) Trueman, Titmus and Statham picked themselves. None of the other bowlers had really looked the part and the selectors went for Knight to pack the batting. Titmus had bowled steadily and batted well and was to be a vital part of the England machine.

Unusually Australia had produced no new players and their side was essentially that which had retained the Ashes in 1961, Grout being the only absentee. Harvey and Davidson were still very formidable but approaching the end of their distinguished careers. The attack seemed to be a bowler short and much would depend on Mackay's ability to keep an end going inexpensively and on Benaud's suspect shoulder holding out. But the side batted very long, with Benaud at No 9, and Australia started favourites, for the first Test at Brisbane.

Benaud won the toss and elected to bat on a very hot day. This meant England needed to make an early breakthrough if Australia were not to make a big score. Trueman achieved this, beating Lawry outside the off-stump a couple of times, before getting him to edge one and give Smith his first catch in a Test. O'Neill made a shaky but lucky start, he might have been run out by Dexter before he scored and then nicked a ball into the slips which both Sheppard and Parfitt touched before it fell to earth. However O'Neill was out soon fending Trueman to short-leg when he had made 19. Harvey settled in, but Dexter fooled Simpson by whistling a bumper past him, then bowled another short ball, a long-hop in truth, which Simpson hooked at and got high on the bat to be taken at mid-on.

At 97 for 3 Australia were in a little trouble at lunch but it was to get worse. Burge and Harvey were out by the time the score had reached 140 and Dexter could congratulate himself on a really good piece of attacking cricket. He would have been conscious though that his bowlers were vulnerable if any batsman got well in, and it was Booth who frustrated him. He and Davidson batted for an hour and when Mackay followed Davidson, the attack was beginning to wilt. This was the first series in which England had to play six hours a day in Australia and they had perhaps the wrong side for it. It was asking a lot of Trueman and Statham to come back after tea and Dexter was very grateful for Titmus and his thoughtful accuracy in the last hour. Booth was not to be contained however, and completed his hundred in under three hours. Titmus finally dismissed him, very well caught by Dexter for 112, just before the end, which came at 321 for 7. It had been an even day finally; the score was less than England could reasonably have expected on losing the toss.

The second day was less satisfactory for England. Mackay and Benaud added 67 more runs before Benaud was caught by Smith down the leg-side off Knight, who made short work of the last two, leaving Mackay not out on 86. Mackay, who, like Harvey and Davidson was playing in his last series, was one of the characters of the era. A remarkably ungraceful left-hander, he had a disastrous time in Laker's year of 1956, being totally unable to cope with the off-spinner on helpful wickets, but in Australia he could be a most frustrating opponent, being a fine timer of the ball with a most uncanny appreciation of the position of his off-stump. Time and again he would leave a ball alone which was missing the stumps by millimetres. It is hard to imagine a cricketer who presented a greater contrast to Dexter and yet there they both were, each playing a valuable part for their sides.

England made a slightly sticky start against accurate bowling and sharp fielding which put their own efforts to shame. But Sheppard and Pullar survived the opening attack and were beginning to settle when Benaud came on and got them both out in two overs. England were 65 for 2 and Dexter's duel with Benaud became not merely a personal struggle, but decisive in the context of the match and very possibly of the series. Dexter rose magnificently to the occasion, cutting, pulling and driving. He scored 40 in 45 minutes, dominating a partnership with Cowdrey, who looked secure enough but content to leave all the aggression to his captain. Mackay contained Dexter with a good probing spell and Cowdrey holed out at long-leg off Simpson. Finally, at the end of the day, in difficult light, Dexter seemed to lose sight of a flighted ball from Benaud and was bowled for an excellent 70. The first battle between the captains had ended in a draw, but England were 169 for 4 at the close and looking vulnerable.

England pulled the game round on the third day, Smith, the night-watchman, made a solid 21 in the first hour and saw off the opening overs of the new ball. Meanwhile Barrington was batting admirably, taking every chance to score and reaching his fifty in under two hours – swift going in the circumstances. Parfitt made a jittery start, but 264 for 5 at lunch represented a real recovery. Benaud appeared to be the only bowler to worry the batsmen once the shine was off the ball, but it was Mackay who first applied the brake with a thoughtful defensive spell. Eventually Barrington lost patience, lashed out at Benaud and was taken in the covers. Then Parfitt and Titmus got rather bogged down, the latter in particular being foot-tied against Simpson, who ought perhaps to have been hittable. Parfitt fell at last to Benaud for 80 and England were all out for 389. It had been a good riposte to Australia's score and a draw was very much on the cards.

The Australian second innings was one of the low points of the tour for England. Simpson and Lawry had been a little lucky to survive five torrid overs on the third evening, but settled in happily next morning against some fairly defensive fields. The hundred came up before lunch and it was very evident that Australia were not going to be bowled out. The most ominous sign was that Trueman and Statham looked distinctly less formidable than on the first day; what would they look like by the end of the series? Two catches went down before Dexter had Simpson caught at the wicket, but this only brought in O'Neill, the likeliest man to force the pace towards an early declaration. Titmus tied him down for a while, but he got going against Knight and Dexter. Lawry went for 98, being caught by Sheppard off Titmus. Harvey came in and the assault continued, but England were glad to get rid of O'Neill when he took one chance too many against Statham. By now the only question was when Benaud would choose to declare, and it was something of a compliment to Dexter that he delayed until the close of play when Australia were 362 for 4, leaving England needing 378 to win. This was clearly an unrealistic target, but if any man in the world was likely to contemplate it and to give the fielding captain a fright, it was Dexter.

England began sensibly and well, taking the runs as they came and not allowing the bowlers to get on top of batsmen intent only on survival. Pullar and Sheppard made 83 in two hours before lunch, slowish going but not unduly so. Pullar was dropped at the wicket, but otherwise they looked safe enough. When Pullar got out at 114, Dexter strode impatiently to the wicket and was at once looking to beat the field. He was more successful against Benaud than against Davidson, who was in the middle of a good spell; he had dismissed Pullar and now he had Sheppard in the gully. Cowdrey had been looking out of sorts for some time and he now looked incapable of hitting the ball off the square. Dexter scored 50, while Sheppard and then Cowdrey at the other end, were making nine. At tea England were 182 for 2, needing 196.

There was still drama left in the game. Cowdrey was out to Benaud, whereupon Dexter who had already hit Mackay off, sailed into Simpson, who went for 19 off one eight-ball over, 11 to Dexter and 8 to Barrington. Understandably, Benaud whipped him off and took the overdue new ball. Dexter was yorked by McKenzie for 99, made in 185 minutes out of 143, and the pendulum swung again. Barrington was caught, as was Parfitt, and Titmus and Knight had to play out time, which they did with no trouble. The match was drawn, very slightly in Australia's favour on figures, but this concealed the very real success of England's batting on this last day. The critics were agreed that Benaud had been mastered on the day and that England had a real chance in the series. E W Swanton, as usual, had a perceptive comment:

Dexter at the moment is a fascinating cricketer. He commands a team of inescapable limitations and one cannot say with hand on heart that his grasp of fundamentals is sure enough always to make the most of what he has got. That side of his performance is maturing, one hopes . . . At the same time, he is probably becoming increasingly aware of the influence he wields as a batsman, not only on his own side, but on the opposition.

The comment on his captaincy is a fair one, but of course, Dexter's lack of experience must be remembered. His batting, as I have said, was the key to the whole series.

MCC played two encouraging first-class matches between the first and second Tests. Victoria were beaten by five wickets, Cowdrey making runs and looking in distinctly better form and Coldwell taking 6 for 49 in the second innings. Pullar was injured while fielding, went in down the order with a runner and scored 91. He would be fit for the Test, but the main effect of the accident was that Parfitt had to open in this game and the next, failed four times and went out of the Test team, which was bad luck for him. Against South Australia Cowdrey regained his batting form in the most dramatic way, making 307, the highest score ever made by an Englishman in Australia. Graveney also made a hundred, which sealed Parfitt's fate.

For the Second Test at Melbourne, played over the New Year, Graveney took Parfitt's place and Coldwell replaced Knight. Australia were unchanged and won the toss. Again they got into early difficulties, and although they recovered England were well in the game at the end of the innings. They would have been much better placed if they had held their catches, but four or five went down making an incalculable difference. Simpson and Lawry were particularly lucky in the opening session. Not only were three chances missed but there was a good deal of playing and missing, this even though Trueman was clearly below his best and operating off a shortened run. Coldwell finally got rid of Simpson with the score at 62 and then O'Neill after taking the score with Lawry to 111, was taken at slip off Statham. Soon after Coldwell dismissed Harvey before he had scored and Trueman had yorked Lawry.

At 112 for 4, Australia were in considerable trouble and looking to Booth once again. He and Burge tried to play their way quietly out of trouble but Dexter faced them with Titmus, who had them both out, sweeping. For a captain who was supposed to have an inadequate grasp of fundamentals, Dexter wasn't doing badly. Arguably he should have kept the pressure on with his fast bowlers, but he preferred to wait for the new ball and with a class off-spinner attacking two left-hand bats, he may well have been right. In fact it didn't come off, and the new ball had been taken some time before Trueman got Davidson to edge to Smith; by this time 164 for 6 had become 237 for 7. Statham now had Benaud dropped twice and Australia finished at 263 for 7, only a moderate score on a good wicket.

The Australian tail fought it out next morning in typical fashion finally reaching 316. England went in with high hopes, but in his very first over, Davidson beat Sheppard all ends up and only missed Dexter's off-stump by the proverbial coat of varnish. Dexter now played yet another fine innings; he lost Pullar to Davidson immediately after lunch, but then added 175 with Cowdrey in the best England stand of the series, quantitatively and qualitatively. They started warily against Davidson, but Dexter hit McKenzie for two fours in an over and when Benaud switched his fast bowlers over, did the same to Davidson. Benaud came on himself and they took 25 off his first 3 overs. Mackay came on and the batsmen took easy singles off him to bring the field in to make room for the fours. It seemed too good to be true. Benaud was forced to bring O'Neill into the attack and he actually induced two chances, although the second, a drive by Dexter, nearly took the bowler's head off. When both men were approaching their hundreds, Benaud came on again and got Dexter to edge one to Simpson when he was only seven short of his century. He had made his third successive score of 70 or more and was certainly ahead on points in his personal battle with Benaud. Barrington came in and saw out the day, protecting the weary-looking Cowdrey who was on 94, out of 210 for 3, at the close.

Cowdrey and Barrington made a good beginning to the day, the former completing his hundred in the first ten minutes and then setting about Benaud, but he mis-hooked McKenzie and was caught and, almost before he was back in the pavilion, Barrington was lbw to a really unplayable ball from the same bowler. England's hopes of a really substantial score faded, and they did well in the end to get a lead of 15. Only Graveney looked at all happy and he was run out by Harvey when he had made 41. Davidson went through the tail and England had forfeited their chance.

Simpson and Lawry started confidently, almost complacently for Australia, and then Trueman looking much sharper than in the first innings, bowled Simpson middle stump and had O'Neill caught by

Cowdrey first ball. Tea was taken with the sides very much on an even keel, and immediately afterwards Harvey tried to take one for the throw to Pullar and was run out by a distance. Once again Lawry was holding the innings together, but he lost Burge at 69, and then in the last over, was himself put down at slip.

At the time, it seemed that this was a very important miss indeed; if Lawry had been out, Australia would have been 105 for 5 and would in all probability have been struggling to make a decent score the next day. I have generally refrained from identifying those who put the catches down, but in the light of the sequel I can perhaps say that the culprit on this occasion was David Sheppard, who had already missed a few close catches on the tour and was now fielding at slip while Graveney was off the field. Dexter was, reasonably, criticised for putting Sheppard there and if the match had been lost, the placing might have gone down in history alongside Maclaren's mis-disposition of Fred Tate. Fortunately, there was to be a happy ending – this time.

Australia started uncertainly on the fourth day. Lawry and Booth survived but could make little of the bowling and had made only 29 in the first 90 minutes, Lawry's fifty arriving after four and a half hours. A few minutes before lunch, it seemed that the one result which had seemed unlikely at the end of the third day – a draw – was on the cards, for Australia were approaching 160 for 4, only 145 ahead and Benaud had already shown that he was unlikely to make a challenging declaration with Dexter about. Almost in desperation, the captain went on himself and, with a touch of real originality, bowled the last ball before lunch round-arm and distinctly quick. It was the sort of thing that Ian Botham was to do in later years, and Dexter's enterprise was rewarded when the ball turned out to be a dead shooter, shot under Lawry's bat and uprooted his middle stump. It was perhaps the decisive ball of the match.

After a brief interruption for fine rain, Booth and Davidson plodded on till Titmus got Davidson to edge one. Mackay failed, and then Cowdrey took a superb rolling catch at slip to get rid of Benaud. McKenzie was out for nought and Jarman entered in a breathless hush, Booth being on 94. Jarman was equal to the occasion, he not only saw Booth to his hundred but added 20 valuable runs with him. They took England's target to 234, a very different matter from 214.

A finish was now almost certain. England had half an hour to bat in which it was important not to lose a wicket. Pullar was a little unlucky and fell to McKenzie's first ball; he brought off a leg-glance, but hit it a little too fine and Jarman dived to make a great catch. Many captains would have sent a night-watchman in at this moment but this was not Dexter's way. He came in himself, striding eagerly to the wicket looking ready to get at the bowlers. It was a positive decision and he deserved to win.

Neither batsman looked to be in any trouble during the next two overs, but the umpires took them off for bad light with a quarter of an hour to go – leaving all to play for next day. It rained in the night, which slowed the outfield down and the skies were still overcast in the morning. Conditions were in Australia's favour and Sheppard in particular must have felt less than confident. He had made a duck in the first innings and had fielded so poorly that his Test future looked doubtful.

Dexter was much more confident and got under way by cracking Davidson for a couple of fours. Benaud came on for two overs, during which he very nearly had Dexter as he tried to cut and instead edged the ball only just wide of the off-stump. Then he changed ends, tossed one up to Sheppard and saw it hammered through the covers for a glorious four, neither Harvey nor O'Neill, both splendid fielders, could move to cut it off. It was an important moment for Sheppard never looked in real doubt again, though he was hard pressed to keep out a couple of dangerous inswingers from Davidson. Dexter looked happy enough against Benaud but found Mackay difficult to get away. The general view of the critics was that he was just a little out of touch and very sensibly adjusting his game accordingly, waiting for the bad ball and hitting it hard. At lunch, he and Sheppard had each scored 44, and the total was 96 for 1, an excellent start.

After lunch Sheppard looked the more fluent and Dexter had a fright when Benaud made a great leap at an edged stroke, got a hand to it, but could not quite hold it. Dexter got over the shock and went to his fifty, but was then sadly and unnecessarily run out when Sheppard called him for a quick single to Benaud fielding at short cover. Dexter responded at once, but the run was never on if the throw was straight and he was out by a foot or so. England were 129 for 2 and in a little bit of bother.

Cowdrey started slowly and Sheppard took time to settle down again. Suddenly they looked vulnerable, as Cowdrey tried to place McKenzie wide of the slips and edged. Luckily for him, Davidson, of all people, put it down. Then Sheppard edged Davidson, and Jarman and Simpson made a mess of it between them. If fielders like Davidson and Simpson were making mistakes, the pressure was getting to them, too.

The crisis passed as both batsmen got hold of McKenzie. The requirement was shrinking fast and at tea it was virtually over, England having made 188 for 2, with Sheppard just four runs short of a memorable century. Five minutes after tea, Sheppard hit Benaud for three and completed his hundred. It had taken him 264 minutes and he had looked the part throughout.It was downhill work now for England. Benaud gave the new ball to Davidson but he looked weary and uninspired, and Mackay came back. Both players now contributed fine strokes and the runs came fast. It was an anti-climax when Sheppard was run out for 113 with the scores level, but it mattered not at all. The match was won by 7 wickets and England one up in the series, would take a lot of beating.

When England batted first in the Third Test at Sydney, Sheppard appeared completely bemused by Davidson. It was as if he had never played that innings at Melbourne. He was beaten several times and it was no surprise when he got an edge and was taken by McKenzie at slip. True to form Dexter played Davidson with much more assurance. This time Benaud won the battle with Dexter, getting him to mistime a slower ball to third man. Dexter had scored 32, and this was his first dismissal for less than fifty. Even so, half-way through the series, Dexter had scored 346 at an average of 69.20, impressive figures. From this point he rather fell away and his poorer form was reflected in the side's decline. Cowdrey batted calmly but unassertively and Pullar was having trouble finding the gaps. On either side of lunch the game seemed to be slipping Australia's way and when Simpson came on, Pullar holed out to Benaud at mid-wicket. Barrington made a brisk start encouraging Cowdrey to look for runs until England had made 161 for 3 at tea and the game was delicately poised.

After tea Cowdrey sailed into both Guest and Benaud, scoring at more than a run a minute. Not for the first time in his career, it seemed that he might be about to dominate a Test. But he fell, just when he seemed under way. He tried to cut the innocuous-looking Simpson and was caught by Jarman off the bottom edge. Simpson followed this by having Parfitt out for nought, pushing sightlessly out and being caught at leg-slip. England at 203 for 5 seemed to have thrown away their advantage. Davidson came back with the new ball – a bold decision by Benaud, when Simpson was getting wickets – and he, and then Simpson again, wrapped the innings up. England finished with 279 and if Trueman had not laid about him for 32, it would have been a good deal less.

Statham and Trueman were unable to make any impression on the batsmen when the Australian innings began and Trueman, who was up and down throughout this season, was distinctly lacking in fire. Coldwell came on and Lawry at once edged him a little too fine, to be caught down the leg side by Murray. Sadly, Murray landed heavily on his shoulder in making the catch and soon had to leave the field with Parfitt taking his place for the rest of the match. Parfitt made a very brave effort, but a substitute wicket-keeper is never as effective as the specialist and the England fielding suffered. Simpson and Harvey batted a little shakily now and Harvey was dropped once, and came close to offering another catch off Barrington.

The cricket was pretty sub-standard in the afternoon session. Trueman was rested and Statham and Coldwell looked pretty plain; only Titmus bowling into the wind, looked a genuine Test bowler and Dexter was virtually obliged to make him the corner-stone of the attack. He and his

88

Dexter's stance: orthodox and aggressive. *Evening Argus*

Dexter taking the field with Sussex. Jim Parks on his right, Alan
Oakman behind. *Evening Argus*

Dexter and Sheppard, friendly rivals for the captaincy in 1962.
Evening Argus

Dexter pulls a ball to the boundary in the Gentlemen-Players match
of 1962, the last time the match was played at Lord's. He was
appointed to lead the side to Australia in the course of the match.
S & G Press Agency

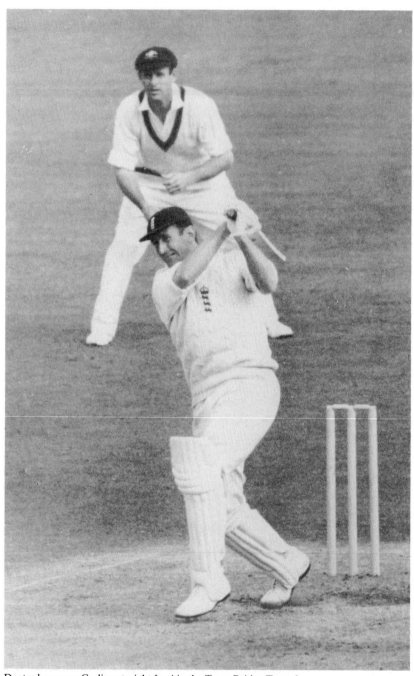

Dexter hammers Corling straight for 4 in the Trent Bridge Test of
1964. O'Neill at slip. *Barnaby's Pic Library*

Susan Dexter, Ted Dexter, Colin Cowdrey and Jimmy Hill.
Tudor Press Agency

Ted Dexter and Richie Benaud. Opposing captains in Australia 1962-63. *Evening Argus*

Dexter in 'retirement', on his favourite form of transport. He is
holding the William Younger Cup, competed for by village cricket
teams, before the final in 1985. *P A Photos*

England Team
B.R. L-R D A Allen, J M Parks, D B Close, F Titmus, M Stewart, J Edrich.
F.R. L-R K Barrington, F Trueman, Ted Dexter, D Shakleton, M C Cowdrey, June 1963.

England v Australia at Lords:
Ted Dexter, England's Captain, bowling during Australia's 1st innings, 20 June 1964.

The Spirit of Festival: Ted Dexter hits another boundary, Hastings.
Gerald Brodribb

Dexter, chairman of selectors, in the troubled series of 1989, with
David Gower (captain) and Alan Knott at Old Trafford. *Patrick Eagar*

fellow-selectors must have been regretting the decision to play Coldwell rather than Allen. None of the batsmen looked happy against Titmus and he had Harvey caught at cover soon after tea. O'Neill looked uncertain, and Simpson, on the edge of his first Test hundred, was obviously very nervous. He was finally out for 91, playing no stroke to the ball from Titmus which bowled him. Almost at once, O'Neill hit all round another well-pitched-up ball from Titmus and was bowled. The score was 187 for 4, the match was in the balance and Shepherd about to come in to play his first innings in a Test at a most awkward moment. The situation became worse still when Booth was caught off Titmus and the close of play score was 212 for 5.

The third day was undoubtedly England's worst of the series though it began well enough when Sheppard ran Jarman out with a deft flick from short leg, as he played forward. Davidson lasted for an hour before Titmus trapped him, meanwhile Shepherd had been batting serenely enough; he was no great stylist, but a solid player who knew his limitations. Benaud then came in and they began to bustle the field with some short runs. With a makeshift wicket-keeper, this was the more possible of course, but Titmus brought this little phase to an end with a smart return catch to send Benaud back. He then had McKenzie, and Australia were only one run ahead with the last man coming to the wicket. Shepherd and Guest, also playing in his first Test, added 39 before Statham bowled Guest. Titmus finished with 7 for 79 and had carried the England effort. Dexter had not bowled at all but he may have felt that he hadn't enough runs to play with, and he did tend to bowl rather less when Coldwell, a similar bowler to himself, was in the side.

It was very soon apparent that what had seemed to be an even position was no such thing. Pullar played a terrible stroke at his second ball from Davidson, pushing at it with no movement of his feet and dragging it on to his stumps for a duck. Dexter looked thoroughly ill at ease for almost the first time in the series, fishing three times at out-swingers from Davidson before getting the edge to one which Simpson took two-handed at first slip for only 11.

Sheppard had momentarily looked as though he were conquering his uncertainties, but he now failed to cover Davidson's swing and was caught by Simpson. At 25 for 3, England were still 15 behind, with half the specialist batting gone. Benaud came on now and before England had cleared the deficit, induced Cowdrey to snick yet again, Simpson finished the job with a fine catch and the match was surely lost.

Parfitt looked terribly insecure, but it was Barrington who went next, playing back to a half-volley, the kind of thing that only happens when a side is in shock. Titmus was taken at leg-slip and Murray, inexplicably, came in next. He could do no more than scrape forward at each ball, but managed to bat out the day with Parfitt. The score was 86 for 6, a sickening score-line for England to contemplate after the euphoria of Melbourne.

Next day, Murray soldiered on painfully, but could only watch as McKenzie and Davidson clinically removed the last four batsmen at the other end. England were all out for 104. Murray was left at 3 not out, he had batted for 74 minutes before scoring and is immortalised accordingly in that odd little list in the record books of those who have batted for an hour in a Test before getting off the mark.

Australia needed only 65 runs and there was a distinct lack of excitement about the prospect. As a final blow to England, a short shower ensured that they would be bowling with a wet ball and that the shine would soon disappear. Trueman, bowling with rather more life than in the first innings, defeated Lawry and Harvey, the latter playing a distinctly absent-minded stroke, but Simpson and Booth saw things through and the match was safely won. England could only be intensely disappointed to be brought back to earth with such a jolt, but the series was balanced and still very much alive. One small compensation was that Lawry had failed in each innings. Dexter has explained in his book that this was the result of a careful plan designed to block Lawry's best strokes and concentrate on his relative weakness, the cut. Characteristically, Dexter almost apologises for closing Lawry down and not cultivating his strokes and it does indicate that Dexter was a good deal more than a dashing playboy as a captain. The plan certainly worked, Lawry's first four innings in the series were 5,98,52,57; thereafter he made 8,8,10,16,11 and 45 not out, the last innings when he was making no serious attempt to score as Australia played for a draw.

England had to bring Smith back in place of Murray for the fourth Test in Adelaide. Graveney was fit again and replaced Parfitt and Illingworth was chosen ahead of Coldwell; this lengthened the batting and also recognised the fact that Adelaide usually took a little spin later in the match. Australia too lengthened their batting, recalling Mackay for Guest, who had played his one and only Test match. Grout was fit at last and came back for Jarman.

Benaud won the toss on a gloriously sunny day, but England struck a quick blow when Simpson glanced Statham and was acrobatically caught by Smith. Harvey came in and played perhaps the luckiest innings of his life, once he got away with a glance at Trueman which Dexter just got a hand to but could not hold. A quiet spell followed until Dexter brought Illingworth on; he bowled Lawry at once leaving Australia 16 for 2. This should have led to a collapse, but in the spinner's next over, Harvey was dropped off successive balls by Cowdrey and then Sheppard. If he had gone, with an out of form O'Neill coming in at 21 for 3, anything might have happened. Harvey now began to play his strokes, but was dropped

90

yet again, this time by Cowdrey. It was rare for him to drop two slip-catches in one morning and it was particularly bad luck that he did so in this vital match. Booth had been batting on, playing and missing now and again until finally after lunch, he got an edge to Titmus and this time Cowdrey held the catch.

In came O'Neill and promptly pushed one straight through Dexter at short-leg. This time Dexter was undoubtedly too close. That was the end of the alarums as far as Australia were concerned and from that moment it was all strokeplay from them and toil for the bowlers. 77 runs were rattled up in the hour before tea, Harvey completed his last Test hundred and turned his attention to nursing O'Neill to his hundred. This duly arrived and then both batsmen fell to Dexter, mostly through sheer weariness and loss of concentration. With Statham and Trueman wilting in the heat – Trueman had to leave the field – the captain had borne more than his share of the bowling, putting in 19 overs. Dexter was never afraid of hard work, and he fully deserved the reward of two wickets. Australia were 322 for 5 at the close and it began to seem that the best England could hope for was to escape with a draw and renew the fight again at Sydney; it would all have been very different if two or three catches had been held.

The second day was an odd one. Australia ought to have gone on to a big score after such a start, but it didn't happen, the last five going down for 71. Davidson and Benaud made a little stand and Dexter brought himself on again to break it. Davidson was the only batsman to make many runs, but he took his time about it and England may not have minded seeing him tiring himself out. Sheppard must have had a nasty moment when, after his previous missed chances, he found himself under a towering skier, but he held it safely, to finish the innings at 393.

Australia struck early getting Pullar quickly out bowled off his pads. Dexter promoted Barrington to No 3, possibly because he himself was very tired after bowling 23 overs, but Barrington was a regular No 3 for his county, which Dexter wasn't, and it was a logical move. Barrington launched into a remarkable assault on Davidson, hitting him for four consecutive fours, three of them over the heads of the slips. It was strong stuff, all right if it came off. In fact it was Davidson who came off, clutching a thigh. He had bowled just 28 balls for 30 runs thanks to Barrington. England had the platform to go on to a good score, but Benaud brought all his great experience to bear to prevent it. He came on himself and tossing one high, had Sheppard going down the pitch and missing.

Barrington had settled down to play a long innings, but Cowdrey was in one of his introspective moods. Suddenly both fell, to Simpson and McKenzie. Dexter and Graveney had a real crisis on their hands at 119 for 4. Dexter was troubled by Simpson for a time, but he was happy to take it out on Mackay. After three-quarters of an hour in which runs had come pretty freely, Graveney fell to McKenzie. There followed a piece of typical Dexter. Graveney was out at quarter to six with Dexter on 25. One would have expected him to shut up shop and concentrate on shielding Titmus, but he protected him in the most effective fashion possible, sailing into Simpson and hitting him for two huge sixes. He doubled his score in the last fifteen minutes and sent everybody home looking forward eagerly to the next day.

Anti-climax followed. To begin with, persistent drizzle prevented any play before lunch, a blow to England even though their hopes of a win were faint enough. When they finally got on, Dexter and Titmus began quietly and the former was on 61 and just beginning to open out when he took a slash at McKenzie and was quite miraculously caught by Grout, flying to his right. Dexter did seem to get out to astonishing catches rather more often than most batsmen, though this may only have been because he was a stroke-player, and catches off him were usually hard ones. It now became a question of how many England could scrape together. Titmus played excellently, very straight and not at all discomposed by the situation or by anything Benaud could throw at him. After two more wickets had fallen, Trueman arrived to play one of his best innings, scoring 38 in as many minutes, including two splendid off-driven sixes off Benaud. England were 328 for 9 at the close and a draw seemed probable.

Statham was quickly out on the fourth morning and Titmus was left not out on 59 with an innings total of 331. England had yet another piece of bad luck when a short shower gave them a wet ball to bowl with, but Trueman soon had Lawry, and Harvey was picked up by Barrington the first time he offered a chance. The score was 37 for 2. Simpson and Booth understandably closed things down, adding just 86 during the afternoon. Dexter tried everything, but failed to part them. Benaud may now have thought that he was pretty safe from defeat and gave Booth orders to go for it, because he made 24 in the half-hour after tea. Dexter now came on, and once again he struck, having Simpson caught as he tried to push the ball between slips and gully and then Booth taken down the leg side.

At the fall of Booth Australia were 237 on and realistically England were not going to have a target unless Benaud declared, which he was not going to do. O'Neill and Shepherd added a few runs and then Dexter came back again and defeated Shepherd. He was having another good day with the ball even if the game was eluding him. Mackay fell before the close, but O'Neill and Benaud saw it out at 225 for 6. Benaud might declare at some point during the morning, but it wasn't very likely. Benaud was himself dropped by Titmus in the first over of the day, but O'Neill fell in the third over and that really ended any chance of Australia scoring fast enough for a declaration.

92

Australia were in fact all out on the stroke of lunch, leaving England needing 356 – too many by any reckoning. Australia were a bowler short and it seemed unlikely that they would manage to bowl England out, but then the openers fell, fishing outside the off-stump in the first ten minutes, and Sheppard in particular seemed to have forgotten that he had ever made a Test hundred. Cricket form is a strange and elusive thing. Barrington and Cowdrey tried to rebuild the innings and they were doing so successfully when Cowdrey tried a quick single to O'Neill, the last man in the world to tilt against, and was narrowly run out. Dexter, realistically, batted quietly, but he always looked more vulnerable to Benaud when he surrendered the initiative, and the Australian captain soon had him, well caught by Simpson for 10. Barrington was now on 76, out of a total of 122 for 4 when Graveney joined him. There was just a chance of an England collapse if Graveney failed, for Illingworth was ill and not fit to bat. However Graveney stood firm and together with Barrington added 101 at a run a minute. Barrington completed his first hundred against Australia in three hours less four minutes, with a huge six. The match thus ended in a tame draw and it was all to play for.

England had the better of a draw with Victoria before the fifth Test. Graveney made a big hundred and Dexter himself scored 35 and 70, maintaining his batting form to the end. The final Test was going to be a most vital one, in a double sense; England needed to win of course, to regain the Ashes, but an attractive match was hoped for too. So far, the series had not come up to the high standard set by Australia and the West Indies two years earliers. This was partly because few batsmen had contrived to turn fifties into hundreds – the scoring rate generally increases when long innings are being played, and so far thirty-five innings of over fifty had been played, but only seven hundreds.

Pullar was injured leaving Dexter with a nice problem to solve; he could use Illingworth or possibly Titmus as the opener, the latter had been admirably consistent in playing all the Australian bowlers. But Dexter did the positive thing and asked Cowdrey to open to keep the scoring rate up. For the first time he included Allen in the side; several critics had been advocating this throughout the tour, but it did mean that he had an unbalanced attack of three off-spinners, two fast bowlers and himself. In the event, Illingworth got only 15 overs out of 203. Australia dropped Mackay again, for the last time, and as an attacking move brought in the more positive Neil Hawke for his Test debut. They also recalled Burge for the unlucky Shepherd, but Burge had been making runs and his experience would be needed in what was expected to be a tight match.

As ever the chances of bright attractive cricket depended as much on the pitch as on the players. Dexter was a shade unlucky that he won the toss and elected to bat. Everybody expects a pitch to be at its best on the first day, but this Sydney wicket was both slow and of varying bounce, furthermore, the outfield was distinctly shaggy. All this being said, the best players can often get the better of unfavourable conditions and England certainly did not bat well. Cowdrey was out immediately, very well caught by Harvey. Barrington again batted third which after his excellent innings at Adelaide was not a negative decision, but he struggled from the start. He lost Sheppard after a very slow 39, then Dexter came in to force the pace if he could. He started with two fours, but after lunch got far too little of the strike as Barrington was unable to score quickly or to push the strike to Dexter. E W Swanton commented that he had never heard Dexter barracked for slow scoring before, but the fault was not really his; he made 47 in something like two and a half hours, even though he wasn't getting his share of the strike. Just three short of his fifty, Dexter fell to O'Neill, who could sometimes get a little bounce when other spinners could not, and for the fourth time in the series Simpson caught him at slip. Graveney was out during a period of poor light (an appeal had just been disallowed) and finally Barrington, looking very weary, holed out at cover. England were 195 for 5 at the end of a rather frustrating day and had a lot of critics to answer.

The second day was only marginally better. Illingworth and Titmus, both good county batsmen, went along at almost a run a minute and when Illingworth was out, Trueman appeared at No 8. It was a good unorthodox move to promote him above Smith and Allen, but Trueman was never a great hitter of the faster bowlers and he made no better progress than anybody else, batting almost two hours for his 30. All that Dexter had achieved was to raise the crowd's expectations, but the intention had been good and the rest of the batting at least made runs, if not swiftly enough. England closed at 321, a position from which a result might at least be possible. Australia were quite as slow as England had been and they soon lost wickets. Lawry, Simpson and Booth were all out before the day ended with the score at 74 for 3. Titmus's figures of 8-2-10-2 tell much of the story, he had used a cross-wind well to tease and torment everybody.

The off-spinners were on very early next day – Dexter was looking for all the help he could find in the wicket and Trueman and Statham had had a long tour. Burge and O'Neill played the bowling with considerable skill, using their feet well and never surrendering the initiative. O'Neill, in particular, produced firm and imaginative strokes. He might have been stumped immediately after lunch, but the mistake was expensive only in terms of time lost, for he added only 3 more runs before Graveney caught him off Allen. Burge now blossomed, while Harvey was settling down; he was dropped behind the wicket when he had made 63 and this was pretty well the last of England's expensive fielding lapses in the series. There were two short stoppages for rain with Harvey out in the interval of play between. Then Dexter got Davidson out before the umpires decided that the light was too bad to continue. It should be said that the umpires, at least, were doing their best to ensure a good finish to the series; they had had little to say to most of the light appeals during the match. Australia had gone on to 285 for 6, leaving poor Burge to a sleepless night on 98 not out and England a lot to do if they were to win.

Australia only added another 64 runs on the fourth day, but they occupied 100 minutes of the time. Burge reached his hundred and was out at once, and then Benaud, as at Adelaide, led his tail-enders in a rearguard action. He was giving the clear impression by now that he was content to leave it to Dexter to make the running. This time Dexter opened with Sheppard and Illingworth, which seemed a little negative, but he was doubtless hoping for some aggression from Cowdrey in the middle order. They responded with the best opening stand since Brisbane; it only amounted to 40, but it afforded a platform of sorts.

Dexter was generally expected to bat next, but when Illingworth was out, he sent in Barrington, who was after all the man in form and he repaid his captain by scoring freely from the start. It was well that he did, for Sheppard was as tied up as he had been in the first innings. Australia, in the person of Lawry, now put a catch down off Barrington, who was beaten by Simpson once, but otherwise looked secure. Sheppard continued to be terribly slow until tea, but afterwards opened out and had hit McKenzie, Simpson and Davidson for fours before he tried to do the same to Benaud and was well caught by Harvey, who was having quite a match in the field. The score was now 137 for 2 and the stage was set for a typical Dexter innings. He hit Davidson down the ground in the most glorious manner, but Benaud had the last word in their personal duel, throwing the ball up to him and having him stumped yards down the pitch when he had only got 6. In fairness to Dexter, one should say that he had absolutely no choice but to go for the bowling, England were fast running out of time and there were wickets in hand.

The light was now getting very poor, but Cowdrey and Barrington simply had to stay on and get whatever runs they could. With seven minutes to go they gave up the struggle and appealed – neither the umpires nor the fieldsmen were in doubt about the answer. England had gone along at better than three runs an over since tea, but they were only 137 ahead and would not be able to declare before lunch.

In the morning Benaud went on to the defensive, bowling himself round the wicket, aiming just outside leg-stump and instructing Davidson to bowl leg-theory also. Barrington and Cowdrey reasoned that England would get runs more quickly once they were well in, than from their successors if they got out. They accumulated 39 in the first hour, but both got out when they tried to accelerate. Barrington was a little unlucky to miss his second hundred in the match – he finished six runs short – but he might well have taken a few more on the fourth day and nobody felt unduly sorry for him. The later batsmen laid about them as the moment for the declaration approached and England had made 103 in the morning when Dexter called it a day. Good, but hardly good enough.

Australia were set 241 in four hours at just a run a minute, without needing to take the slightest risk. If they got runs without losing wickets for the first hour and a half, they might consider a gesture, but not otherwise. No criticism is implied; it is a Test captain's job to win the series or to retain the Ashes if he holds them and this must always be his priority. Simpson was shot out by Trueman without scoring and that effectively settled the matter. Benaud restored Harvey to the No 3 position for his last innings and he started pleasantly, but Lawry was totally uninterested in runs – his job was to make Australia safe. Allen came on and bowled Harvey, who was roared from the field in tribute to a great Australian Test cricketer, at that stage second only to Bradman on aggregate. Allen got O'Neill too and when he bowled Booth for nought, Australia were 70 for 4, with more than two hours to go. It was the last crisis of the series, but it was a tall order for England to get six more wickets on this slow pitch. Burge started with the utmost solidity and the small crisis passed. When the occasional bowlers came on, Burge flailed about, but nothing disturbed Lawry's approach and he was only on 45 made in four hours when the end came with Australia on 152 for 4, and still in possession of the Ashes, which they were to retain for another eight years.

Dexter was very harshly criticised at the end of the series, not so much because he had failed to regain the Ashes, but because it had not been a very thrilling tour. This was rather hard on him. He had gone out with an ill-balanced side, which only reflected the general state of English cricket at the time, and he was certainly not solely responsible for any slow play in the series. There was practically nothing to choose between the over-rates of the two sides and England had scored faster than in any series in Australia since Gilligan's tour of 1924-5. Benaud was, of course, a great publicist and he had persuaded the critics that his team was playing positive cricket when it was not, or not consistently. If England had held their catches, particularly at Adelaide, the story would have been different.

Although Dexter personally had done by no means as well in the second half of the series as in the first, he had emerged with an enhanced reputation as a batsman. Barrington, thanks to his fine batting in the last two Tests had the figures, but Dexter remained the man that opponents feared most.

	Innings	N.O.	H.S.	Runs	Average	100	50
1962/63	10	—	99	481	48.10	—	5
To date	66	5	205	3054	50.06	7	18

11 New Zealand epilogue

The programme for the New Zealand tour was not well arranged and one of its worst features was that England had to begin the first Test at Auckland just three days after the end of the fifth Test against Australia in Sydney. Into a two-day break, they had to crowd not only the customary end-of-series celebrations, which had an extra degree of fervour as Harvey and Davidson took their leave, but their packing, travelling and more importantly, their re-grouping. Four of the party – Allen, Graveney, Pullar and Statham – returned to England, which left Dexter with just thirteen men; it was reminiscent of those early tours organised by Alfred Shaw, when a party would traverse Australasia with only twelve men, plus anybody they could pick up on the way. At least in those exciting far-off days, they didn't have to play Tests in New Zealand and moreover the captain, unlike Dexter, could call on the services of the manager as a player!

Dexter had not only to re-organise his team, but to keep up their motivation. Pullar's departure effectively committed him to use Illingworth as the Test opener with Sheppard, but they were both out by the time the score was 45. Barrington, in prime form, batted at No 3, and Dexter joined him when Illingworth got out. He may have expected easier runs than he had found against Australia, but he missed out this time, being caught off Yuile, the slow left-arm bowler, for 7.

England were 63 for 3 and in a little bit of trouble, but this was not a very formidable New Zealand bowling side and the batsmen, despite being weary, were equal to the occasion. Barrington made his third century in his last four Test innings, the missing score having been 94, and Parfitt and Knight also made centuries, adding 240, which still remains the England sixth-wicket record. Dexter declared at tea on the second day at 562 for 7 and turned his bowlers loose. Trueman was unfit for this match which gave an opportunity for Coldwell and Larter. They took it well, reducing New Zealand to 7 for 3, then Titmus chipped in with a wicket and New Zealand were badly placed at 66 for 4 at the close.

On the second day John Reid the New Zealand captain, who had spent most of his Test career shoring up collapses, began the recovery. Yuile and

Motz two unlikely batting heroes, made 95 for the eighth wicket. Dexter managed his slightly makeshift attack well and two run-outs put the seal on a very fair performance in the field. New Zealand were all out for 258 and following on were skittled out for 89 by Larter and Illingworth. Beating a weakish New Zealand side, even by an innings, might not appear to be a great achievement, but in the circumstances it was something to be proud of. England had had to pick themselves up amidst a storm of criticism after that disappointing match at Sydney with little time to get it right.

England went into the second Test at Wellington after only one day off. Trueman was fit for this game and Dexter on winning the toss put New Zealand in. There was nothing in the wicket but he was relying on *their* low morale, and Trueman's reputation and skill, to do the trick for him. It did. Playle, who had failed as an opener in the first Test, was able to stay this time, but he couldn't get on top of the bowling, and the other batsmen tumbled to Trueman and Knight. New Zealand, 96 for 7 at one point, were salvaged by another unexpected hero, Bob Blair, the fast-medium bowler, who made 64 not out, his highest Test score, but they were still all out for 194, no sort of a score at all.

Blair then bowled Sheppard for a duck, but Illingworth and Barrington began to right the ship. Dexter came in at 77 for 2 but as in the first Test, he looked to be short of form and concentration. He had had a long and testing tour and there was after all plenty of batting to come. Dexter made 31, and England were not in fact making the most of their opportunities when they fell to 197 for 6. This was in measure a misleading score, for Cowdrey, who had injured his hand in the field, came in at No 8. His injury didn't trouble him and when Alan Smith joined him at 265 for 8, they set about all the bowlers with a will. Smith's best Test score to that date was only 21, but he was a very competent county batsman, and he played everything the bowlers could send down with his own brand of quiet authority. Meanwhile Cowdrey was quite simply in his best form – and nobody looked better than him when he was really on song. Dexter was able to delay his declaration until they had added 163, breaking the Test ninth-wicket record made sixty-eight years earlier by Blackham and S E Gregory. That record may have been made in more testing circumstances, but players can only deal with the opponents they are faced with.

New Zealand 234 runs behind, faced a hopeless task. They lost some cheap wickets, but Playle battled it out for 65. He was a steadfast player who over his whole career was often unsupported, and he deserved better luck than he got. Dexter relied chiefly on his spinners and was able to afford the luxury of giving Barrington a good bowl. This was not a matter of giving New Zealand the chance of a few runs – Barrington took 3 for 32 – but of investing for the future. There would be other occasions when Barrington's fiercely spun leg-breaks would be needed by England and

98

Dexter wanted to accustom himself to directing such a valuable weapon. England won by an innings and 47 runs.

England won by an innings again in the only non-Test fixture of their visit and, still with little rest, went into the final Test at Christchurch. It was the nineteenth first-class match of the tour and by its conclusion, the tourists would have played on ninety-eight days. It might or might not be more strenuous than an English season, or a nineteenth-century tour, but it was demanding enough, and Dexter would have been concerned when he lost the toss. However Trueman did him excellent service by taking 7 for 75 as New Zealand were bowled out for 266. In the course of the innings, Trueman overtook Statham's record aggregate of 242 Test wickets; Dexter was to see him to greater triumphs yet.

Dexter's own contribution, apart from his skilful husbanding of Trueman's strength, was to put in a good tight spell of bowling himself, with figures of 9-3-8-0.

The England batting faltered again and the scoreline rather suggests that the batsmen were running out of steam. Four men, including Dexter, reached forty, though none of them went on to fifty, and all the New Zealand bowlers took wickets. It looked like a collective loss of concentration and England were 13 behind at the end of the first innings. New Zealand had never beaten England and must have been hoping that their hour had come, but apart from Reid, their batsmen were not equal to the task. They were all out for 159, Reid making exactly 100, one of the most heroic innings ever played for New Zealand or for anybody else for that matter. He batted for just four hours, striving all the time to keep the strike, working to get all the runs he could off some excellent bowling. Titmus with 4 for 46, was the most successful bowler, but Dexter again put in an inexpensive spell.

England needed 172 and were still not quite out of the wood. Illingworth was sick so Barrington opened with Sheppard. They made 70 for the first wicket, and the game was safe. Dexter was content to let his other players get the runs – he kept his feet up in the dressing-room, prepared to come in if there was any trouble, but there wasn't. England won by 7 wickets; it had been a highly successful epilogue to a tour which had had more than a few ups and downs, but had certainly not been the disaster that Dexter's detractors alleged. He was, at all events, now firmly established as the captain.

	Innings	N.O.	H.S.	Runs	Average	100	50
1962/63 (N.Z.)	3	—	46	84	28.00	—	—
To date	69	5	205	3138	49.03	7	18

12 A classic innings, and a classic match

The West Indian tourists of 1963 were eagerly awaited. English cricket enthusiasts had read all about the tremendous series in Australia in 1960 and were anticipating more of the same. But it takes two to make a great series and too often the teams are not matched in such a way that skillful, exciting cricket results and the pitch too is important. Worrell certainly had a fine, well-balanced side at his command; two really impressive forcing batsmen in Kanhai and Sobers and a forcing opener in Hunte, well supported by Worrell himself, Butcher and Solomon. The bowling had genuine, frightening pace in the hands of Hall and Griffith, Gibbs and Valentine were world-class spinners and Sobers of course was a man of many parts. The only possible weakness was that there might be no really effective partner for Hunte because McMorris had seen his best days and Carew was notoriously inconsistent. Allan was expected to be the Test wicket-keeper, but Deryck Murray, only nineteen when the team arrived, was said to be enormously promising.

Just as Benaud had been expected to get the better of Dexter strategically and tactically, so Worrell was expected to be much too experienced for him. This time, expectations were realised, but probably more because of the sheer quality of the West Indian side, than because of Worrell's superior cricketing brain. A captain, generally speaking, is only as good as his material.

The tourists made a good start, having the better of draws with Worcestershire and Lancashire and beating Gloucestershire and Cambridge University, but they came to grief against Yorkshire, being well beaten by 111 runs. Hunte, Gibbs and Hall were not playing, but the revelation was Trueman who had a magnificent match, taking 10 for 81, as well as scoring 75 for once out. He had evidently suffered no ill-effects from his strenuous tour, and England would be expecting a great deal of him. The West Indies recovered well to defeat MCC – this time they were at full strength and the MCC side led by Cowdrey, was not a strong one – and they went on into a rich vein of form during which they inflicted an innings defeat on both Somerset and Glamorgan. Going into the first Test, all their players were in pretty good form and they were favourites for the match.

100

Meanwhile, Dexter had had an average start to his season. He began with 118 and 77, but then perhaps his exertions in Australia caught up with him and he failed to pass fifty in his next nine innings. Nevertheless, he was rightly appointed to lead England in the first Test. England had some changes forced upon them. Sheppard had returned to his pastoral duties and Pullar was sidelined with the knee injury he had suffered in Australia. England opened with Stewart and Edrich of Surrey followed by Barrington at No 3; this was the first time that three men from the same county had taken the first three places in the Test team at home.

Close came in for Graveney who had started the season uncertainly, and the four bowlers who had done well in Australia – Trueman, Statham, Titmus and Allen – were retained. Keith Andrew came in as wicket-keeper for only his second Test, the first having been on Hutton's tour, eight and a half years earlier. Andrew was regarded on the county circuit as the best keeper in England, but he was not notably better than Murray and his inclusion did weaken the batting. His chance of surviving for the series largely depended on the batting performance of the bowlers.

Worrell won the toss and chose to bat on a really good wicket. His only problem was that the Manchester skies were overcast and the light would not be good, but against that, England could expect to have a wet ball to bowl with at some time during the day. The West Indies took a chance on Carew, who had just made a hundred at Cardiff, and surprised everyone by picking Murray, who thus began a most distinguished and eventful career. Hunte looked solid from the start, but Carew played and missed once or twice before Trueman had him taken at the wicket. This brought in Kanhai, who played the first of several brilliant innings of the series. He scored 90 in 160 minutes and hit ten fours, while Hunte proceeded solidly at the other end, punctuating periods of defence with some fine hitting.

The England off-spinners were steady enough but the wicket held little for them and, while Trueman attacked with plenty of fire, Statham seldom beat the bat. Kanhai's great innings was concluded by a sad misunderstanding between the batsmen as Allen made a good stop at mid-on, Kanhai running and Hunte refusing. The West Indies kept up the pressure with Butcher making 22 and Sobers then batting out the day with Hunte. The forecast rain duly arrived and an hour was lost, but the West Indies were 244 for 3 at the close and well placed for a win if the wicket should take spin later.

Hunte and Sobers started the second day as if they had never left off, though circumspectly against some off-theory from Trueman, but Sobers opened out in the second hour, hitting two sixes before hitting a towering catch to Edrich off Allen. It was 359 for 4 and still plenty of batting to come. Opinions of Dexter's captaincy in this dire situation varied; some critics thought he handled his bowling well, but Swanton sharply commented that 'one felt that Dexter was setting his men to work on a rota and waiting for something to turn up.' To which I would reply, as no doubt would Dexter, that there comes a time on the second day of an innings, when the work simply has to be shared evenly.

England's fielding weaknesses were beginning to recur; Worrell was put down twice, off Trueman and Statham when the new ball was taken. Worrell had come in to join Solomon when Hunte was at last out for 182 made in 500 minutes. Worrell against this weary attack recaptured the zest of his youth and topped up the innings with 74 in 95 minutes, including fifteen fours. It was a scintillating finale and it was an aggressive move when he declared at 501 for 6. This left England with an awkward fifty minutes to bat which Stewart and Edrich survived without serious trouble. Edrich got the few bad balls and took toll with four fours. It was a totally different story in the morning, Hall bowled with fire and accuracy and had Edrich at once. Barrington remained in the No 3 spot but was not in his Australian form, he never looked entirely happy and, like Edrich, was taken at the wicket. Dexter sent Cowdrey in at No 4 and saw him fall to the fast bowler, who bowled him for 4.

England were in all sorts of trouble at 67 for 3 and a big innings was needed from the captain. The wicket was now beginning to offer the bowlers a little help and Dexter needed to be positive and indeed he batted brilliantly. He soon lost Stewart, who had batted doggedly for 37 in 160 minutes until he gave Gibbs his first wicket. Dexter hit Gibbs for two enormous sixes, to long-off and long-on, but then Close, who had been going well, tried to emulate him and was very well taken by Hunte at long-off. That was virtually the end of the innings, for Gibbs and Sobers were much too good for the later batsmen. Dexter continued to play his strokes, but fell to a magnificent popping googly from Sobers which went off his glove to Worrell at slip. Throughout his career, Sobers retained the knack of producing the unplayable ball when it was most needed and he usually reserved them for the best players. Dexter had scored 73 in 195 minutes and had looked a class above his team-mates, but England were now following on and had to bat steadily for the better part of two days if they were to save the match.

Stewart and Edrich batted really well in the second innings seeing off the opening attack and playing Gibbs with some skill when he came on. It seemed that they would last until the close, but Worrell came on himself and had Edrich caught by Hunte with a juggled catch at short-leg. Dexter was not much given to using night-watchmen but this was one occasion when the ploy was justified, and Andrew came in and played out time. He batted bravely on the Monday, staying in for almost an hour and absorbing the first attack of the fast bowlers. Sobers then came on and dismissed him, to start a nasty collapse. Barrington failed and then Stewart who had

102

played the slow bowlers really well, always prepared to use his feet, tried to chop Gibbs and was caught by Murray, who was having a dream of a match on his first appearance.

Cowdrey also fell to Gibbs and only Dexter and Close stood between the West Indies and an easy win. Dexter again batted well, going for his strokes. There was no need to be defensive, there was plenty of time and the weather was good. Dexter usually looked much safer when playing his natural game and even now with the ball spinning like a top, he scored 35 in quick time before making room to cut, he was taken at the wicket, to give Murray his sixth catch of the match. Wickets now fell quickly, and it was only a beefy little innings from Trueman who hit both Sobers and Gibbs for six, that forced the West Indies to bat again. The scores were level when Griffith bowled Statham and there followed one of those episodes which make non-cricketers smile, when thirteen players and two umpires trooped solemnly on to the field. Hunte tapped the only ball bowled for a single and they all went off again! Gibbs had taken 11 for 157 in the match.

England made two interesting changes for the second Test at Lord's. Statham had not looked at all dangerous at Old Trafford and was replaced by Derek Shackleton. Shackleton was thirty-eight and had not played at home since 1950, but he had been one of the most consistent bowlers in county cricket for years and at the beginning of the 1963 season had taken over 2,000 wickets at an average of about 19. He was perceptibly slower than in 1950 and indeed, looked innocuous from the ring, but batsmen soon found that he was not. He was essentially a 'wobbler', the ball deviating late in its flight in the most disconcerting way. The theory behind his selection was that the West Indians were quite used to fast bowling and anyway England had no bowler of great pace – it was better strategy to face them with something different. It worked too, though it was noticeable that the batsmen played him better as the series went on and it might have been clever to make another change once they got used to him. The tail had not batted well at Old Trafford and this decided the selectors to go for a wicket-keeper who could bat well. Having got this far, they went the whole hog and picked Parks, a wicket-keeper who was making a lot of runs for Sussex. The only change in the West Indies team was McMorris for Carew.

The second Test turned out to be one of the most thrilling Tests ever seen in England. It was played on a thoroughly good wicket which encouraged stroke-play but always offered the bowler something. Worrell won the toss again and Hunte got the game off to a cracking start by hitting Trueman's first three balls for four. This rate of scoring was not maintained, Shackleton doing the job he had been selected for by restricting the batsmen to less than two an over. By lunchtime, the score was only 47 for 0, made in 100 minutes (there had been a brief shower, which delayed the start) and afterwards Trueman got rid of both the openers.

Sobers and Kanhai in partnership were always good value and they now added 63 in even time. Allen parted them and Butcher didn't last long, but Solomon supported Kanhai in another good stand. The batsmen never looked like getting hold of Trueman and Shackleton and the score at the close was only 245 for 6. On the second day Murray and Hall were able to make a few, but the side were all out for 301, which promised a result. Shackleton, who had bowled wonderfully well on the first day without taking a wicket finished off the innings by taking 3 wickets in 4 balls. He had the remarkable figures of 50.2-22-93-3 and his recall had been a distinct success. Dexter had not had many decisions to make – it had been very largely a matter of turning Trueman and Shackleton loose and using his other bowlers to relieve them. Dexter himself had bowled twenty overs, looking to exploit the pitch as Shackleton had done, but the ball was not running for him and he took no wickets, though he kept the runs down.

Griffith got the West Indies off to a terrific start, shooting the openers out for a total of 2 runs, and this was the cue for one of Dexter's greatest innings. Dexter wrote, after the tour, that he was convinced Griffith threw some, if not all of his deliveries and he may well have been in a rage when he came in; he certainly made haste to the wicket. He drove the fast bowlers as they had seldom been driven before and when they dropped short, he hooked and cut them. The crowd, West Indian and English supporters alike, were in raptures. Dexter reached his fifty in eleven overs; he had taken 49 of the 65 balls bowled, which speaks volumes for Barrington's unselfishness and skilful management. Dexter went on to make 70 in 81 minutes and when he was leg-before to an unplayable googly from Sobers, the crowd gave a collective sigh of disappointment before applauding him every yard of the way to the pavilion. It was the second highlight of his Test career, after that great innings at Old Trafford in 1961.

The bars around the ground resumed business and the mere mortals continued the match. Cowdrey fell to Gibbs and Close failed, but Barrington and Parks added 55 before Barrington was out for a very worthy 80. England were 244 for 7 at the close, and if they were behind on points, they were still very much in the game. Anything could happen from this position.

This was a game that continually threw up new heroes and the next to take the stage was Fred Titmus. Not out overnight, he began to walk calmly across his wicket to play on the leg-side, used his feet to the slow men, and farmed the bowling with all the skill and confidence of a man in form. He was on 52 when Shackleton was out and had hauled England to

104

within four runs of the West Indian score. The game was almost back on an even keel already and when Shackleton and Trueman sent the openers back for 15, it had swung England's way.

Dexter was off the field on this Saturday; he had taken a couple of knocks on the knee during that marvellous 70 and was wisely resting; runs would certainly be needed from him some time on Monday or Tuesday. Kanhai and Butcher struggled against tight bowling from Shackleton, Trueman and Titmus and they seemed to be emerging from the tunnel when Kanhai edged Shackleton straight to Cowdrey, who took his sixth catch of the match. Almost at once, Sobers was out to Trueman and Solomon to Allen and the game had turned completely round to 104 for 5.

Worrell, the coolest man on the ground, survived one or two near-misses, and began to play Trueman with something like comfort and suddenly Butcher, who had been quite restrained, started to play his own game much as Dexter had done the day before. He hammered Trueman for five leg-side fours, and when he drove Allen for two towering sixes, the crowd realised that the game had been turned yet again. In the last hundred minutes of the day, Butcher and Worrell added 110 and Butcher reached the only hundred of the match and went pounding on to 129 out of 214 for 5.

There had been little that Cowdrey could do about this onslaught; Shackleton had just finished a long spell, and Butcher was carving into all the other bowlers alike. Dexter would have been just as helpless had he been on the field, except that his own bowling would have been available – but would he have dared to put himself on? The West Indies were now 218 ahead, and 250 always took, and still takes, a lot of getting in the fourth innings at Lord's, and it seemed that the West Indies would put the game out of England's reach in the first hour of Monday. But not at all. Trueman's third ball of the day popped, Worrell fended and Stewart took a smart short-leg catch at the second attempt. Murray and Hall made only two apiece, Butcher, trying to get what he could while he could, swung at Shackleton and was lbw and the West Indies were all out for 229. They had lost 5 wickets for 15 runs. Hall replied with a fiery spell in which he got rid of both Stewart and Edrich and then Worrell pulled off a master-stroke. For a long time, Dexter could get little of the strike and when he had to face the bowling Worrell confronted him not with Hall, but with Gibbs. Impatient to get on with it Dexter tried to force the off-spinner, hit over the top of the ball and was bowled for 2. England were 31 for 3, and it seemed, yet again, that the match had taken its final turn.

Cowdrey and Barrington batted calmly after lunch, Cowdrey looking in particularly fine form; but the light was getting extremely poor. England were reluctant to come off – more rain was forecast, and it would be as well to leave as little to do on the morrow as possible. Then at 72 Hall bowled the fateful ball. It was short, but not a bouncer. In those days there was no sightscreen at the Pavilion end at Lord's – it would have deprived too many members of their view – and Cowdrey clearly never saw the ball. It rose sharply and hit him just above the wrist with an impact clearly audible all over the ground. His arm was broken and he was escorted from the arena in great pain. The following year sight-screens were installed – a classic case of locking the stable door after the horse had bolted. The horse in question – Hall – continued his onslaught on Barrington and Close, who set their teeth and battled on in the murk. Barrington took his frustration out on Gibbs by hitting him for two sixes. At last they had to acknowledge that it was too dark to play. England at 116 for 3, were nearly halfway there, but of course they were really 116 for 4 and a tremendous amount depended on the two not-out men.

England had a stroke of bad luck the next day; light rain fell in the morning and it was impossible to make a start before lunch. In the ordinary way this would not have been crucial; three and a half hours would be long enough to get 118 runs, if they were to be got at all. But Worrell was relying on his fast bowlers to do the job and he was not such an apostle of brighter cricket that he would shrink from slowing down the over-rate if that proved necessary. The fellows with the slide-rules had already worked out that England had scored their runs a great deal faster than the West Indies in the first innings and the visitors were about to demonstrate that they could bowl at a slower rate too. Bright cricket will always take a poor second place to red-blooded conflict, and so it should. Hall and Griffith got through only 13 overs in the first hour, a funereal rate at that time. In that same hour, England scored only 14 runs and lost Barrington. 130 for 4 was a different matter from 116 for 3 and all the pressure was on Close.

Close had had a curious Test career to this point. This was only his ninth Test, though he had first played fourteen years earlier at the age of eighteen. He had a habit of performing well then blotting his copybook and being cast out of the fold – and there were thirteen more years of this before him. A highly talented batsman, he never scored a Test century, but the innings he was playing now would rank as highly as many centuries. He took almost all of Hall's bowling, playing the ball only when he had to and often content to let the ball hit him; photographs of his rib-cage, taken the next day, were spectacular. At the other end Parks tried hard to get on to the front foot and managed to play some authentic cover-drives but he was living dangerously and before tea, he was lbw to Griffith, trying to turn him to leg. At 158 for 5, time and wickets were beginning to run out for England. Titmus kept the scoring going with the odd single, but Hall was desperately hard to get away on the leg-side. After tea, Close began to try to swing or lap him away on the leg-side. It was dangerous work, the ball usually went in the air and mostly towards long-leg. Surely he would hole out soon, but the gamble had to be taken – there was nothing to be had off the front foot.

The 200 came up and England were getting close, then Hall got at Titmus and had him in the leg-trap. In came Trueman to hit his way to glory perhaps, but the first ball was beautifully aimed, just outside the line of the off-stump and Trueman edged it to Murray. 203 for 7, effectively 203 for 8, and yet again England had lost their grip. Close now, in desperation, began to run down the wicket to Hall who was disconcerted but plugged away, still short of a length, and Close was unable to find the ball regularly. He did swing both Hall and Griffith for fours, but he was not connecting often enough, and Allen seemed unable to get the ball away at all. At last, in an impossibly tense atmosphere, Close swung once too often at Griffith and Murray took a catch off the bottom edge.

England still needed 15 and Allen and Shackleton were no Hirst and Rhodes. Shackleton had begun life as an all-rounder, but his sight had deteriorated to the point where he had scarcely any vision in one eye and little could be expected from him. Yet he and Allen stood firm, taking the occasional single, but seemingly unable to make firm contact. Meanwhile the exhausted Hall and Griffith were equally unable to conjure up the fast yorker that would surely do the business. Eight runs were needed when the last over came; the news had seeped from the England dressing-room that Cowdrey would bat 'if required', but his part would surely be to block and not to hit. Allen and Shackleton hit two singles, then Shackleton played one to short-leg and ran – desperately. Worrell picked up and with unearthly calm, ran to the bowler's end and whisked off the bails with Shackleton just out of his ground. If he had risked a throw, it might have gone for four overthrows and the scores would have been level. Fortunately as the batsmen had crossed, Cowdrey did not have to face the last two balls. Allen settled for the draw, playing the last two balls quietly back.

The idealists said that the game had been such a good one that neither side deserved to lose, but Dexter didn't agree, and neither do I. England were the moral victors, they had played more positively and scored faster; if Cowdrey's arm had not been broken, they would surely have won, and the West Indies only prevented them from winning by some fairly blatant time-wasting. Still there it was, England were one down and had to regroup to cover Cowdrey's absence.

The selectors decided to recall Peter Richardson, who had not played for England since the tour of Pakistan. He was an experienced player and they were hoping that he would make more of this excellent West Indies attack than had Edrich. The replacement for Cowdrey was Philip Sharpe, who was having only a reasonable season for Yorkshire, but was a slip catcher of the very highest class, one of the best in cricket history. Finally, Lock came in for Allen to lend variety to the bowling. The West Indies continued the alternation of Carew and McMorris, but needed to make no other change.

Dexter won the toss and batted on what looked a very flat Edgbaston wicket, but the England performance was disappointing. The wicket gave Hall and Griffith nothing at all, though Hall defeated Richardson for 2 by sheer pace. Sobers came on as first change, bowling in his quicker style, and very soon had the batsmen in trouble. He found something in the air that helped him to swing the ball – he usually did – and dismissed all the front-line batsmen, except Richardson and Sharpe. Dexter batting at No 3, had driven each of the fast bowlers for four, but Sobers beat him for pace and bowled him as he played across the line for 29. Stewart and Barrington also went cheaply, but Sharpe made a promising start to his Test career, helping Close to add 40, and then Parks and Titmus each stayed with Close while he made 55.

Rain prevented any play after tea on the first day and almost washed out the second. In the time that play was possible on the Friday, Hall and Griffith swept away the tail and England were all out for 216, Sobers taking 5 for 60.

The third day was also ruined by rain and it was beginning to look like a draw. Only two and a half hours play was possible, but England made the most of it. At this stage of his career, Trueman would often bowl off a shorter run relying on swing and cut rather than pace, if the wicket was soft, and this was his method here. Hunte took most of him but fell playing back to a half-volley. Carew made 40, hooking several balls firmly, but then went through with the stroke too quickly and gave Trueman an easy return catch off the splice. Dexter now put himself on and bowled a splendid tight spell. Kanhai was finely caught by Lock at short-leg and then Dexter had Solomon leg-before. The shortened day ended with West Indies on 110 for 4 and beginning to struggle.

The weather cleared over the weekend and Monday provided a full six hours of exciting cricket. Butcher and Sobers fell early and the West Indies never recovered from 130 for 6. Trueman continued to trouble everyone with his cut and Dexter bowled as well as he had ever done in a Test. He took 4 for 38 in all, off 20 overs and nobody played him confidently. Trueman took 5 for 75, and the West Indies were all out for 186, 30 runs behind. Griffith struck at once getting rid of Richardson and Barrington, who batted third to rest Dexter after his bowling stint was bowled by Sobers. Close came in next but made only 13 before Griffith had him caught, and when Stewart who had batted doggedly for 105 minutes was caught at the wicket, England were 69 for 4, only 99 ahead.

Dexter and Sharpe were now together and one of them was going to have to make a score if England were to set any sort of a target. Together they rose to the challenge, concentrating on defence and taking time to fathom a pitch which was beginning to offer the bowlers variable bounce. Dexter actually batted for an hour before hitting a boundary and this may well have been the only innings of his first-class career in which that happened. The reconnaissance proved well worthwhile; after tea, Dexter changed gear and set about all the bowlers. He hit one magnificent pull to the mid-wicket boundary and, in the words of E W Swanton, one straight-driven four sailed perilously close to Worrell's 'illustrious head'. He seemed to be in complete command when he played forward to an off-break from Gibbs which went straight through the gate to be stumped by Murray for 57. It was the first stumping of the series and by all accounts a very good one.

Three wickets now fell quickly to the spinners, but Lock came in and played with total confidence, cover-driving Sobers and scoring 23 of the last 37 runs of the day. Sharpe was still there at the close, when England were 226 for 8.

The new ball was taken immediately on the last morning but it didn't trouble Lock and Sharpe. Lock, in inspired mood, reached his first fifty in his forty-fifth Test, and the timing of Dexter's declaration was all-important. Some thought he delayed it too long; Mr Swanton with his usual delicacy wrote that 'no one thought the captain had been too rash, but the critic does have an easier job than the captain.' Well said. Dexter in fact declared at 278 for 9 when Lock was out, leaving poor Sharpe on 85 not out; happily, he did make a hundred against New Zealand before the end of his Test career.

The West Indies were set to make 309 in 280 minutes and the declaration was not at all an unreasonable one. Trueman and Shackleton soon put victory out of the batsmen's minds by each taking a wicket before lunch by which time the score was 55 for 3, Dexter having chipped in with Butcher's wicket. His plan was probably to bowl Shackleton at one end in the afternoon and to alternate himself with Trueman at the other, but Trueman, finding a wicket which responded to his leg-cutter made nonsense of all predictions by bowling the West Indies out in an hour. Only Kanhai played him with any confidence, and Trueman actually took the last 6 wickets in 24 balls. The visitors were all out for 91 and England had won by 217 runs. Unexpectedly England were back at one-all and although the West Indies eventually won the series comfortably, one should not forget that at this stage on July 9, England had had at least an equal share of success. Dexter, Barrington, Close and Sharpe had all shown that they could play this very formidable hand of bowlers and

Trueman and Shackleton were proving hard to score off. Generally, the cricket had been tight but full of interest.

England made one change for Leeds by bringing in Bolus, the Nottinghamshire opening batsman, for Richardson. McMorris had made his highest first-class score – 190 not out – against Middlesex, and he came back again to replace Carew. Worrell won the toss and batted and once again the England bowlers got off to a good start. The wicket offered that bit of help to the seam bowlers early on and Trueman, Shackleton and Dexter each got a wicket before lunch. This brought together Kanhai and Sobers, easily the best batsmen in the side and they responded with their best batting of the series. They began carefully but soon picked out the bad balls and put them away. Noticeably they got little to hit from Shackleton, but they were seldom beaten by him and he looked to be a riddle that had been solved. Dexter was criticised for not bowling Lock during the afternoon session, some critics with hindsight pointing to Lock's dismissal of Kanhai for 92 soon after tea, as proof positive that he should have come on sooner. Dexter may well have been remembering that game at Lord's in the previous year, when he had put Lock on at a time when the faster men had the game by the throat and seen him collared. Truly, as Mr Swanton wrote, the critic has the easier job. Sobers completed an excellent hundred after Kanhai was out, but Lock got him too with a wonderful return catch off a firm stroke, leaving West Indies at 294 for 5 at the end of a good day's play.

Next day the Tourists added 103 for the last five wickets, Trueman and Lock getting two wickets each. 397 was a formidable score and it looked even more impossible when Griffith tore into the England batting taking 4 wickets as they tumbled to 34 for 5. This was one of those days when English players were most suspicious of that Griffith action; short balls and yorkers were alternated with no perceptible change in the action or angle of approach. There was more than a feeling that some of the batsmen were letting their uncertainty and frustration about his action get the better of them. Dexter hit rather over the top of a long half-volley and played it on when he had made 8, and only Barrington of the specialist batsmen got past twenty. The collapse continued to 93 for 8, but Lock, coming in when Griffith was tiring, again played his strokes and he and Titmus were still there at the close having taken the score to 169. However both fell quickly the next day and England were 174 all out, 223 behind.

There is no record of Dexter's having protested about the bouncers, he was generally content to leave that to the umpires. He was of course concerned about Griffith's bowling action, and it is undoubtedly easier to throw a bouncer than to bowl one; or to put it another way, if a bowler inadvertently does throw occasionally he will be likely to do so when he is putting in the extra effort required for a bouncer.

110

If Worrell had enforced the follow-on, he would no doubt have won the match, but there was just the faintest chance that England would make a big score and get his side on a wearing wicket on the last day. He had all the time in the world and decided to bat again. This was the popular decision from the point of view of a huge Saturday crowd who wanted to enjoy either some lively batting or a West Indies collapse. They got both. Trueman soon disposed of Hunte and McMorris and yet again, the West Indies openers failed to get away to a good start. Their opening partnerships in the series had been 37, 51, 15, 42, 2, 28 and now 1, much about the same average partnership as England's. Kanhai and Butcher were unconcerned by the reverse and made 65 in 39 minutes. Butcher and Sobers made 96 in 72 minutes, before Butcher was out for a rapid 78. The West Indies continued in the same Saturday-afternoon spirit but found Titmus a difficult bowler to treat lightly. He took 4 for 44 in 19 overs as they were all out for 229, scored in 210 minutes. Dexter had had little to do, but to keep his tighter bowlers on and wait for the inevitable mistakes.

The West Indies were a massive 452 ahead with two days and one session to go. It was just a matter of time. Sobers and Griffith opened the bowling and the left-hander bowled Stewart at once. Dexter played a stroke or two, then played back to Griffith when perhaps he should have pushed out, and was lbw for 10. Bolus, shaping well in his first Test, and Barrington added a few runs but Sobers had them both before the close which came at 113 for 4. It had been a highly eventful day, with 347 runs and 16 wickets for the crowd to enjoy. Close fought it out on the Monday; he made 56 and Parks 57, but nobody else did much and England were all out very soon after lunch for 231, defeated by 221 runs. The margin of victory could have been much more if the West Indians had batted more seriously in their second innings, but it had been a comprehensive defeat.

England were left with few selection options for the final Test at the Oval. The middle-order batsmen had done neither well nor badly, but there were no obvious replacements waiting in the wings. Smith, Parfitt and Graveney were the likeliest candidates, but none was obviously better than the men in possession. The opening batsmen were more suspect, but the only possible replacement was Geoffrey Boycott, who had worked his way up the Yorkshire order in the course of the summer. In the event he may have been lucky not to be selected, the Australians would provide rather easier opposition in the following year.

The selectors decided to bring Statham back into the party, took a look at the wicket on the day of the match and left out Titmus. As it happened the wicket gave nothing to either Gibbs or Lock and they were probably right. The West Indies tried a new opener in Rodriguez, who had come over as the team's leg-spinner, but had had some knee trouble. He had been tried as an opener against Yorkshire and had made 93 and on the strength of this, in he went. At the last moment, another change was forced on England when Stewart fell ill and so Edrich was recalled on his home ground.

Dexter had so far won only one toss out of four and was due to win one, and he did, choosing to bat on what looked to be the best pitch of the five. Bolus and Edrich made a solid start and Hall resorted to some pretty fierce bowling by the standards of the day (it would have passed unnoticed in the nineteen-eighties). Syd Buller, the umpire, intervened at once after he had hit Edrich and bowled two consecutive bouncers at Bolus, and gave the captain an unofficial warning. The situation quietened and the batsmen went on to pass fifty for the first time since the first Test. Then Sobers dismissed them both in consecutive overs. Consistently in this series, Sobers broke partnerships when things were looking critical for his side. He dismissed Dexter four times in the series with Griffith and Gibbs each getting him out three times.

Dexter and Barrington stayed until lunch, but afterwards having driven Griffith handsomely for two fours Dexter offered him a sharp return catch and was out for 29. Barrington was out to Gibbs, caught round the corner by Sobers, and England at 115 for 4 had again failed to take advantage of a good wicket. Once again it was left to Close and Sharpe to pull the game round, adding 101 in a long slow partnership. However when the new ball was taken Griffith mowed down the rest of the side, and they were all out for 275. The mowing down became almost literal at one point as he began to bowl short, and this time Buller warned him direct telling him that there was no quota of allowable short balls, it was in the hands of the umpires. Worrell later said that he was entirely happy with Buller's action but was content to leave the umpires to decide such questions, an attitude not shared by some captains of more recent times.

The West Indies had bowled England out just before the close and began their reply the next morning. Rodriguez did no better than his predecessors, being out for 5, but Hunte and Kanhai settled in and took the score to 72 before Lock bowled Kanhai. Hunte and Butcher added another 80 before Hunte gave Shackleton his last Test wicket. When the West Indian score stood at 185 for 3, it looked as though they would gain a long lead, but two unusual dismissals turned the game back towards England. Butcher was terribly unlucky; he was backing up quite correctly when Sobers hammered a drive back at Lock the bowler. Lock managed to get a hand to it and deflected it on to the stumps with Butcher well out of his ground. Thirteen runs later Solomon and Sobers went for a quick single and Close threw the stumps down with a fine throw to run Sobers out. England had regained the initiative and Trueman and Statham, who were bowling together in a Test for the last time, finished the batting side off for 246. England had a most unexpected lead of 29 and seemed to have a real chance of squaring the series.

Yet again England failed to capitalise on the efforts of their bowlers, allowing Griffith and Sobers to make early inroads into the batting. Both the openers had gone with the score at only 31. Dexter batted in a curiously restrained way, but justifiably so as Barrington and Close went cheaply. Dexter and Sharpe took the score from 69 for 4 to 121. Both were missed off Sobers, before Dexter sparred at Sobers for the last time and was caught by Murray. The West Indian keeper had had a wonderful first series, taking twenty-two catches and making two stumpings. Sharpe, also having a good series on his debut, fought on alone and was at last out for 83. No Englishman made a hundred in this series, a most unusual feature, but Sharpe came very near in two matches and probably would have made one if he had been more strongly supported. England were all out for 223, leaving the West Indies wanting 253 to win. Dexter had made 27.

Disaster struck England on the fourth day. Trueman had damaged an ankle in the first innings and he broke down after bowling only one over. He was by far the most successful English bowler in the series, taking a record number of 34 wickets in a series between England and the West Indies and his departure was the final blow. Hunte and Rodriguez were able to settle in gradually and were in no hurry to score off Shackleton and Statham. It was left to Dexter to break the partnership when they had made 78 and set their side well on the way to a win. Kanhai batted brilliantly, scoring 77 in even time, and when he was out, only 62 runs were wanted. Hunte reached his hundred before the end, thus closing the series as he had opened it, his century sealing a decisive win. The West Indies deserved their win, even if their tactics in the field had not been as scintillating as some of their batting.

The series had two important outcomes. Appalled at the thought that on the programme of tours already arranged, the West Indies would not be seen again in England until 1971, the English authorities responded to an inspired suggestion that some tours might be 'twinned' and this created the present pattern, although any suggestion of the West Indies themselves having only a half-tour has long since been abandoned. Secondly, the events at Lord's really began the long struggle between legislators trying to provide a minimum amount of cricket every day and players who sometimes seem to be full of ideas for offering as little play as possible. Hence fines, minimum overs, rules and all that.

What of Dexter? It was generally agreed that as captain he had done as well as could be expected with the material available, neither batting nor bowling having quite measured up to the tough West Indian challenge. As a batsman, Dexter had done as well as anybody, except Sharpe, but he had failed to produce the one big innings which would have set his mark on the series. He had bowled usefully and effectively, often in difficult situations.

	Innings	N.O.	H.S.	Runs	Average	100	50
1963	10	—	73	340	34.00	—	3
To date	79	5	205	3478	47.00	7	21

13 A fateful hour

England made a short tour of India in 1963-4, but Dexter decided to take a rest, after two strenuous winter tours in succession, and M J K Smith led the side. Dexter was taking something of a risk; he had failed to regain the Ashes and had lost to the strong West Indies side, and if Smith should turn out to be an inspirational captain, Dexter might find himself supplanted. However the tour wasn't an easy one and Smith had little time to make an impact, and, just possibly, Dexter might not have minded losing the captaincy – he was to relinquish it quite happily a year later.

In the event, Smith did very well, with a weakish side, and in difficult conditions. All five Tests were drawn with none of them coming close even to a conclusion. Over the whole tour, he led with intelligence and understanding – he has been described as a 'player's player' – and Cowdrey, who had originally been unfit to tour because of his broken arm, had agreed to join the team in their distress and had made two centuries. Thus, both he and Smith were in credit with the public, the press and the selectors and although Dexter, as the man in possession, would be appointed as captain against Australia in 1964, he would be expected to win, or to pay the penalty.

It looked as though the series should be winnable. Australia, under Simpson, were regrouping. They had lost through retirement three of the all-time great players in Benaud, Harvey and Davidson, as well as the very talented Mackay, and the only formidable newcomer was Ian Redpath, a workmanlike batsman who has been rather overlooked by historians. McKenzie was going to have to carry a very heavy load. They lost a lot of useful practice time at the outset, the weather being unusually bad even for an English April, and the early matches had to be used for acclimatisation. Nevertheless, Simpson had the side well in hand by the time of the traditional fixture against the MCC who were well beaten. Dexter, who had had an indifferent start to his season, failed once and succeeded once in this match, as did Boycott, who had just come to the fore and was widely fancied to come in as one of the openers.

Boycott was duly selected for the first Test alongside Edrich, Cowdrey, Barrington and Sharpe. England brought Coldwell back to partner

Trueman and reintroduced Flavell, who had not played since the 1961 series. Coldwell and Flavell were having a tremendous season for Worcestershire, who won the Championship for the first time in 1964, owing a lot to their seam attack. Titmus and Allen were also in the twelve, and it is likely that either Flavell or Allen would have been left out, but a most unfortunate mix-up resolved the dilemma. On the day before the Test Edrich trod on the ball at practice and twisted an ankle. He didn't take this very seriously and warned nobody that he might be unfit. When he reported on the morning of the match that he could not play, there was no reserve batsman on the ground. Titmus had to open the batting at the head of an ill-balanced England side. No harm resulted and Edrich escaped with a caution, but one wonders what would have happened to him if England had lost! Australia played the expected side with just four specialist bowlers supported by Simpson and O'Neill.

Dexter won the toss and batted on a cloudy morning with rain about; play started 25 minutes late, and it was obvious that they would not get a full day's play. Boycott had two or three escapes early on, playing and missing at McKenzie until at 25 he was lucky to be dropped at slip, but he began to look increasingly better as the shine wore off. There was an unusual and heartening incident when Titmus going for a quick single, collided with the burly Hawke, fell, and was still well out of his ground when the ball was thrown to Grout; the wicket-keeper quickly realising that Titmus had been impeded, simply threw the ball back to the bowler without stressing his own sportsmanship. It got the series off to a good start. Australian virtue was rewarded when Titmus was caught two minutes later. Dexter came in but had scarcely got going when the rain returned and washed out play for the day.

Dexter fell early on the second morning, pushing out to Hawke and being well taken by Grout. He had made 9. Boycott, on the edge of a fifty in his first Test innings, got an edge to Corling and was brilliantly caught by Simpson diving far to his right. The score was only 90 for 3, but there was a lot of rain about and it was beginning to look as though 250, say, would be a winning score, if there was to be a finish at all. McKenzie was out of form and for the moment the Australians looked vulnerable, but the other bowlers were well on target and England had only reached 216 for 8 when rain brought Friday's play to an early end. Saturday was completely washed out and Dexter had little choice but to declare on Monday morning and put Australia in, to see what they could make of a cranky wicket. They made very little. Sharpe dropped a slip-catch early on, a rare sight, but Lawry didn't profit very much from this. After batting for more than an hour for 11, he was out to a bat-pad catch off Coldwell. Redpath had already fallen to Trueman and Australia were 37 for 2. O'Neill had looked more secure and assertive against Trueman than had the openers,

116

but he fell to a ball from Allen which really turned and gave hope that there might be a finish. This looked like an even better bet when Booth starting on a suicidal run, was sent back by Burge and thrown out by Trueman. 216 began to look like quite a big score.

Simpson could only dig in. He looked distinctly safer than Burge, who was hit on the body before being lbw to Trueman. Veivers used his considerable reach, pushing out at fast and slow alike, although Dexter seemed reluctant to use Titmus and didn't bowl himself at all preferring to keep the bowling tight. It was a blow when Boycott fractured a finger and had to leave the field, but quick runs, and not too many of them would be wanted in the second innings. Veivers now fell to Flavell and McKenzie, rather out of his depth at No 8, to Coldwell. Titmus had come on at last and it was he who dismissed Simpson, caught at mid-on for a brave 50.

The Australians were all out for 168 at five o'clock; England probably had not the time to force a win, but Dexter made the obvious attacking gesture by going in first himself. He began to hit at once, was dropped at the wicket, but went whole-heartedly for all the bowlers, taking 14 in one over off Corling. Titmus was less assertive and it might have been better to have opened with Cowdrey, but Dexter was aware that he was reduced to only four specialist batsmen and could yet get into trouble. England were 71 for 0 at the close with Dexter on 56 made in 75 minutes. In the circumstances, the *Yorkshire Post* headline the next day, reading 'Dexter Excels as Boycott's Deputy' was entertaining as well as being literal.

Dexter got out early on the last day, wonderfully well caught at cover while still playing the right game for his side. He had made 68 and when Titmus followed him for 17 England supporters looked for attacking play from Barrington and Cowdrey but neither were to get going. Eventually, they began to go for their shots and had made 52 in an hour when Barrington was out. England were 195 ahead and Dexter could think about declaring, but Cowdrey could still not accelerate as the situation demanded and when he was sixth out at 180, he had made only 33 in 115 minutes. At lunch England were 234 ahead, with 210 minutes to play. It wasn't enough, a mad half-hour from O'Neill and Burge could soon put Australia ahead and it is a priority not to go one down at the start of a series. The England tail added only 7 more runs after lunch, but Australia were now set 242 in 190 minutes, a less likely proposition. England, with the exception of Dexter, had thrown away a good chance of victory.

As so often it all ended in anti-climax. Lawry was run out in the first over, this might have inclined Simpson to shut up shop for good but O'Neill hit four Trueman long-hops for boundaries and the crowd could hope for a fight. Redpath was caught at the wicket and then sadly O'Neill was twice cracked on the finger and had to retire. Burge and Booth had already settled for the draw when, for the last time, the rain returned and put an end to the drama. Australia would almost certainly have escaped with little bother, but they had been the worse of two moderate sides. England had bowled well and Dexter had directed them well enough, but the batting had yet again let them down.

England produced a more balanced side for the second Test, but it had an odd feature. Dexter had been appointed as captain only for the first Test and he was now appointed only for the second. Was there an heir apparent? He was asked, or volunteered, to open the batting, which seemed strange. In his autobiography, Boycott suggests that this was to keep the place warm for him until he was fit again, but if so, it was ill-advised, there were plenty of competent county openers about. Dexter thus opened with Edrich with Parfitt taking the vacant batting place. Gifford, slow left-arm and playing in his first Test, replaced Allen in the twelve. Australia were unchanged.

The weather continued to be absolutely awful. Nothing could be done on the Thursday or the Friday; it didn't rain on the Friday but, not for the first or the last time, the drains at Lord's were not up to the demands made on them by the drenching on the first day. England left Flavell out of their twelve, reasoning that, in a three-day match, four bowlers plus Dexter would be enough; Dexter won the toss and put Australia in, a fighting gesture not often made in those days.

Trueman got Lawry out with an inswinger in this third over and put Australia on the defensive at once but Redpath and O'Neill batted confidently enough. Dexter was soon switching his bowlers about, trying Trueman at both ends desperately seeking for whatever life there might be. But he took the first wicket himself, coming on at the Nursery end and persuading O'Neill into a hook which Titmus caught safely. A quarter of an hour later he trapped Burge lbw and Australia, at 58 for 3, were looking vulnerable. Those who had described this as the worst Australian side of the century began to look smug and, if there had been official betting on cricket then, anybody would have got good odds against Australia's winning the rubber. Redpath and Booth played patiently out of the immediate crisis, but immediately after lunch Trueman destroyed Booth with a beautiful outswinger and, with no addition to the score, Redpath fractionally mis-hooked Coldwell and Parfitt made a very fine catch. 84 for 5.

Simpson survived a loud appeal for a catch at the wicket but then failed to get right on top of a cut and Parfitt made another sharp catch. With all the specialist batsmen gone and McKenzie batting at No 8, it seemed impossible for Australia to make many more, but McKenzie defended desperately, relaxing only to pull Coldwell for a vast six, while Veivers used his considerable reach to stifle the good balls and to hit the bad ones.

Dexter entrusted the attack to the spinners in this crisis and he collaborated in the wicket that resulted, making a fine running catch off

118

Gifford to get rid of Grout. Veivers now had to go for quick runs and Gifford bowled him for a heroic 54. Corling was bowled by Trueman and Australia were all out for 176 – not enough, but more than it might have been.

Dexter wanted to look for quick runs when he opened with Edrich, but he didn't stay long enough to make his intentions known. He played back to a well-pitched up ball from McKenzie and was bowled for 2. Edrich and Cowdrey had no choice but to regroup and quietly play out time. England were 25 for 1 and a draw looked certain now.

Monday was cloudly but dry and Hawke seemed likely to be the dangerous bowler, seaming and cutting the ball after the manner of Ken Mackay. Cowdrey was taken at slip at 30 and McKenzie had Barrington lbw at 42. The odds against Australia began to shorten. Edrich was battling in his own individual dour defensive way with an occasional thumping hit when the bad ball was served up. Parfitt on joining him, flashed once or twice at off-side balls, but played some fine drives too, and they were beginning to look dangerous when Parfitt fell lbw to Corling. Edrich and Sharpe batted until lunch, when the score was 110, with Edrich past his fifty.

Hawke struck again to have Sharpe lbw at 138, Edrich went doggedly on, emerging again from defence to pull Simpson for six. Parks went at 170 and in defiance Edrich hit another six. He arrived at his invaluable century after batting for 287 minutes; he made 120, and England were all out for 246. Hawke had bowled well, but the novice Corling, with 4 for 60, had the best figures. The experiment of opening with Dexter had not been a success and the selectors would have to choose two regular openers for the next Test, whether or not Boycott was available. Dexter was simply too valuable to be sacrificed to a theory.

Lawry was out before the close caught by Dexter in the bat-pad position, but Australia batted out time and England would be hard pressed to get them out on the last day and have time to knock off the runs. By the morning the wicket had lost all its unpredictability and Redpath and O'Neil had taken Australia into a narrow lead before O'Neill, incomprehensibly in the circumstances, mis-hooked at Trueman and saw Parfitt take another catch. Burge batted with his customary imperturbability and he and Redpath looked likely to save the game for Australia, even if the weather did not. But Redpath fell lbw to Titmus and Burge, after making a solid but by no means wholly defensive 59, was well caught by Dexter at silly mid-on. Australia were only 83 ahead at lunch, with four wickets down; the game was by no means safe. Unfortunately weather had the last word when a steady drizzle descended at half-past two preventing further play.

England could count themselves unlucky, they had had the better of what play there had been and would almost certainly have won if there had been, say, a further full day's play; whether they would have won in the remaining three and a half hours if it hadn't rained, is much more doubtful. England had looked the better side during these first two Tests but the weather had frustrated them, and touring teams tend to be at their best in the middle of the series when they are working as a machine and before they begin to feel tired and homesick.

Boycott was fit again for the third Test on his own home ground at Leeds and replaced Sharpe, allowing Dexter to return to his proper place in the order – perhaps he had been keeping the place warm for Boycott after all. Coldwell, who had not looked very sharp at Lord's, was replaced by Flavell. Australia planned to make no change. However, on the day of the match, both Cowdrey and O'Neill were declared unfit. Cowdrey was replaced by the very in-form Taylor of Yorkshire and Cowper, making his first Test appearance, came into the Australian side. Simpson would move up to open the innings, allowing Redpath to take O'Neill's slot at No 3.

Dexter won the toss for the third time and batted on a good-looking pitch. It was a bitter day, not one to relish fielding on. Boycott made a very good start, taking 12 runs off an over from McKenzie, but Edrich failed to get hold of an attempted hook and was easily taken by Veivers. Dexter began as if determined to play the long innings that he and England needed; he played himself in with the utmost care and then went over to whole-hearted attack, hitting four fine boundaries in one over from Hawke. Boycott too was in good form, driving both Hawke and Corling for four, but at 38 the opener got the faintest of touches to an outswinger from Corling, and Simpson took the catch. It was totally unexpected – Boycott had looked unbeatable – but England were 74 for 2. Dexter continued in fine form, crashing McKenzie straight down the ground for four.

Barrington looked edgy, but they were 112 for 2 at lunch and it seemed that a big score was in prospect. It was not to be. Dexter chopped at McKenzie and was caught at the wicket for 66; it had been a fine innings, but there were many critics of his cavalier approach to a five-day match. It is worth quoting two of the kindlier comments. Mr Swanton wrote:

Dexter made the Australian bowling look, by the highest standards, second-rate. Is it over-critical then to make much of the lapses that cost him his wicket so regularly when he has the enemy almost on their knees, and only concentration seems required to bring the richest rewards?

Swanton seems to be saying 'Play your strokes but don't get out', but it's a little deeper than that; he is suggesting that a great batsman knows when to

120

stay on the right side of total abandon. The *Times* correspondent was even more explicit with his pretty fair description of Dexter:

His batting, once he was launched, was positively contemptuous . . . With tolerance he could have had them at his command. Yet with him there are no half-measures . . . he must make his runs as he wants to, or not make them at all. He looks at once gloriously and dangerously unaware of the perils of batting.

Things went from bad to worse. Barrington was yorked by McKenzie and Taylor fished at Hawke and was taken by Grout. England were 163 for 5, a losing position unless Parfitt and Parks could do something about it. They stayed and struggled together until Parfitt fell, again to Hawke, at 215. The irritating thing to English eyes was that the bowlers were not bowling particularly well, McKenzie had some fire about him, but Hawke and Corling looked quite ordinary and there was no spin in the wicket for Veivers, but still the England batsmen found ways of getting themselves out. Parks began to play his strokes, clearly reasoning that he would soon be left high and dry if he did not. He scored 68 in 160 minutes, a good if seldom classical innings. The last four batsmen mustered only 13 runs between them and England were all out soon after six o'clock, for 268. The Australians appealed successfully against the light before a ball could be bowled.

Lawry obviously felt he was overdue a good score and began with fierce determination, missing few opportunites to score, but showing the broadest of bats to anything on the wicket. He lost Simpson at 50, as the captain chopped a ball from Gifford onto his stumps, but Redpath offered a firm defensive bat to everything. Dexter rung the changes with his bowlers, but seemed curiously reluctant to use Titmus, who was only put on shortly before lunch. Australia were 95 for 1 at the interval with Lawry on 59. Redpath continued to bat extremely slowly after lunch, causing the crowd to comment very audibly. Lawry was run out when Redpath pressed him to a quick single to Boycott, he had responded slowly and was out by yards, having made 78 runs. As soon as Burge came in, Redpath was bowled by Gifford. Titmus was now on, proving almost impossible to get away, and Australia were bogged down. Gifford bowled on and had Booth stumped. Cowper, never comfortable, was bowled leg-stump, by Trueman, not a happy start to his Test career. At tea, Australia were 172 for 5 and marginally behind. Burge was on 30.

The final session of the day was to prove decisive, in this series and, in a sense, in the historical assessment of Dexter as a captain; it deserves extended analysis. When it began, the new ball was only a few overs away. The Australians had not shaped very well against the spinners before tea, but neither had they played Trueman with any confidence at Lord's. The conventional tactic would be to take the new ball, but there was a case for leaving it till, say, quarter to six, on the 'two bites at the cherry' principle; that is, to get wickets that night if he could, but still have some shine to work with in the morning. But, of course, Dexter was hoping to have Australia out before then. He began with Titmus and Taylor. The latter was an odd choice at this stage, being a fairly occasional bowler and certainly England's sixth man on the day. It was further evidence that Dexter intended to take the new ball and was filling in time. Titmus, however, got rid of Veivers and McKenzie with only 6 runs added and it is on these successes that those who believe that Dexter should have persevered with the spinners rest their case. He seemed to consider it, replacing Taylor with Gifford, but in the eighty-ninth over, be brought Trueman on. The considered view of the better-informed of the newspaper writers was that it was a perfectly reasonable thing to do, that the decision was a finely-balanced one.

Alas for Dexter, both Trueman and Flavell bowled very indifferently. Burge recognised this and took the fight to them immediately, his part is too easily forgotten in what followed; he batted very well and could have been equally successful against Titmus. He took several fours off both bowlers and Hawke joined in with a boundary off Flavell. 51 runs had come in as many minutes before Dexter took Trueman off, switching Flavell to the other end. This was the point at which the 'quality' critics parted company with him, not only because he kept Flavell on, in the teeth of the evidence, so to speak, but because he went on himself at Flavell's end. He did, in fact, get Hawke to offer a chance which was put down, but this was rather overlooked by next day's critics.

Australia were past 250 before Dexter brought the spinners back and of course Hawke was by now well-established. Nevertheless, the point must be made that Titmus and Gifford made no impression on him and Burge was now in full sail for his hundred. At last Dexter brought Trueman back again at the other end, and after Burge had completed his hundred with a square-cut off him and a quiet push to the off-side, he had Hawke taken at slip. This was the end of the day's play. Australia were 15 runs on, in theory an even position, but they had won the moral advantage.

The skies fell on Dexter's head next day, but it is difficult to see why. Almost any modern captain would have taken the new ball when he did; he could not have foreseen how badly Trueman and Flavell would bowl. However the popular papers enjoying the wisdom which hindsight brings, denounced him with one voice. The more thoughtful acknowledged his difficulty, but were critical of his refusal to cut his losses, and here they have more of a case. If he had gone back to Titmus when the score was, say, 230, he might well have had Australia out that night. It is fair to say that Dexter's preference throughout his career and afterwards, was for speed and seam. This time he was let down, and that is really all that can be said.

Dexter compromised in the morning, opening with Trueman and Titmus, then replaced Trueman with Flavell. Grout, no mean batsman to be coming in at No 10 (his career average was 22.56) played both speed and spin calmly and Burge was by now looking invincible. Flavell left the field with a strained achilles tendon, and it was already known that Taylor had chipped a finger while batting. The omens were poor indeed, but worse was to come. When Titmus changed ends, he bowled short enough for Burge to square-cut him for two fours, but at last he trapped Grout lbw; the eighth and ninth wickets had added 194. Burge now had a hit and made the most of it until he had made 160 in 314 minutes, then he was caught by Rees, the substitute for Flavell. It had been a match-winning innings, though he had been helped by some very poor bowling.

Boycott was out at once for 4, caught by Simpson off Corling for the third time in three innings, the whole of his Test career to date. Parfitt took his first ball on the glove, it damaged a finger and he retired hurt. England were effectively 14 for 2, with Taylor injured as well. Barrington came in ahead of Dexter and the Surrey partnership prospered for a while. They certainly didn't attack, but the runs kept ticking along and at tea they had brought the score to 88 for 1, 33 behind.

The very first ball after the break was edged by Edrich to Grout and Dexter entered to a first-class crisis. He played an odd little innings, driving at McKenzie without getting to the pitch of the ball and then going right on to the defensive against Veivers. Barrington looked much more positive, cutting McKenzie and playing Corling sweetly off his toes. He made all but 16 of the first 50 runs of their partnership. Dexter had made 17 and then propped at Veivers – it couldn't be called a drive – and was caught by Redpath at silly mid-on, something that seldom happened to him. Soon after Parks joined him, Barrington fell lbw to Veivers, he had made 85 in 189 minutes, good going in the circumstances. Gifford came in as night-watchman and saw out the day. 157 for 4, or just 36 ahead. Surely it was all over.

Gifford was very soon out on the Monday and although Taylor seemed to be playing without too much discomfort, he seemed absentminded. Parks went next, offering Booth an easy catch, and then Taylor making room, was bowled by Veivers. Parfitt joined Titmus, but had obvious difficulty in timing the ball and soon fended Hawke to Redpath. Trueman and Titmus played a few vigorous strokes, but the innings closed for 229. Australia needed only 109 to win.

The sad thing was that if Australia could have been set just a few more – say 150 runs – they would have had to struggle. Titmus got a good deal of turn which no batsman was happy with. However, Trueman got the first wicket when Lawry reverted to his tentative style and edged him to Gifford, who had to reach high to take it. Simpson and Redpath went quietly along, but the runs came very slowly and Titmus in particular was almost impossible to get away. Only 2 runs were scored off him in 10 overs when Simpson tried to stun a ball from him, and didn't quite get over it. Barrington made the catch at silly mid-off. Burge, not the tiger of the first innings, made only 8 in 38 minutes before Titmus bowled him. But it was all too late, when Burge was out the score was 64 for 3, and an assertive Redpath saw Australia through without trouble. England, after having much the better of two draws, were one down and deservedly so.

Dexter's position was safe – he had been appointed captain for the series after Lord's – but there was a crying need for some new bowlers. And England did indeed import a whole squad of new bowlers for Old Trafford. Out went Trueman, Flavell and Gifford; Titmus stayed and in came Price of Middlesex, Mortimore of Gloucestershire, Cartwright of Warwickshire and Rumsey of Somerset. Mortimore and Cartwright were accomplished batsmen and with Parks keeping wicket, the selectors could afford to gamble with only five specialist batsmen. Australia simply brought O'Neill back in place of Cowper.

The wicket looked an absolute beauty and, if England were to have any chance of winning, Dexter must win the toss. He didn't of course. This was undoubtedly the best toss of the five to win and it was the one that Dexter lost. Right from the beginning Lawry and Simpson looked very comfortable, they took their time, scoring 17 off the first 7 overs, then suddenly in an ominous moment Lawry hooked Price to long-leg for six. Cartwright, reputedly the most accurate and economical bowler in England, came on and away he also went for six, something that didn't happen to him very often in county cricket. Simpson who had continued cautiously, now began to come down the wicket to Titmus, and he made up ground on Lawry.

Australia were 84 for 0 at lunch and looking good for lots more. Thereafter, the two batsmen simply accumulated runs and the day can be recorded statistically. The 100 came up in 131 minutes; the 150 in 200 minutes; Lawry's century in 235. The Australian first-wicket record of 180 was left behind, and then when it seemed that a wicket would never fall again, Lawry called for a run to mid-on, not realising that Mortimore had fielded the ball. Simpson refused and Lawry was out by the length of the pitch. Unfortunately this brought no relief to England. Redpath batted solidly against all the bowlers he faced, though he was dropped at 223. Dexter had taken the new ball in the hundred and fourth over; this time he seemed to be trusting his spinners, but on this pitch, all came alike. Cartwright had Redpath lbw before the end of the day which came at 253 for 2, with Simpson and O'Neill going serenely along and the Ashes halfway back to Australia.

Next day Dexter was shuffling the cards again, though surprisingly he didn't bowl himself at all, probably because he realised he had to conserve himself for a big innings. O'Neill was out for 47 before lunch, by which time Simpson had passed his 150, with absolutely no change in his demeanour or his scoring-rate. This was Simpson's first Test century, in his thirtieth Test and he was determined to make it a memorable one. The crowd finally lost patience with him after lunch and began to slow-handclap, this was like water off a duck's back to Simpson, but it did upset Burge, who went for a real cowshot against Cartwright and holed out at square-leg. The score was now 382 for 4 but Australia had seen no need to curtail their batting line-up and Booth was a formidable player for England to see coming in at this score.

The fall of Burge had mollified the crowd, who sat back and applauded the milestones as they were achieved; it was a surprise that the previous highest individual score in a Test at Old Trafford was Bill Edrich's 191 in 320 minutes in 1947. Simpson had been going for close on ten hours when he passed the score, but the circumstances were very different. Simpson accelerated after tea, taking his score from 198 to 265 in the final session. Booth was 82 not out at the close and the total 570 for 4.

Optimists looked for an overnight declaration from Simpson, but he was committed to enforcing the follow-on if he was to win and needed all the runs he could get. He took a net in the morning and went on to bat much more briskly on this third morning. As for Dexter, he was by now reduced to rotating his bowlers in short spells and conserving the energy of his batsmen if he could. He, Boycott and Barrington bowled only five overs between them in the whole innings. He took the *fourth* new ball at 616 and entrusted it to Price, who had already dismissed Booth on 98 with the old one. Simpson passed his 300 and then lashed out at Price and was caught for 311. He had batted for 762 minutes, almost as long as Hutton at the Oval in 1938. *Still* he did not declare and it was Rumsey who picked up two cheap wickets at the very end. It was a pity that Cartwright, who had been much the most economical bowler, sending down 77 overs for 118 runs, could not be on when wickets were on offer, and the crowd applauded sympathetically when his figures were announced.

England's batsmen had now to think their way into a long-term batting groove, putting their physical exhaustion out of their minds. Edrich did not manage it, he was out at only 15, and Dexter who had much more to occupy his mind, had to bat after putting his feet up for only forty minutes. It would not have been at all surprising if he had failed, but he came in and batted with grace and charm. He and Boycott were together at lunch, when the score was 43, and they were still together at tea, on 123. Each man had reached his fifty; in Boycott's case it was the first of the sixty-four he was to make over a career lasting eighteen years. He fell eventually after tea having made 58, bowled by McKenzie, and England were still very much in the woods.

Barrington, ever dedicated to England's cause, was the right man for the job, and he was still there when bad light ended play at 5.40pm, England being 162 for 2, Dexter 71 not out. He had batted circumspectly but without looking pedestrian, playing classical strokes with an air, whenever he deemed it safe to do so. The Prime Minister, Sir Alec Douglas-Home, was on the ground for part of the day. Dexter had already said that he would be standing as a Conservative in the General Election when it came and the wits and cartoonists had a good time at the expense of them both.

On the fourth day Dexter and Barrington battled on. Simpson selected Veivers and O'Neill to open the attack in the interlude before the new ball could be taken, which was some indication of what he thought of the pitch. This was to be Simpson's opportunity to break the partnership but the batsmen acccelerated scoring 51 in the first hour, in the situation positively breakneck speed. Mr Denzil Batchelor commented that Barrington's aggression and Dexter's discretion were equally to be praised. In fact the batsmen were helping and supporting each other, which should always be a feature of a big partnership. Dexter's hundred took almost five hours, it was the first he had made in his last twenty-eight Test innings, though he had gone as near as he could on one occasion. When he had made 108, he hit a ball to Burge in the covers which nobody could be certain that Burge had taken on the full. The umpire, very properly, gave Dexter the benefit of the very real doubt. At lunch, the score was 247 for 2 and afterwards the batsmen cut loose for a spell, taking 22 off two consecutive overs.

Barrington, who was actually going marginally faster than Dexter, completed his hundred soon after. England would undoubtedly save the follow-on, equally undoubtedly Australia would have nothing like enough time to rattle up quick runs and declare. 111 runs were scored between lunch and tea, a very fine rate of scoring indeed, but at 5.5pm, Dexter inexplicably missed a straight ball from Veivers and was bowled. The ball appeared to do nothing off the pitch, and it must have been that after eight hours' batting, his concentration had simply lapsed for that one ball. It didn't matter by then – the score was 372 for 3, Dexter had made 174. Nothing was more certain than that England would make the 85 runs they still needed to avoid the follow-on. Parfitt started slowly, almost fearfully, and Barrington took time to play himself in again. A few of the certifiable began to slow handclap – what do such people expect? O'Neill came on again and this got both batsmen going. McKenzie and Corling took the

126

third new ball, but they looked as weary as Barrington and nothing came of it. At the close, England were 411 for 3, and the match was dead.

England had to be cautious at the start next day until the follow-on was saved and even more so when Parfitt was out to McKenzie; but Parks batted securely and the magic 457 was reached before noon. Barrington was expected to relax now and play his strokes again, but he looked desperately tired. His second hundred took some ninety minutes longer than his first, and he could clearly not hope to rival Simpson's score at this rate of progress. Parks was slow too, but he completed his 50 in some two and a half hours before falling to Veivers, who was in the middle of a marathon spell without precedent.

It was 560 for 5 in mid-afternoon and the crowd would have appreciated it if England had thrown the bat a little. But Dexter remembered, if no-one else did, that Simpson had batted on into the third day and would be in no hurry to expose his bowlers to more hard work on this wicket. Titmus fell at 589, and then finally Barrington went; his patience snapping at last, he aimed a hearty pull at McKenzie and was lbw. He had batted for 685 minutes, for 256, the highest score made for England against Australia since Hutton's 364 in 1938. The last three wickets went down cheaply after tea and England were all out for 611; McKenzie had taken 7 for 153 and Veivers had bowled for the whole of the last day, amounting to 51.1 overs. Overall, he had bowled 95.1 overs, second only to a marathon performance by Ramadhin in 1957, and he had taken 3 for 155.

A final touch of farce was added as Australia had to bat for just two overs to complete the allotted time. Typically Simpson and Lawry opened – no nonsense about giving Hawke and Corling a knock because they hadn't batted in the first innings. Nor did the batsmen lash out, all was solemn duty to the last and 4 runs came from 2 overs.

Well, there it was, a predictable draw and Australia had retained the Ashes. Was there anything Dexter could have done about it? Short of winning the toss, probably not. He had managed his bowling as well as possible, until in the later stages, it had become a matter of conserving energy and no more, but the plain fact was that the Australian batting, and the wicket, had been too good. There would have to be changes for the Oval, where the rubber was still to be decided, but there were no very obvious new candidates for bowling places, so somebody might have to be recalled. With the bat, Dexter and Barrington, heroically supported by Boycott and Parks had done wonderfully well and would be retained.

In the event, the selectors made few changes. Cowdrey returned, in the place of the bowler Mortimore, not a very attacking gesture. Trueman came back instead of Rumsey, which lent the game some statistical interest, for his Test aggregate stood at 297 wickets and he had an excellent chance of becoming the first bowler ever to take 300 Test wickets. The third change was more surprising, Edrich was included in the squad, but was made twelfth man on the day, an odd demotion for the hero of Lord's, but in picking Bob Barber to open the selectors were thinking of his leg-spin bowling, as well as hoping that he and Boycott would give the batting a positive start. Australia made no changes.

Dexter won the toss and batted on a wicket that promised to have some life, though not enough to justify putting Australia in. Boycott looked solid but Barber was lucky when Burge dropped him early on and again when Veivers almost got to a difficult one round the corner. It did him no good, for he played over a ball from Hawke and was out for 24. Dexter came next and there was an amusing incident when he pushed out at Hawke and his bat split vertically and neatly, the offside half flying out to cover-point. But the smiles quickly faded from English faces when Hawke bowled Boycott with a leg-cutter. 61 for 2. Cowdrey was slow to get started, but Dexter seemed to be in prime form, taking firm fours off McKenzie and Corling. Cowdrey was dropped by Veivers before lunch and Dexter just afterwards; but it was a surprise when Dexter was the first to go, hooking at a shortish one from Hawke and skying it to mid-on for 23. The first three batsmen had each reached twenty and none had gone on past thirty, and the critics were beginning to mutter that this was not what one expected in a Test. It is generally reckoned that the first 20 runs are the difficult part and that thereafter it *should* be a question of concentration. Life and cricket are not always as simple as that.

With Cowdrey batting slowly, a lot depended on Barrington and he started well, but he lost Cowdrey caught down the leg-side, when the score was 111. Yet another batsman had made 20 and gone no further, but the next, Parfitt, was even less successful, bowled by McKenzie for 3. There was no recovering from this horrific start. Barrington soldiered on to make 47, but wickets fell steadily at the other end, and England in their worst display of a pretty poor batting season were all out for 182. It was far from clear that the pitch was responsible. Few balls had seemed to misbehave, but Hawke, who had taken 6 for 47, had certainly been able to get a little cut on the ball. It was time to see what England's bowlers could achieve.

Not much more could be done on this first evening; the Australians appealed against the light after just two balls and although turned down, it got steadily darker and they were off for good after four balls. The light was little better when play began in the morning and Simpson began the day with an appeal but it was rejected and the light improved at once as if by magic. Simpson and Lawry, with plenty of time in hand, made a circumspect beginning, but Simpson fell at 45, after Dexter had switched Cartwright to the Vauxhall end.

It was a distinct plus point for Dexter's captaincy that he was always ready to try the switch, if the bowler was agreeable, and this is very often a

128

productive move. A bowler can seem like a totally different proposition when he changes ends. O'Neill started brightly, but Cartwright got him too, with his outswinger. Australia were 57 for 2 and it looked just possible that England would climb back into a match that had looked lost on the first evening – providing they could get rid of Lawry, he had made only 24 by lunchtime, but was looking very safe indeed. Burge went next, missing an attempted pull at Titmus and being plumb lbw. Just after this, Parfitt narrowly failed to bring off what would have been a marvellous catch to dismiss Lawry. It's unfair to blame him, but if he had held it, the Australian fat would have been well in the fire.

This incident initiated a period of extremely slow play, no runs at all being scored for half an hour. Booth was unable to get off the mark and Lawry, who had never really come out of his shell, was all suspicion. Trueman came back about half an hour before tea and this got things going again, Lawry hooking him for four. Dexter was reluctant to break the spell by risking Barber's leg-breaks, but gave him the last over before tea, after the manner of a captain of the nineteen-eighties. The new ball was due after tea and Dexter took it at once, but Trueman and Price failed to beat the bat. Dexter took the ball himself, bowling first at the Pavilion end and then switching to the Vauxhall end. Once again, the switch was successful, as Lawry played him quietly into the hands of short-leg. The ball had undoubtedly got up a little and Dexter's reactions may have been mixed. Australia were certainly going to get a sizeable lead, and England might be batting to save the match on the Tuesday. Lawry had made 94 and Australia were 202 for 4. Booth now attacked Dexter's bowling, driving him for a couple of fours. Dexter's response was to ring the changes with his bowlers and he was rewarded at last when Price had Booth caught by Trueman in the final over. The wicket came just in time, Australia on 245 for 5 were 63 ahead and England needed quick wickets.

Trueman had made no progress towards his elusive wicket. So far he had bowled 19 overs for 55 runs and to be truthful had not looked like getting anybody out. Dexter opened with him and Cartwright on the Saturday morning, but initially Trueman looked no more inspired than on the day before. He came off after half an hour and saw Cartwright bowl Grout for 20. The crowd were torn – they wanted to see Australia finished off, but they also wanted to be there when Trueman reached his landmark. Conceivably, if he didn't do it on this day, he wouldn't do it at all, for he was beginning to look like a man nearing the end of a great career. The crowd need not have worried. Veivers began to bat like an attacking No 4 batsman. He drove Titmus for four and swung him to leg for a six, while Redpath pottered along at the other end looking totally safe. They saw Titmus off and Dexter replaced Cartwright.

Veivers had just overtaken Redpath who had had a long start, when Dexter brought Trueman on for just two overs. There are two versions of this. Some onlookers thought this a clever piece of captaincy. Trueman, with the 300 in his sights, would give it everything and might do the trick. When Trueman tells the story, he takes the ball away from an indecisive captain, making the decision for him; but these stories are apt to improve with the telling. In any event, Trueman *did* give it everything, and in the second over, bowled the best ball of the match, an outswinger which came back after pitching – it totally defeated Redpath and bowled him. McKenzie edged his first ball to Cowdrey at slip and Trueman was on 299 wickets and a hat-trick!

At this dramatic moment they all went to lunch and one wonders whether Trueman or Hawke, the next batsman, ate anything at all. It would be a climactic moment in keeping with Trueman's whole career if he could seal the record with a hat-trick, but of course it didn't happen, the first ball going wide of the off-stump. Hawke and Veivers batted for some forty minutes while Trueman toiled on. He took the new ball, beat Veivers without hitting the stumps and finally got at Hawke, induced an edge from a well-pitched outswinger and saw Cowdrey take a safe two-handed catch. It may not have been very relevant to the match, but it was a great moment. Trueman had Corling at slip too, and finished with 4 for 87. England were 197 behind and would need a massive batting effort if the match was to be won.

England clearly needed to establish a good start before going all out for runs, and this Boycott and Barber gave them. Looking back at the stand, it is surprising to note that Boycott scored almost twice as fast as Barber, but Boycott was somewhat more free than he later became and Barber had not yet acquired the confidence which came to him a year later. They scored 80 in a little under two hours, before Barber was lbw to McKenzie; there was just a suspicion that he was reacting to a call of 'no-ball' from somebody in the crowd, in any case, he was out, and Dexter was coming in for his last innings of the series. He batted brightly, even fiercely, but even more than usual there was the feeling that he was skating on the edge of destruction, and it was not altogether surprising when he slashed at a McKenzie outswinger without getting over it and was inevitably caught by Simpson for 24. It was the Australian captain's tenth catch of the series and a very important one.

Titmus came in as night-watchman and played out time without scoring. This may have been a tactical error on Dexter's part, England were going to need quick runs the next day and Titmus, sound batsman that he was, was not the fastest of scorers.

Monday dawned overcast and an early shower delayed play, but the ground staff did really well to keep the lost time down to fifteen minutes.

130

Boycott opened in excellent form, but Titmus was unable to get started, he clearly had no orders about getting on or getting out and only 30 runs came up in the first hour, nothing like enough. When Veivers came on however, Titmus set about him joyfully, as one off-spinner to another, and hit him for a four and a six in one over. Even so, only 67 runs were made in the 105 minutes of the morning and England were only just ahead.

Boycott reached his first Test century, a very sound one, but after several maiden overs after lunch, he failed to get out to the pitch of a ball from Simpson and was caught at slip for 113. 200 for 3. Cowdrey was in passive mood, clearly very doubtful about the wicket and, as so often, he looked more vulnerable when he allowed the initiative to pass to the bowlers. Halfway through the day, England had added only 100 runs and it was increasingly clear that there would be no opportunity for a challenging declaration. Grateful as England supporters were to Titmus for his fighting batting, they could only be more grateful still when he got out for 56. Let there be no misunderstanding – it wasn't Titmus' fault that he scored slowly, he was going as fast as he was capable of going, but somebody else should have been at the wicket for those four hours or so. Barrington for a time looked to have no more sense of urgency, though he did get less than his share of the bowling, and Cowdrey made only 42 in the two hours between lunch and tea.

The two batsmen revealed their opinion of the prospect of a finish by appealing against the light at four o'clock, not a sensible decision. Fortunately the umpires turned them down. I cannot think that the appeal would have had Dexter's support. In the last hour of the day the bowlers began to tire and lose concentration and the batsmen were able to score at a run a minute but only 249 runs had come in the whole day and England 184 ahead, had forfeited their slender chance of a win. It was all rendered irrelevant when the last day was completely washed out, but that in no way invalidates the argument that England should have got on with the scoring on the Monday.

Australia thus finished the series as the winners by one match to nil. In a close-fought series, the work and decisions of the captain are scrutinised with particular care. Was this defect in any way Dexter's fault? He had, most of the time, been tactically astute – I have tried to show that, in the matter of the really crucial decision at Leeds, there were strong arguments on both sides – but as strategists, he and the selectors had been out-thought by Simpson, and they had failed to exploit the relative inexperience of the Australian attack.

On the credit side, England had found a new batsman in Boycott and Barrington had progressed to the point where he was perhaps the most *reliable* Test batsman in the world. As a batsman, Dexter had had an average season; if his huge innings at Old Trafford is subtracted, his figures are a little unimpressive, but that innings in adversity made up for a lot. This was, unexpectedly, Dexter's last Test as a captain. His final record reads: Played 30, Won 9, Lost 7, Drawn 14. Not very impressive, certainly nothing like as good as May's record, or Brearley's, but it should be remembered that he encountered a very good West Indian side and a pretty good Australian one, in 1962, and also that he played on some very easy wickets.

	Innings	N.O.	H.S.	Runs	Average	100	50
1964	8	—	174	384	48.00	1	2
To date	87	5	205	3862	47.09	8	23

14 Cardiff to the Cape

The cricket world at least was amazed when it was announced that Dexter was going to stand as a Conservative candidate in the autumn 1964 General Election. He had never exhibited any strong political views and indeed he didn't see himself as a particularly political person. He voted Conservative – I imagine that most county cricketers do – but when he agreed to stand it was in response to an approach from others. He saw it as the kind of challenge which he always loved to respond to in each new phase of his life. The fact that he would be opposing the Chancellor of the Exchequer, Mr James Callaghan in the safe Labour seat of Cardiff South-East made the challenge that much more stimulating for him.

The upshot of this venture was that Dexter was unavailable for the captaincy of the England side to tour South Africa that winter. However it was by no means definite that he would have been asked to captain the side anyway, even if he had wanted to. He had failed in two series to recapture the Ashes and Mike Smith had done a good job as tour captain in India the winter before and must have been in the running to take the side to Australia in 1965-6 anyway. Dexter did announce though that if he wasn't returned at Cardiff – and politics is no more a foregone conclusion than cricket – he would be free to join the side as a player. In the event he joined the tour only a week after the first match.

The side as a whole had a few weaknesses; neither Trueman nor Statham went and Trueman had a good deal to say about his omission both at the time and later. He had not had a very good season in 1964, but then neither had Price who supplanted him – and didn't do very well. The other opening bowlers were Thomson, Cartwright and Brown, none of whom did very well either. Nicholson of Yorkshire was originally picked but a back injury compelled him to withdraw and Thomson replaced him. Poor Nicholson never did get a Test cap. The Test attack relied on the spinners Titmus and Allen, Barber the all-rounder and Robin Hobbs, a young leg-spinner who was taken to learn experience but wasn't seriously expected to bowl his way into the Test team, and didn't do so.

Apart from Smith, Dexter and Barber, the batsmen were Boycott, Barrington, Parfitt and Brearley. The latter would have to do sensationally well in the early matches to displace any of the others. Brearley started well enough, but didn't force his way in and his batting deteriorated. Parks and Murray kept wicket.

The tour began well with four first-class wins and a draw very much in MCC's favour. They were harshly criticized for not winning this last match, against Western Province – Dexter who was captaining this match, delayed his declaration a little too long – but in truth it hardly mattered. The important thing was that all the team were fit and in good heart. The pitch for the first Test at Durban was likely to take some spin and it would be important to win the toss. Smith did just that and of course batted.

South Africa were just a little between sides at this time. Of the great side with which they were to bow out of Test cricket, Barlow, Lindsay and the Pollock brothers had arrived. Richards and Procter had not. Of the side of the recent past, McGlew had gone, Goddard, McLean and Waite were going. Bland was still very much present. The side looks a little better on paper than it was; or perhaps it played as well as it was allowed to.

Boycott and Barber got off to a splendid start. They scored 19 off the first 14 overs, but Barlow and Pollock applied the brakes and at lunch England were 79 without loss, Barber on 52. Afterwards, they progressed smoothly until Goddard, the South African captain and a notable defensive bowler, bowled Barber with his slower ball. Barber had made 74 out of 120 – his first real impact in a full-strength Test for England. Dexter followed him and played a quiet little cameo innings. He batted pleasantly, but never dominated and got rather less than his share of the bowling before hitting out at Seymour, to be smartly caught and bowled for 28.

Boycott fell lbw, for 73, soon after tea and Parfitt went for a duck; local opinion had it that the ball as usual began to swing at high tide. If the batsmen had been fed this legend, they fell for it, though it would have been unlike Geoffrey Boycott to be psyched out. Anyway, once the tide had turned, Barrington and Smith batted unambitiously to the close. At 260 for 4, it had been an even day on a placid pitch with a slow outfield.

The batsmen made a steady start next day and had just about drawn the teeth of the opening attack when Smith was out. Barrington batted too placidly for the crowd but he was clearly playing to instructions and the wicket was going to take spin, sooner rather than later. Parks was livelier and the score moved along steadily enough. Barrington completed his hundred in five hours and, when Parks made his hundred, Smith declared at 485 for 5, Barrington on a splendid 148.

A tired and slightly demoralised, South Africa lost three wickets that night, all top batsmen, and one each to Price, Thomson and Titmus. Dexter just missed what would have been an excellent catch at short-leg, just before the end, but it mattered very little; the game was effectively

134

won. On the third morning the spinners were soon on and getting turn. Allen beat Bland and had him caught with his first ball of the day, and he soon had Pithey, too. Lindsay and McLean had a bright little stand, but it was too rich to last and Barber separated them at 120. This was the end, the three spinners, in rotation, finishing them off for 155.

Smith asked South Africa to follow on – there was so much help for the spinners that he was confident of his victory and unconcerned about the remote possibility of a huge score and England being dodged out on the last day. Price had only four overs but got Barlow's valuable wicket, and then Titmus and Allen were at it again. Titmus took two quick wickets and there followed an entertaining interlude by Pithey and Bland. During it, Dexter dropped a catch at long-on and misjudged another high hit. There were a few barbed remarks; Dexter was clearly concerned about suggestions that he was less than whole-hearted. Supplanted captains always are so vulnerable, but there was never any question of Dexter's commitment. Pithey and Bland saw out the day at 122, but with two days to go, it was clearly a matter of time and no more.

Five minutes after the morning restart, Pithey hit a huge drive in Dexter's direction. He made ground to it easily and took the catch cleanly – no lack of attention there, and the stories died as easily as they had been invented. Bland was taken in the leg-trap soon afterwards and South Africa's slide to defeat was delayed only by some effective leg-side play from Seymour. They were all out for 226 and England had won by an innings and 104. Allen had taken 7 wickets and Titmus 6. In the circumstances, Dexter didn't get a bowl, but he took three catches.

The pattern of the rubber became depressingly clear. Smith had not been given a well-balanced attack, but he was one up. Unless he came across another spinner's wicket he would be able to hang on to his lead, as he had the batsmen to keep the scores high. The spectators would have to hope that his more exciting batsmen would also be the successful ones. In the second Test at Johannesburg Smith's plans worked out well enough, England were unchanged and South Africa likewise – they had clearly put the defeat down to the wicket.

Smith won the toss again and batted. England lost Boycott at 10, so Dexter took the stage early. However, it was Barber who took the eye in the morning session, scoring 75 to Dexter's 42, and playing his strokes all round the wicket. Englad scored at a run a minute, even though South Africa bowled only 16 overs an hour, a slow rate for the times. Barber seemed set for a big score, but Seymour trapped him with a slower ball as he tried to swing him for the four which would have given him his hundred. Dexter had been happy to lend Barber support, but he now began to open out himself, and he and Barrington took the score to 222 by tea, leaving the bowlers on their knees. Dexter came to his hundred soon after tea after an awkward little pause on 99, and then he fairly dismantled the attack, hitting nine fours in 27 balls. Barrington, seeing his mood, gave him as much of the strike as possible and Dexter was 167 out of 329 for 2 when bad light ended play. England were already in a position from which they could hardly lose.

To the general disappointment of the crowd, Dexter was out next day before he could settle. He had made 172 in 330 minutes with twenty-seven fours and, as it turned out, the last of his nine Test centuries, at least one of which had been scored against each other country.

Charles Fortune, doyen of South African cricket, was enraptured, writing:

Dexter's was a display that satisfied the wildest wishes of the hundreds of eleven-year-olds who swarm to the Wanderers', and should silence for all time the ever faithful followers who gather at the top of the stand each week to re-affirm that cricketers today are not in the mould of yesterday's heroes. Dexter's innings was a classic: an innings without a flaw and a memory for posterity to cherish.

This is typical of many contemporaneous accounts of Dexter's finest innings, over and over again, he called to mind the heroes of bygone times and was hailed as a reincarnation of the Golden Age. It wasn't a comment often made about his team mates.

Barrington now took charge and completed his hundred before lunch (413 for 3). After lunch, he hooked at the elder Pollock and was caught at long-leg by the younger. Smith soon holed out and England had made rather fewer than they might have done. Peter Pollock kept up a good pace and disposed of most of the later batsmen. Parfitt batted through the collapse without managing to take charge and England were all out for 531, when they may have been hoping for 600. Rain brought play to an early end, while England were pressing for a breakthrough, but to no avail.

Both opening bowlers seemed to be a little out of sorts on the third day and Titmus was on by the eleventh over. It took him much longer to get a wicket but he eventually bowled Goddard at 78. Pithey was soon showing that he was in form and when Smith boldly put Barrington on immediately after lunch, he went for 29 in 4 overs and bowled no more in the match. It was Titmus who again came to the rescue, this time with two wickets, his second scalp that of Graeme Pollock, caught at short-leg. Titmus had now got the brilliant Pollock out three times in three innings. He seemed to have a firm grip on him, but he didn't dismiss him again in the series. Pithey and Bland had now to play South Africa out of a real crisis, they did so so cautiously that they practically ground to a halt. Smith and Price responded by undertaking a bouncer attack, with a string of short-pitched balls. Price shifted Bland when he tried to hammer a yorker slipped in among the bouncers and was taken at mid-off, but such a one-man assault could be seen off and duly was. Barber had McLean lbw as he tried to hit him to leg, and South Africa were 261 for 5 at the close, with the last two specialist batsmen together. Only Pithey, a solid and much under-rated player, stood between England and the imposition of the follow-on.

Allen bowled Pithey very early on the fourth day and South Africa subsided to 317 all out. England had a great chance to go two-nil up in the series and things looked better still when Allen had first Barlow well caught by Dexter close in and then Pithey cheaply. Goddard had been much freer than Barlow during their opening stand and went to an excellent 50 but was then well taken by Smith at short cover. McLean, still very much out of form, was bowled by Titmus, and at 109 for 4 it seemed that South Africa had lost the game.

Inexplicably this was the turning-point of the match and in a way of the series. It may have been that Smith had overbowled Allen and Titmus – they shared 79 overs in the first innings and had bowled 68 overs by the end of the fourth day. South Africa, led by Bland, batted out the rest of the fourth day and the whole of the fifth, and they never looked like being beaten in the last three matches. It is also true that they never looked like winning either, and that England therefore won the series, but they were able to tour England in confident mood the following summer and win the last series to be played between the two countries.

Play was curtailed a little on the last day by rain at the start and at the finish, but South Africa would in any event have saved the match. Bland batted for four hours for 144, starting slowly, and then dismantling the attack piece by piece; it was one of those innings which have a profound effect on a whole series. Neither Price nor Titmus was quite the same bowler again. Dexter bowled 8 overs during this phase of the match and conceded 33 runs, though he did pick up Varnals' wicket. South Africa were 336 for 6 at the close, and had comfortably saved the match.

South Africa were understandably anxious to get back into the series and introduced three new bowlers for Cape Town. Burke – fast-medium, Bromfield – off-spin and Hall – leg-spin, to replace Partridge, Seymour and McLean, who had thus played his last Test.

It is worth dwelling for a moment on Roy McLean who was South Africa's nearest counterpart to Dexter. A glorious attacking batsman, he scored five Test centuries, every one a gem, but he could be over-impetuous, and the South African selectors were as wary of him as the England selectors have sometimes been of brilliant players, such as Dexter, Graveney and Charles Barnett. McLean can never have felt that his place was entirely safe, but he is still remembered with immense pleasure by all who saw him.

The playing of three bowlers in place of two bowlers and a batsman had changed the balance of the side, in a daring bid for victory in the third Test at Cape Town. The gamble paid off in that South Africa made plenty of runs. England were unchanged. Goddard won the toss at last and embarked on what was to be a pretty bad-tempered day. In extenuation, it can be said that there had only been a two-day break since the second Test and the players were tired and hot. Goddard and Barlow got off to a good beginning by scoring 44 in the first hour, during which Dexter bowled his only 2 overs of the innings, and pretty inaccurate ones at that. For almost the first time in the series, the batsmen were getting the better of Titmus, when he bowled Goddard with his arm-ball, just before lunch. 80 for 1.

Not long afterwards came the incident which soured relations between the sides for the rest of the game, though they put it behind them before the next Test. Barlow played at a ball from Titmus which was caught by Parfitt in the gully. It undoubtedly hit his bat and then his leg, it may then have hit the ground before Parfitt took it. Anyway the batsman got the benefit of the doubt, but the England side thought he'd been caught cleanly and should have walked. He and Titmus had a sharp altercation at the end of the over and when he reached his hundred, the Englishmen with the exception of Smith, refrained from applauding him, making their feelings even clearer by congratulating Pithey on his 50 in a very ostentatious way. It was all rather childish, but it didn't affect the competitive Barlow and he was 138 not out at the close, when his side were 252 for 1.

Barlow was soon out the next day and it is sad that Charles Fortune remarks that Dexter was seen to join in the applause for him, the implication being that most of the other fielders did not. Pollock and Pithey added another 61 before Allen had Pollock caught. Bland and Pithey now attacked with a will and Pithey had made 154, his first Test hundred, before Allen had him caught in the deep. The score was now 430 for 4 and South Africa were not going to miss the extra batsman. Goddard declared at 501 for 5 but not before Dexter had run out Bland, himself a great fielder and fine runner, with a fast accurate throw. Barber and Boycott had their problems, but survived the day, on 24.

The England manager, Donald Carr, called a Press conference on the Sunday to convey apologies and regrets for the Barlow incident, but clearly the England players were still unhappy. Barber batted brightly when play began on the Monday but lost Boycott at 72 and was himself out at 80. Dexter and Barrington, the two senior batsman in the side, had some rebuilding to do, and Barrington looked the more confident. Bromfield bowled particularly tightly, but it was Peter Pollock who defeated Barrington and precipitated part two of the 'incident'.

138

Barrington got a very faint edge and was caught by the wicket-keeper. The umpire made no move, either to accept or reject the appeal, and Barrington stood stock-still for several seconds before giving himself out and walking slowly away. Press opinion was mixed. Many thought that Barrington had simply done the right thing, but others felt that if he were going to 'walk', he should have done so right away and that he was, in effect, embarrassing the umpire by giving him a chance to get it wrong. If the umpire had, in fact, given the batsman not out then Barrington was technically retired out, but it seems more probable that the umpire who was standing in his second (and last) Test, was simply so paralysed that he didn't react to the appeal at all. It all left rather a nasty taste. Dexter, who played no part in the incident but must have been a baffled observer at close range, soon followed Barrington, caught and bowled by Bromfield for 61, one of his less memorable innings. England were still in danger at the end of the day, on 240 for 4.

The last two days were distinctly odd. Parfitt fell very early, but Smith and Parks made the game completely safe by adding 117 and saving the follow-on. The South Africans attacked Smith's off-stump, but found him as adept on that side of the wicket as on the other and he made 121 before getting out at the very end of the innings to Bromfield, who had the remarkable figures of 57.2-26-88-5. England were only 59 behind and there was nothing for South Africa to do but to bat out the match. This they just failed to do, first losing two quick wickets, and then much later collapsing before, of all people, Boycott (3 for 47) and Barrington (3 for 4). Dexter had a long bowl, taking 1 for 64 in 17 overs, and he, Parfitt, Boycott, Smith and Barrington bowled seventy overs between them; it was hardly vintage Test cricket, but Titmus and Allen needed the rest. By the end of the match the two teams must have been rather tired of each other and it was as well that the next Text was sixteen days away.

The pitch for the Johannesburg Test looked as if it might have a little life, so England decided to bring in Cartwright and drop the unlucky Allen. Dexter had made a sparkling century against Border (as had Cartwright) and seemed to be due for a big score. South Africa recalled Partridge, and brought back Waite to keep wicket. Van der Merwe came in for Varnals, and he was destined to captain the side in England a few months later, for Goddard announced his retirement from Test cricket during this Test. The left-arm spinner, McKinnon, who had toured England in 1960, came in for Hall.

Having left Allen out, Smith elected to put South Africa in when he won the toss. The gamble didn't come off and he was severely criticised. Yet again, Goddard and Barlow made a very good start, Barlow particularly went at a good rate, reaching his 50 off 62 balls. Much of this was to be laid at Dexter's door, Barlow taking 17 off one over from him, with four fours, two on each side of the wicket. The hundred came up in the twenty-fourth over, breakneck speed on the first day of a Test. Price went lame before lunch and could not bowl again that day. There was universal disappointment when Goddard was run out by smart work from Barrington and Boycott. South Africa were 134 for 1. Bland came next and they had taken the score to 161 when play was halted by a cloudburst. The ground dried very rapidly and play was resumed with an hour to go, time for Barlow to get out, very well caught and bowled by Cartwright. At 192 for 2, South Africa were well placed.

Soon after the start of the second day Smith took the second new ball and Price had Bland out and then had Pollock splendidly caught by Parks. At 226 for 4 England were back in the match, but Pithey and Waite consolidated and although unable to take command they steered South Africa to a better position at lunch and made exactly 100 between lunch and tea. Then Waite got cramp and asked for a runner, Bland came on and amazingly managed to be run out – the greatest natural athlete in world cricket had been involved in two run-outs in successive Tests! Even after a record fifth-wicket stand, South Africa still hadn't enough runs.

None of this made much difference, for another storm took the players off at 390 for 5 and Goddard was obliged to declare overnight. England seemed to have no problems, they had only to avoid the follow-on to be safe. Boycott was soon out edging Partridge to slip, which meant that Dexter was exposed early. He began quite splendidly with strokes all round the wicket even outscoring Barber, which few people did, but Barlow came on and tied him down and then Goddard defeated him when he was on 38 with a little outswinger which Waite took behind the wicket. 78 for 2 and a minor crisis, but both Barber and Barrington were put down, and Waite missed a stumping chance. The batsmen made the most of this and took the score to 144, before McKinnon, who had seen the chances go down off his bowling, had Barber lbw. Barrington was now at his most assertive and going well and together with Parfitt added exactly 100 runs before he was run out on 93. Smith and Parfitt kept the score moving in the last hour and England had made the very good score of 297 for 4 by the close.

Smith was out soon on the fourth morning and Parks and Titmus failed, but Parfitt kept going, picking up fours off the bad balls as they came along, and he was 122 not out when the innings ended at 384, only 6 runs behind. A draw seemed certain, but Barlow made a rapid 42 out of 65, and then Goddard took up the running, hitting Cartwright for two sixes and was 89 not out at the close, out of 171 for 1. Perhaps he was going to make that hundred at last – it would be the most popular event of the season if he did, his retirement had by now been made public and perhaps there would be a challenging declaration and an exciting finish.

140

The hundred arrived to enthusiastic applause after about half an hour, it had taken 235 minutes, or putting it another way, 62 innings. Pithey had got out before the century was achieved and Pollock was now in, and forcing the pace. Goddard was out for 112, but Barber while catching him at long-leg damaged his finger very badly and was able to play no more on the tour. Bland and Pollock had nothing to lose now by having a real crack and they scored at 6 runs an over until the declaration came, Goddard leaving England to score 302 at 79 an hour, difficult enough, but par for the course for a Test match challenge.

Smith showed what he thought of the declaration by opening with Boycott and Titmus. If he had been making a serious attempt, Dexter would have gone in first. Titmus almost survived the opening burst from Peter Pollock but he got out, and then sadly Dexter was taken by Graeme Pollock with a fine catch at short-leg before he had scored. Barrington went cheaply and at 33 for 3, that was the end of any thought of England winning. Pollock pulled a thigh muscle and that finished South Africa's chance, though McKinnon and Bromfield put in a long probing spell. Boycott batted for the rest of the day to score 76, a triumph of concentration and character. Parfitt, Smith and Parks all kept him company for a while and England were 153 for 6 at the close. It had been a close-run thing but not quite as close as it looked, Cartwright was a sound player and England were probably good for another hour or two.

England had selection problems going into the last match at Port Elizabeth. With Barber injured England had to field a new opening bat. Brearley was hopelessly out of form, but Smith experimented with him and John Murray in the two matches between the Tests. Brearley did marginally the better, but Smith still banked on Murray.

It is fascinating to speculate on what might have been. Just suppose that Brearley had played and, against all the odds, had made some runs. He might have been selected for the next Test in England and his career *might* have got under way eleven years earlier than it did; but if he had had a short career of say, four or five not-too-successful matches, the 1976 selectors might have been less inclined to pick him in their crisis. He would have been one of 'yesterday's men'. It can sometimes be more profitable *not* to be picked. Price was injured and so were Brown and Cartwright, the other opening bowlers in the party. Fortunately Kenneth Palmer of Somerset was coaching in Johannesburg and he was recruited to partner Thomson. They were not the most formidable pair of bowlers ever to open for England, it must be said. Allen returned, of course. Peter Pollock was fit again and to partner him South Africa introduced Macaulay, in place of Partridge.

Goddard won the toss and his batsmen took full advantage of the English makeshift opening attack. One or two strokes might have gone to hand but did not, and the lunch score was 88 for 0. It would have been more, but the outfield was extremely slow. Smith surprised everybody by using Boycott as his first-change bowler rather than Dexter, but Boycott could be very hard to get away and Dexter had shown himself vulnerable to the stroke-players once or twice. Anyway Boycott bowled with great steadiness, starting with four maidens. Palmer had bad luck when a chance went down off him after lunch, but Allen broke the opening stand when he had Goddard caught. Bland came in and played a rich little innings full of strokes, some of them edges, but none going to hand. Barlow went just before tea, caught off Boycott, but this simply brought in Pollock to continue the attack. He lost Bland, and then Pithey seemed to get rather more than his share of the strike. Nevertheless, 262 for 3 was a good day's work and offered hopes of a finish.

Pithey was out early on the second morning and Waite was very soon run out by a fine pick-up and throw from Palmer, making his first impact on the match. With van der Merwe, the last specialist batsman, coming in South Africa were in anything but a sound position, but he settled in and batted doggedly, while Pollock at last showed his true quality. They added 113, of which Pollock made 76, his off-driving being the glory of his play. When he reached his hundred, he had scored hundreds against both England and Australia before his twenty-first birthday, a remarkable feat. When he was out for 137 his brother came in to partner van de Merwe. The elder Pollock was unable to force the pace, but his partner simply accelerated and took over the leading role. It was a fine piece of strategic batting. South Africa were all out for 502 and could throw everything into attack to try to salvage the rubber. Once again, Titmus and Allen had been the most effective bowlers and poor Palmer emerged from his first Test innings with only 1 for 113. Smith had not used Dexter at all, but had bowled Boycott for 26 overs. Nevertheless, the Yorkshireman showed no sign of strain when he opened with Murray, batting calmly and resolutely for more than an hour and putting the occasional loose balls away for four. It seemed that Murray, too, would last out the evening, but he went to Macaulay just before the close.

Titmus, the night watchman, was out early on the third morning and Dexter entered. He might well have set his sights on survival, but some loose bowling from McKinnon got him started and he had made 40 runs by lunchtime out of 63 while he was in. It looked very much as though he was in for another long innings, but he was run out in the first over after lunch. Opinions differ about the responsibility for the misunderstanding, but Dexter ran for a stroke of Boycott's and the batsmen found themselves at the same end, with Graeme Pollock taking off the bails at the other. It made little difference to the course of the match, but Dexter had looked in excellent form and he might well have made a lot of runs.

142

Boycott and Barrington batted very solidly for most of the rest of the day until, with Boycott now well past his hundred, Barrington was caught at short-leg. For the second successive day, Smith used a night-watchman – Thomson, this time – and had thus committed himself to having Parks come in ninth and possibly be left high and dry. The night-watchman survived but Boycott did not, he too was taken at short-leg, for 117 and England were 277 for 5, with just a slim chance of a good finish.

Thomson batted pretty well next morning and certainly looked as comfortable as Smith, as well as rather more enterprising. Pollock was not at his best, and Thomson hit him very convincingly through the covers. They put on 69 before both of them and Parfitt too, were out at the same score, 346. Two of the wickets fell to Barlow, the quintessential partnership-breaker in the South African side, and if he could have taken one more wicket, South Africa would have regained valuable time, but Parks and Allen, experienced Test hands who had coped with crises in the past took the score to 410 before Barlow made the breakthrough. England finished on 435, just 67 behind and South Africa had only eight hours in which to force a win.

It couldn't be done; Goddard went early and Barlow and Bland were quite unable to get on top that evening. Next day, Bland was soon out and then Pollock played another wonderful innings. He made 77 off exactly the same number of balls and produced every stroke in the book. For the first time, Titmus was played with freedom, but of course it was only for a short spell, and the other batsmen were unable to pierce Smith's defensive fields, Pollock's 77 was scored out of 109 made while he was at the crease. Goddard made a challenging declaration, as indeed he had to. England were asked to make 245 at about a run a minute, but the rain came soon after Boycott was out. Dexter was at the wicket with 5 not out, when they came off for the last time.

It had been an interesting series, even if the excitement came only in spasms. More to the point, as far as I am concerned, Smith had acquitted himself well as the captain for the second time on tour and would certainly be the leader at home. Dexter had supported him loyally, but he wouldn't be back as captain unless and until Smith failed. It was fairly generally agreed that Dexter had been a shade unlucky as a batsman, holing out every time he miscued. His average looked fairly impressive, but exactly half his runs had come in that one big innings at Johannesburg. He and Barber had been distinctly the most exciting batsmen on view.

	Innings	N.O.	H.S.	Runs	Average	100	50
1964/55	7	1	172	344	57.33	1	1
To date	94	6	205	4206	47.79	8	24

15 The end of an era

1965 was the first year of the twin tours instituted as a result of the West Indies' great popular success in 1963. New Zealand and South Africa were the first visitors under the new arrangement. After the successful tour of South Africa, Mike Smith was the obvious choice to lead England and it didn't seem that Dexter had much chance of being re-appointed to the captaincy. However he was expected to be one of the mainstays of the batting along with Barrington, Boycott and possibly Cowdrey. It didn't work out like that. Dexter had a very moderate start to the season, but was nevertheless selected for the first Test at Edgbaston. It was a tribute to his great authority, for he had only passed fifty once in the season and any other batsman would have been left out on that lack of evidence of form.

New Zealand were already a fairly tired side before they reached England, having completed seven Tests in India and Pakistan since leaving New Zealand in February. Moreover they had played three Tests against Pakistan *in* New Zealand, immediately prior to this. Of these ten Tests played over three months, they had lost three and drawn seven, which indicates that they were pretty short of bowlers, although they had a good opening attack in Motz and the youthful prodigy, Collinge. Their batting was strong enough, although their star, the great Bert Sutcliffe, was somewhat past his best. They had made a moderate start in England, although the batsmen had done well against a pretty strong MCC side.

The first Test started on the unusually early date of May 27, and it was played in miserably cold conditions – hot drinks had to be served on the field during play! In such cold weather it's a distinct advantage to bat first – fielders can easily strain frozen muscles and ligaments and be unfit to bat – and Smith was pleased to win the toss. Boycott and Barber failed to take full advantage of the conditions and Motz had them both out with the score at 76 for 2. Dexter played a pleasantly relaxed innings scoring 57 in just over two hours, hitting eight fours, before Motz had him too, and he was able to return to the probably not unwelcome warmth of the pavilion.

Barrington had not been much slower than Dexter, but he now seemed to lose his touch altogether and batted very slowly for the rest of the day. He was much criticised for this and attracted even more fire when he made

144

only 76 in four hours on the second day. This is not considered unduly slow in the eighties, but in 1965 England batsmen were expected to knock the New Zealand bowling about and Barrington was actually dropped by the selectors as a disciplinary measure. This was a pretty tough decision; the selectors and the public were glad enough of Barrington's doggedness when England were in trouble at Old Trafford in 1964 and it seems unreasonable to expect a batsman to play to order at all times, especially when he is out of touch.

After being 300 for 3, England were all out for 435, and one does wonder how many they would have got if Barrington had thrown his wicket away. At all events Dexter's innings passed unnoticed in the general furore; unlike Barrington he had done precisely what was expected of him, although it is worth noting that, out of form as he was, he had risen to the occasion in a Test match.

New Zealand batted like tired men. The opening attack made no great impression on them but Titmus was soon among the wickets and sadly Sutcliffe ducked into a bouncer from Trueman and took a nasty knock on the head. He tried to carry on, but had to go off after a few minutes. He came back at the fall of the ninth wicket, but was clearly unfit to be on the field and retired again. New Zealand followed on, 319 behind. Titmus had been the chief wicket-taker with a 4 for 18 in 26 overs.

The openers, Dowling and Congdon, gave New Zealand a positive start, but as so often happens when a side is down they suffered a bizarre accident when Congdon fell over as he tried to sweep Barber, and was hit in the mouth. He too retired, and although he was soon able to resume, it did disrupt the batting order. However, this final misfortune seemed to inspire the later batsmen and led by Vic Pollard they fought it out all the way. Sutcliffe had recovered over the weekend, and he joined with Pollard in some stout resistance. It is pleasing to be able to record that Trueman scrupulously kept the ball well up to him, making no attempt at all to intimidate him. He might well have done had the match looked like slipping away – and Sutcliffe wouldn't have complained if he had – but the match was pretty well settled by now. It was Dexter who came on to have Sutcliffe lbw; it was his first first-class wicket of the season and also the last of his Test career.

England needed only 95 to win and Boycott and Barber made all but three of them before Barber was caught off a skier. Dexter came in, but the batsmen had crossed while the ball was in the air, and he had only to stand and watch while Boycott hit the next ball for four.

Sutcliffe was injured again before the Lord's Test and New Zealand decided to strengthen their bowling by bringing in Taylor, an all-rounder. England picked John Snow for the first time and he made his first Test appearance in Trueman's last match. Rumsey and Trueman made a three-pronged pace attack, which meant that Dexter wouldn't get much bowling. In fact, the ball moved so much for Rumsey in the first hour, when he took 4 for 7 in 8 overs, that Smith used Dexter rather than Snow, as first change. It was an interesting compliment to Dexter, but he didn't break through the defences of Reid and Pollard and it was Snow and Trueman who finished the job Rumsey had begun. New Zealand were all out for 175 leaving England well placed.

Boycott and Barber got out cheaply, but Dexter and Cowdrey batted out the day and put England well on the way on the second day. Dexter played a very robust innings, hitting twelve fours in his 62, and Cowdrey made a rather more sedate 119. Collinge put in a fine spell to have England all out for 307, which although not a winning position, was a strong one. The wicket was getting slower, though, and Trueman and Rumsey could do nothing with it in the New Zealand second innings. Dowling and Sinclair made good scores and Pollard again revealed his fighting qualities by making 55 before he was run out, trying to keep the strike with the last man in. This time Smith didn't use Dexter at all, using instead his three spinners, Titmus, Barber and Parfitt to wheedle the batsmen out.

The match had been interrupted by showers, and time was running short when England went in to make 216. Boycott and Barber made a sound start but Dexter went in with England needing 152 in three hours. New Zealand, with an attack made up for the most part of fast-medium bowlers, were likely to maintain a slow over-rate – there was then no requirement for a minimum number of overs – and some forcing batting was called for. This was a situation made to order for Dexter and he picked out every loose ball and hammered it in a flawless stand of 126 with Boycott. He hit ten fours in his innings of 80 not out and the match was won with time to spare.

It seemed that Dexter was well and truly established again as the country's leading batsman and perhaps a candidate even yet for the captaincy if Smith should falter, but two days later he had the accident which effectively ended his first-class career. Cricketers everywhere were appalled to hear that he had sustained a serious fracture of his leg and would be out of cricket for the rest of the season. It was all so unnecessary too. Dexter ran out of petrol while driving home from the West, got his car off the M4 in time and then injured himself while trying to push his car off the road. Ultimately, he decided not to return to Sussex in 1966 and this seemed to be the end of his career. There was to be a further instalment, but at the time the general verdict was that he had gone out on a high note with that forceful match-winning innings at Lord's.

	Innings	N.O.	H.S.	Runs	Average	100	50
1965	4	2	80*	199	99.50	—	3
To date	98	8	205	4405	48.94	9	28

146

16 An unexpected coda

Dexter played in only four first-class matches in 1966 and 1967 and it seemed that his active career was at an end, but there was to be a curious little epilogue. England's cricket took an erratic course after his enforced withdrawal in 1965. John Edrich returned for the third Test and made an extraordinary 310 not out, playing and missing a good deal but never actually holing out, and hitting five sixes and fifty-two fours in a spectacular innings; he was partnered by a restored Barrington who under very different circumstances, managed to mollify the same selectors who had dropped him. South Africa then defeated England at Nottingham and drew the other two Tests – their new side looked formidable indeed. Barrington and Cowdrey made runs in the middle of the order and after their own fashion were plugging the gap left by Dexter. Smith failed to get going in any of the Tests that summer, which was distinctly worrying.

Smith was nevertheless asked to lead England to Australia and the series subsequently followed a similar pattern to that of 1962-3. The first two Tests were drawn, each side having the best of one game; England won the third by an innings, thanks to a glorious century from Barber, strongly supported by Boycott and Edrich, and a good all-round bowling performance. Australia bounced back to win the fourth Test by an innings, thanks to a huge opening stand of 244 by Simpson and Lawry reinforced by devastating bowling from McKenzie and Hawke. The final Test, just as in 1962-3, ended in a disappointing draw, but Barrington again finished the series in prime form. Cowdrey, Boycott and Barber all made runs but Smith did not and he was clearly vulnerable. The Tests against New Zealand were all drawn in England's favour.

The West Indies were in England again in 1966 and had very much the better of things. They won the first Test by an innings, during which Smith failed again with the bat and lost his place, to be succeeded by Cowdrey returning as captain. England lost two of the next three Tests, the match at Lord's being drawn, and Cowdrey in his turn was sacked. Brian Close was brought back as captain. England won an extraordinary match by an innings and suddenly Close, normally cast as the villain, was the hero of English cricket. The most successful England batsmen during the series were Graveney and two newcomers, Milburn and Basil d'Oliveira, the coloured South African who had come to Worcestershire by way of league cricket and now made the Test team at the age of 34, in romantic circumstances.

Close led England to victory against both India and Pakistan in 1967, but lost the captaincy after indulging in a piece of time-wasting in a critical county match and declining to express regret. Cowdrey was reinstated. With Graveney and d'Oliveira still to the fore and Barrington returning to his best form, England had not been short of runs. Boycott, like Barrington two years earlier, had been disciplined for making a lot of runs too slowly – another very odd decision – but he was back in the side which went to the West Indies, the selectors presumably taking the view either that he had repented of his sins or that it would be quite all right if he scored slowly in front of West Indian crowds. England won the series, thanks in part to a challenging declaration from Sobers that didn't come off; Barrington, Graveney and Cowdrey all batted well in the middle of the order.

I have dwelt a little on the progress of the England team in these Tests because it leads on to the final episode in Dexter's Test career. Cowdrey has told in his autobiography *MCC* how, when he was recalled in 1967, he conceived a Five-Tour Plan, to put England back on top of world cricket. He hoped to lead England to victory over the West Indies (1967-8), Australia (1968), South Africa (1968-9 and 1970) and finally Australia (1970-1). In the event, he was frustrated in this grand design by a variety of obstacles, but in the early summer of 1968, he had achieved the first objective and was considering every possible angle to achieving the second. England picked a rather odd side for the first Test against Australia with only three specialist bowlers. Australia made a good start to the match, Lawry and three newcomers to England, Walters, Sheahan and Ian Chappell, all making seventies and eighties. England collapsed on a two-paced pitch and Australia went smoothly to a win, only d'Oliveira batting to his potential. It was going to be difficult to come back and win two matches of the remaining four under English conditions and it was at about this stage of the season that Cowdrey suggested to Dexter that if he chose to play in some county games and recaptured his form, there might be an England place for him. Dexter was never the man to refuse a challenge and he began to organise his summer accordingly, planning to play for Sussex in July.

Meanwhile, England were terribly unlucky at Lord's, losing time on the last day when they had Australia on the ropes; the scores were England 351 for 7 declared, Australia 78 and 127 for 4. They were on top again at Edgbaston, where Cowdrey made 104 in his hundredth Test leaving Australia badly placed when the rain returned on the fifth day. Four days after this Test finished, Dexter played his long-awaited first match of the season for Sussex against Kent, and scored 203 in 330 minutes. He was immediately drafted into the England side to replace Knight for the fourth Test at Headingley. Ironically, Cowdrey was injured and stood down at the last moment and Graveney took over the captaincy. Sharpe was called up from Yorkshire's match at Westcliff, but it was Fletcher, already in the squad, who played instead of Cowdrey – a fateful decision. Boycott was also injured and Prideaux came in for his first Test match, partnering Edrich. The rest of the team were Barrington, Knott, Illingworth, Snow, Brown and Underwood. Australia were also without their captain Lawry, and were led by Jarman, the wicket-keeper. Their attack was based on the seamers, but Dexter might be threatened more by Gleeson, a leg-spinner whom he had not seen.

Jarman won the toss and batted. Cowper and Inverarity, a new combination, opened and Snow soon bowled Inverarity. Snow bowled with great fire, and several chances and near-chances went begging; unfortunately most of them were in the general vicinity of Fletcher. Accounts vary and it is impossible to say how many of them were carrying, but the Headingley crowd naturally asserted that Sharpe would have caught the lot. Fletcher was never well-received in Yorkshire from that day to the end of his distinguished career. Cowper batted slowly, but Redpath was in fine form and unusually enterprising. Walters and Chappell also went well, but the predominant impression of the first day was of some rather indifferent England fielding. Most of the chances dropped were difficult ones, but even Knott was having a bad day.

Australia were 258 for 5 at the close and might well have been all out although Redpath had held the side together with 92. Next day, England took a firmer grip with Underwood finishing off the tail in quick time; he took 4 for 41 in all, in 27.4 overs, a fine piece of bowling in the circumstances. Australia were 315 all out and England's new opening pair, Edrich and Prideaux, made an excellent start. Prideaux was driving and hooking as though he hadn't a care in the world, while Edrich batted in his usual style, taking no risks but never missing a scoring chance and keeping pace with his flamboyant partner. They made 123, the only century opening partnership by either side in the series, before Prideaux mis-hooked Gleeson and was marvellously caught by Freeman, who held one of those difficult chances with the ball dropping over his shoulder. Dexter came next and was faced with the fast bowlers. Unusually for him, but predictably enough given his lack of practice, he was tied down and, for once in his life, barracked. The crowd probably had nothing to do with it, but he played over a ball from McKenzie and was bowled for 10. Edrich also went before the close of play, which came with England at 163 for 3.

149

It still looked as though England should get a lead, but there was a sorry collapse on the Saturday, only Barrington (49) resisting a fine spell by Connolly. England were 241 for 9, but Underwood at No 11, played a fine robust innings of 45 not out and together with Brown saw England to 302. The match was very open but time was beginning to run out. The wicket was losing some of its pace and taking spin, and Illingworth was the most effective bowler in the Australian second innings. They had lost Cowper and Inverarity by the weekend and batted slowly on the Monday; this is entirely understandable since they were the holders of the Ashes and it was up to England to take all the risks, but this did not prevent some English critics making barbed remarks. An hour's play was lost to the rain on this fourth day and Australia scored 191 more runs for 4 more wickets, Chappell and Walters heading the resistance. England needed to make a very quick end to the batting on the final day, and they did thanks to Illingworth (taking 6 for 87) and Underwood knocking over the last 4 wickets in an hour.

England were left with the difficult task of scoring 326 in 295 minutes. It was just possible if they got a good start, but Prideaux was out immediately and it was asking a lot of Dexter to play in his form of 1961 when he had had so little practice. He made a most valiant effort and together with Edrich added 77 in even time, but Dexter was bowled by Connolly for 38, and Graveney and Barrington failed to manage the acceleration. Looking back at the match, it is a little difficult to understand why the England batsmen didn't 'go for broke' – they finished on 230 for 4, half an hour before the possible scheduled close and Illingworth and Knott never picked up their bats. However teams were less accustomed to chases then than they are today and bowlers were better at closing the game down than in the Golden Age, whenever that was. The fifties and sixties were arguably the era in which a target was least likely to be attempted, in spite of what had happened at Port-of-Spain earlier in the year. Anyway, England had failed to make the runs and the Ashes remained with Australia. Dexter had seen them lost in 1958-9 and he was not destined to assist in their recapture.

England were still desperately keen to win at the Oval. They felt, reasonably, that they had now had the better of three Tests in a row and that they should be able to square the series. Barrington, still sadly out of form was dropped and Milburn came in to boost the scoring rate. Cowdrey, leading the side again, replaced Fletcher, then had second thoughts about the strength of the attack on a wicket which seemed likely to help the medium-pace bowler if it favoured anybody. He persuaded the selectors to call up d'Oliveira as the all-rounder. It is unlikely that d'Oliveira would have played, but Prideaux fell ill and d'Oliveira replaced him, with Milburn moving up to open. It was a fateful decision, for reasons well outside the scope of this book. Lawry came back into the Australian side and Mallett came in for his first Test, Cowper being injured.

Cowdrey won the toss, following which the England innings took an erratic course. Edrich was soundness itself, but Milburn went for 8, and once again Dexter was exposed early on; one wonders if it would have been wiser to have batted him further down the order in these Tests – he had still only played three innings for Sussex – but doubtless he would have rejected the idea. This time he did fall to Gleeson, for 21. Cowdrey also went cheaply and England were 113 for 3. Graveney and Edrich added 125, d'Oliveira came in, struggled momentarily and then settled. England were 272 for 4 at the close and in a strong position. Edrich was out at last for 164, but by now England were 359 for 5, with d'Oliveira approaching his hundred. He went on to 158 out of an England total of 494.

Lawry was the backbone of Australia's reply, but apart from Redpath, he got little support. It was a typical Lawry innings – dour defence and thumping hits when the rare bad balls came along. He was 135 not out on Saturday night, and Australia were 264 for 7, but he was out first thing on the Monday, though he didn't think much of the decision and seems to have said so to the umpire – dissent is not a new phenomenon. Mallett batted courageously for 43, but Australia were all out for 324, 170 behind. There followed some of the best cricket of the series as England went hard for the runs against some good bowling and marvellous athletic fielding. In an hour, England were 67 for 3, and Dexter was out for the last time having scored 28; he had sacrificed his wicket in a good cause, though, driving at Connolly. England had nothing to lose – but nor had they had anything to lose at Leeds. This time they hammered away to the end, scoring 181 in three hours, Cowdrey and Knott were the only men to pass thirty. Australia had to make 352, or realistically, to stay in for six and a half hours – if the rain held off.

Lawry and Redpath were out that night and it seemed that England's task was halfway to being achieved, but there was still drama to come. Wickets fell quickly in the morning and Australia were 85 for 5 when a torrential downpour flooded the ground. It seemed, as it had seemed at Lord's, that Providence was an Australian after all. But the sun came out and the ground-staff began to do heroic work with brooms and squeegees. The ground authorities, with what I have always considered to be doubtful justification, called for volunteers from the crowd to assist in the drying process. One wonders whether the same appeal would have been made if Australia had been in a winning position, but Lawry apparently raised no objection. Play resumed at 4.45 pm, with 75 minutes to go. Inverarity, who had opened, was still there, and he and Jarman held out for 40 minutes, until d'Oliveira the fifth bowler tried, got through Jarman's defensive push and bowled him. Underwood finished the innings off with the help of two good catches by Brown; a dramatic photograph of the finish shows nine England fielders crowded round the bat as Inverarity is given out lbw, after heroic resistance.

So Dexter left the field of a Test match for the last time, victorious against Australia. He only had this particular notable experience three times, and it was very fitting that his last Test should be a happy one. Who can say whether it was a wise decision to bring him back? England would have won the final Test if someone else had been in his place and would probably not have won the fourth if he had been replaced (though Sharpe, if playing, might conceivably have held a couple of those elusive slip catches . . .). Dexter was aware that this was his last Test and his feelings may be imagined. Most men playing in their last Test are unaware of the fact; Bradman and Hobbs were exceptions, but for example, the Leeds Test of this year was Barrington's last, and Milburn was to play his last in Karachi a few months later; a heart-attack and a road accident, respectively, cut each off in his prime. Dexter's final retirement passed pretty well unnoticed, firstly because he had already retired once, but more importantly, because the cricket world was at once overturned by the uproar about d'Oliveira's omission from the team to go to South Africa, his subsequent reinstatement and then the cancellation of the tour.

	Innings	N.O.	H.S.	Runs	Average	100	50
1968	4	—	38	97	24.25	—	—
Final record	102	8	205	4502	47.89	9	27

17 Summing him up

This really was the end of Dexter's Test career and he played no more for Sussex after 1968. In fact, apart from an unofficial tour to South Africa, he didn't play again in first-class cricket. He plunged headlong into journalism, public relations work and other business ventures, and played a lot of golf at the highest amateur level. However he was never far from cricket, whether instituting a nationwide search for fast bowlers or initiating the computer-based Deloittes ratings, and he became the chairman of the Test selectors, the effective supremo of English cricket, in 1989. More of this in a moment; but let us first try to sum him up, as a cricketer and as a captain.

Some of Dexter's contemporaries thought he had the potential to be the greatest batsman of his generation, probably the greatest English batsman of the post-war era, if only he had applied himself. As they saw it, he had all the technical gifts and if his figures didn't match the ability, there must have been a mental or psychological flaw. The facts don't really bear out this last argument. In Test cricket, he was seldom out playing a casual stroke and he was certainly not a reckless hitter. True, he was a batsman cast in the Corinthian mould. Like Maclaren and Jackson, he believed that he had a bat in his hands in order to hit the ball with it, but Maclaren and Jackson each had a good defensive technique, and so had Dexter. One need only look at his long innings at Edgbaston in 1961 and at Old Trafford in 1964, to appreciate that he was a batsman with patience and sound application. The interesting thing about Dexter in these situations was that, even under extreme pressure, he never became negative – he was always ready to hit the bad ball, preferably hammering it to the boundary.

It is always tempting to look at a fine player, and to say 'if only he had had this, or that attribute, how much greater would he have been?' But there has never been a perfect batsman, though Bradman and, in his time, Hobbs came very close. Others have had identifiable faults. Hammond could be pinned down by a leg-stump attack; Cowdrey yielded to fits of diffidence and self-doubt; Hutton, possibly because of his war-time injury, was vulnerable to the off-break; Gower can be a little loose outside the off-stump. The list is endless and when one man – Bradman – came along who seemed to have no Achilles heel, the cry went up that he was ruining the game, and a strategy had to be devised to contain him which did very nearly ruin the game, and we are still suffering its after-effects. Dexter's temperamental fault, if he had one, was that he was a little too ready to try to get on top too soon – that he admitted no man to be his master. This is not at all the same thing as carelessness or casual play but is the true master-batsman's assertiveness carried a shade too far, but this is a fault very much on the right side.

Although Dexter was not, on figures, the most successful England batsman of his generation, he was certainly the one most feared by the opposition. A comparison of his figures with those of Barrington and Cowdrey, from the beginning of the West Indies tour of 1959-60 to Dexter's last Test in 1965 is revealing:

	Innings	N.O.	Runs	Average
Barrington	82	11	4301	60.57
Cowdrey	62	8	2810	52.03
Dexter	88	8	4135	51.58

Cowdrey missed two tours during this time and Dexter one, but Barrington went on them all though he missed most of the Tests in 1963-4 because of an injury. Dexter was the most consistent of the three, which again runs counter to that image of carelessness. He never had a really bad series and was never left out when he was fit and available. It would be fair to say that each of the other two could be pinned down by the bowlers and be made to look incapable of breaking out of the net; this never happened to Dexter for very long. *Wisden's* comment on the 1962-3 tour is in point:

Dexter was a complete contrast to Barrington. A thrill went round every ground when he strode majestically to the wicket, and most bowlers feared the punishment they were about to receive . . . The tremendous power of his driving and his fast scoring were fine to see, but as the tour progressed and the tension of the Tests mounted, he began to play more carefully, and as a result lost much of his effectiveness.

Leslie Smith, *Wisden's* correspondent, was therefore in no doubt; Dexter was a fine, intimidating player, who actually did better when he played his natural game. Those who think that Dexter would have done better if he had 'got his head down' are vulnerable on two counts; he did on most occasions apply himself with care, but when his approach became too careworn, his figures suffered.

One could argue indefinately about whether Dexter would or would not have made more runs, had he approached the business differently, and the argument is a pretty sterile one; what is not in doubt is that he was a highly exciting player. He came along when England was short of stylish, forcing

154

batsmen, and he filled the gap left by the premature retirement of Peter May. After Dexter's own retirement England had some pretty dull batting sides – it would be invidious to mention names, but after Milburn's accident and Graveney's enforced departure, the next really assertive batsman was Tony Greig and everybody knows why he wasn't with us for long.

It was natural, in the nineteen-seventies, to look back at Dexter with a nostalgic sigh, but I don't think our vision of him has been overly romanticised. He *was* a positive and attractive batsman. 'Great' is a difficult word to use in this context; I wouldn't classify him as a 'great' batsman if the standard is to be set by the likes of Hobbs, Bradman, Hammond and Compton, but he was certainly a very, very good bat indeed, and takes an honoured place in the next group, so to speak. In his day, he was the epitome of fine batting and the man everybody wanted to watch and this has been said of very few cricketers either before or since.

What now of his captaincy? As we have already noted, he won only nine of the thirty Tests in which he led England, but this performance is by no means as bad as it might appear. He encountered some very strong opponents, on some wickets on which it was hard to get a result of any kind. He was generally regarded by his contemporaries as a dashing and enterprising captain, but one who was a little inclined to lose interest on the duller days – to 'let the game run on'. I think this is rather hard on him. He was too often given sides containing too many bowlers of a similar kind – the party which went to Australia in 1962-3 comes to mind – and when teams like that get into difficulties, there is little to be done. Sometimes, he appeared to be mistrustful of his spinners, but this could be said of most of the captains of his day – they were nearly as blinkered as the captains of the nineteen-eighties; although one should except from this criticism Richie Benaud, who knew a good deal more about the spinning business than the others, and the various captains of India, who had to rely on their spinners because they had no other weapon.

Dexter himself believes that he mismanaged David Allen in Australia, trying too hard and too long to persuade him to buy his wickets by bowling outside the off-stump. If this were so, it at least showed that Dexter was prepared to play on the batsmen's strengths, to foster attacking cricket, and he would, as I have indicated elsewhere, have been in tune with the English cricketing establishment of the time. With hindsight, it seems that Allen might well have had more Tests on that tour than he had, but this brings us back to the original selection of the party; Dexter had been given three off-spinners and Titmus, who was batting well and was a vital member of a well-balanced side. Decisions like this are always much easier after the event.

I have tried to analyse Dexter's decisions on the occasions when he was most fiercely criticised, as at Leeds in 1964, and have come to the conclusion that he generally had a perfectly good reason for what he did. At Leeds his bowlers let him down; that happens sometimes and there isn't a lot that the captain can do about it, he has to make the best of what he's got, on the day. Dexter always gave of his best and was always ready to contribute with a spell of bowling when the conditions were against his top-liners; and, whether or not the tales about his practising his golf-strokes in the field are true of his earlier days, there is absolutely no evidence that he failed to lead by example when he was in charge.

Off the field he may have been a bit patchy. He was by no means the easiest of mixers, and it may have been that people made the mistake of thinking that somebody who batted freely and attractively would be, must be, a sparkling conversationalist and ready listener. It doesn't work like that. Lindsay Hassett, a dour and defensive batsman in Test cricket, was the liveliest and jokiest of men off the field; Frank Woolley, handsomest of attacking batsmen, was shy and reserved in company and there are hundreds more examples. Dexter was, it seems, relatively introspective, and if he cut somebody dead in the hotel or in the pavilion, it was because his thoughts were elsewhere, and not because he was trying to upset them. We are all as God made us, and Dexter was unlucky in that nobody seemed to want to make any allowances for him. Nevertheless, his tours were happy ones, and he didn't miss many tricks on the field. A good captain, without being one of the game's great leaders.

After being in and around the game for some twenty years following his retirement, Dexter became the chairman of selectors in 1989. The job in recent years has been much more than just that of selection; it ranges from picking the Test side from the available talent to being the man most responsible for seeing that there is a steady flow of available talent, and this has been taken to encompass responsibility for the whole structure of the game from youth level upwards. Dexter had already demonstrated a deep interest in the grass roots, notably in his search for young fast bowlers, and when the time came to seek a new chairman to replace Peter May, whose unhappy reign had been far from successful, it was logical for cricket's managers to look to Dexter. He made it clear from the outset that he saw his remit as a very wide one, going much further than the simple selection of a Test-winning team, and the implication of that was that the reconstruction would not be quickly achieved. Nevertheless, he is bound to be judged by results on the field and in an Australian year he had a pretty disastrous time.

To get the events of 1989 into some sort of perspective, we should first look at the immediate past. When Dexter took over, England's cricketing prestige had never been lower; she had actually won only three of the last

156

thirty-four Tests and had had, for a variety of reasons, four different captains in the previous disastrous summer. For one reason or another, all those four captains had reason to feel that they had been harshly treated by the governing body and Dexter needed a new broom, without much assurance that any of the brooms in the cupboard were likely to be effective ones. The touring team were Australia – the old enemy – and curiously enough they looked to be more vulnerable than most of the other countries; of those three wins in the previous four years, two had been against Australia and one against Sri Lanka.

Dexter was therefore going to be expected to produce a side which would either win, or at least give a good account of itself. In many ways, it would have been easier for him if the visitors had been the West Indies – at least nobody would expect England to beat them – they hadn't done so since 1974. But to make matters worse a side had to be picked to go to the West Indies at the end of the summer, and players who are the right ones to face Australia in England – fast-medium swing bowlers for example – might well be quite the wrong ones for the Caribbean. It was a daunting prospect for Dexter and there was yet one more hazard. South Africa, banned from official contact with the rest of the cricket world for some twenty years, were desperately trying to put together another unofficial England tour, and offering, it was understood, very sizeable inducements. The players were made fully aware of the consequences of accepting the rand, but those who were either disaffected or nearing the end of their Test careers were sorely tempted. It wouldn't make for a happy dressing-room. Dexter was a brave man to take the job on, but he has never run away from a challenge in his life and he didn't run away from this one.

As we know it all went wrong and Dexter must at times have felt that he was back in 1964 when, with the benefit of hindsight, the critics were taking him apart for that new-ball decision. He and his fellow-selectors recalled David Gower to lead the side; they had no real alternative, but Gower had at least decisively defeated the Australians in 1985 and there seemed every chance that he would do so again. This was no more than even chance though – the Australians had a very fair side, with several players who were manifestly still improving – but it did seem that it would be a close and exciting series. England easily won the one-day series, went confidently to Headingley to find a spotty-looking wicket and took what might have been the crucial decision of the summer, to go in without a spinner and, a logical corollary, to put Australia in if they won the toss. Australia also went in without a spinner, but we shall never know whether Border would have put England in, because Gower did win the toss.

From then on the story needs no re-telling. Everything went wrong for England. The batsmen couldn't cope with some excellent seam bowling, the bowlers couldn't get rid of some good, orthodox batsmen. Gower

157

plummetted from being the hero of the popular press to being an incompetent captain almost overnight and of course the finger of blame was pointed at Dexter. What can one say? It indicates the respect in which Dexter was still held, twenty-one years after his retirement, that he was expected to reverse a tide which had been flowing against England for years: but he had made it very clear to anyone who would listen to him that there was a good deal to be done to reorganise the structure of the game, and that it *wouldn't* be the work of a single season.

However, he would, I am sure, agree that things went a good deal worse in 1989 than he expected and not only because the Australian side played well above their own expectations. Dexter had hoped to build a side gradually, making the minimum number of changes, but several usually reliable players performed very much worse than anyone could have expected; others, notably Botham, Gatting and Lamb were injured at crucial times and of course the South African party was duly assembled and causing all sorts of bad feelings generally. All this meant that twenty-nine players appeared in the Test, and the squad never became a team.

This book is not intended to be an apologia for Dexter; it has to be said that he made the occasional mistake both as a player and as a captain and he and his fellow-selectors made mistakes in 1989. But I am firmly of the view that England would have lost the series against this very strong Australian side brilliantly led by Border, whatever decisions had been made by selectors or captain, and for the fundamental reason that county cricket as a whole has taken too many wrong turnings. Too many mediocre bowlers are taking wickets on helpful pitches; too many batsmen have forgotten how to play cricket strokes and to await their opportunities with the bad ball, under the pressures of limited-overs cricket.

It was apparent before the Australians destroyed England that the rehabilitation was going to be a long job. Dexter may be the man to carry it through or he may not, but no better candidate is offering. In my view, he should be allowed the time and the scope to show what he can do. He was a presence of unutterable awe at the crease – and he may well have the character and the ability to inspire and teach the cricketers of another era. If he has not, we are in a bad way.

Overall Dexter was and still is a considerable presence in the game, certainly one of the most important figures of his era and nobody who watched him bat will ever want to forget him.

Opponents	Innings	N.O.	H.S.	Runs	Average	100	50
Australia	35	—	180	1358	38.80	2	8
South Africa	16	1	172	585	39.00	1	3
West Indies	19	1	136*	866	48.11	2	5
New Zealand	10	2	141	477	59.62	1	4
India	12	2	126*	467	46.70	1	3
Pakistan	10	2	205	749	93.62	2	4
Total	102	8	205	4502	47.89	9	27

	Balls	Runs	Wickets	Average
Australia	1582	742	23	32.26
South Africa	608	310	7	44.28
West Indies	958	397	12	33.08
New Zealand	402	142	4	35.50
India	726	311	7	44.42
Pakistan	1041	404	13	31.07
Total	5317	2306	66	34.93

Dexter's 94 dismissals came about in this way:

Bowled	30	(32%)
lbw	5	(6%)
Caught	52	(55%)
Stumped	3	(3%)
Run out	3	(3%)
Hit wicket	1	(1%)

The bowlers who dismissed him most often were:

McKenzie	9 times
Benaud	7 times
Sobers	5 times
Adcock	4 times
Davidson	
Borde	
Hall	} 3 times
Gibbs	
Griffith)	

In his turn, Dexter dismissed Butcher 4 times, Lawry, Harvey, O'Neill and Simpson 3 times each. It will be seen that it was generally the best bowlers who got him out; and he got some very fine batsmen out himself.

INDEX

161

Millman, G *63, 66, 72*
Milton, C A *12, 14, 15, 17*
Misson, F M *47, 48, 49, 50, 52*
Mortimore, J B *17, 18, 124, 127*
Moss, A E *25, 33, 39, 41*
Motz, R C *98, 144*
Munir Malik *74, 75*
Murray, D L *100, 101, 103, 104, 105,*
107, 109, 113
Murray, J T *7, 46, 47, 52, 55, 56, 59,*
61, 63, 66, 72, 74, 79, 88, 89, 90,
100, 134, 141, 142
Mushtaq Mohammad *64, 72, 76, 77*

Nadkarni, R G *21*
Nasim-ul-Ghani *73, 75, 77*
Nicholson, A G *133*

O'Brien, R *8*
O'Linn, S *38, 41, 43*
O'Neill, N C *13, 14, 17, 46, 47, 48,*
51, 53, 55, 56, 57, 60, 77, 80, 81, 83,
84, 85, 87, 89, 90, 91, 92, 93, 94, 96,
116, 117, 118, 119, 120, 124, 125,
126, 129, 159

Padgett, D E V *43*
Palmer, K E *141, 142*
Parfitt, P H *63, 68, 70, 72, 74, 76,*
79, 81, 83, 84, 88, 89, 90, 97, 111,
118, 119, 121, 123, 126, 127, 128,
129, 133, 134, 136, 138, 139, 140, 141
Parkhouse, W G A *21, 22*
Parks, J M *31, 34, 35, 38, 39, 41, 103,*
104, 106, 108, 111, 119, 121, 123,
124, 127, 134, 139, 140, 141, 143
Partridge, J T *139, 140, 141*
Peebles, I A R *18*
Philpott, P I *13*
Pithey, A J *135, 136, 137, 138, 140,*
141, 142
Playle, W R *98*
Pollard, W *145, 146*
Pollock, P M *134, 136, 138, 141, 142,*
143
Pollock, R G *134, 136, 138, 140, 141,*
142, 143

Prasanna, E A S *67*
Price, J S E *124, 125, 129, 133, 134,*
135, 137, 140, 141
Prideaux, R M *149, 150*
Procter, M J *134*
Pullar, G *21, 23, 25, 29, 30, 31, 34,*
35, 38, 39, 41, 43, 44, 46, 48, 50, 52,
53, 54, 56, 58, 61, 63, 65, 66, 67, 69,
72, 76, 77, 79, 80, 82, 83, 84, 85, 86,
88, 89, 91, 93, 97, 100

Ramadhin, S *25, 28, 29, 34, 35, 127*
Read, H D *6*
Redpath, I R *115, 116, 117, 118, 119,*
120, 121, 123, 124, 129, 130, 149,
151
Rees, A *123*
Reid, J R *97, 99, 146*
Rhodes, H J *22*
Rhodes, W *107*
Richards, B A *134*
Richardson, P E *7, 12, 13, 16, 17, 63,*
65, 69, 107, 108 110
Roberts, Ron *73*
Robertson-Glasgow, R C *11*
Robins, R W V *35, 57, 59, 74*
Rodriquez, W *11, 112, 113*
Rorke, G F *16*
Rumsey, F E *124, 125, 127, 145, 146*
Russell, W E *63, 64, 66*

Saeed Ahmed *75, 77*
Scarlett, R *30, 33*
Seymour, M A *134, 135, 137*
Shackleton, D *103, 104, 105, 107,*
109, 110, 112, 113
Sharpe, P J *107, 108, 109, 112, 113,*
115, 116, 119, 120, 149, 152
Shaw, A *97*
Sheahan, A P *148*
Simpson, R B *13, 15, 48, 49, 51, 54,*
55, 57, 58, 80, 81, 82, 83, 84, 85, 88,
89, 90, 91, 92, 93, 94, 95, 96, 115,
116, 117, 118, 120, 121, 123, 124,
125, 126, 127, 128, 130, 131, 147,
159
Singh, C *27, 28, 33*

163

164